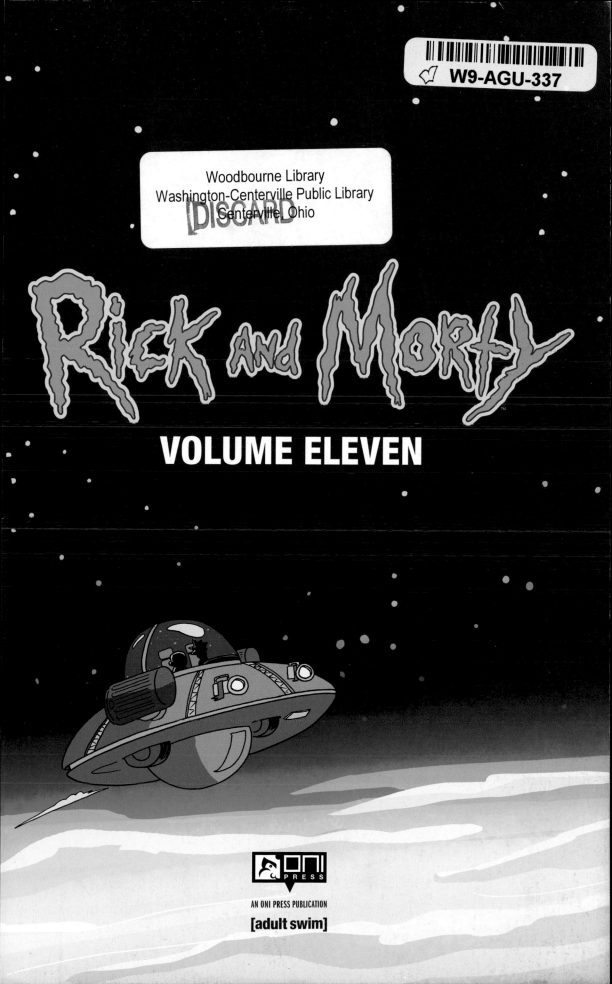

Rick and Morty ™

VOLUME ELEVEN

ONI PRESS

AN ONI PRESS PUBLICATION

[adult swim]

Rick and

VOLUME ELEVEN

RICK AND MORTY™ CREATED BY **DAN HARMON** AND **JUSTIN ROILAND**

RETAIL COVER BY
MARC ELLERBY AND **SARAH STERN**

ONI EXCLUSIVE COVER BY
JULIETA COLÁS

EDITED BY
SARAH GAYDOS

DESIGNED BY
SARAH ROCKWELL

ONI PRESS

[adult swim]™

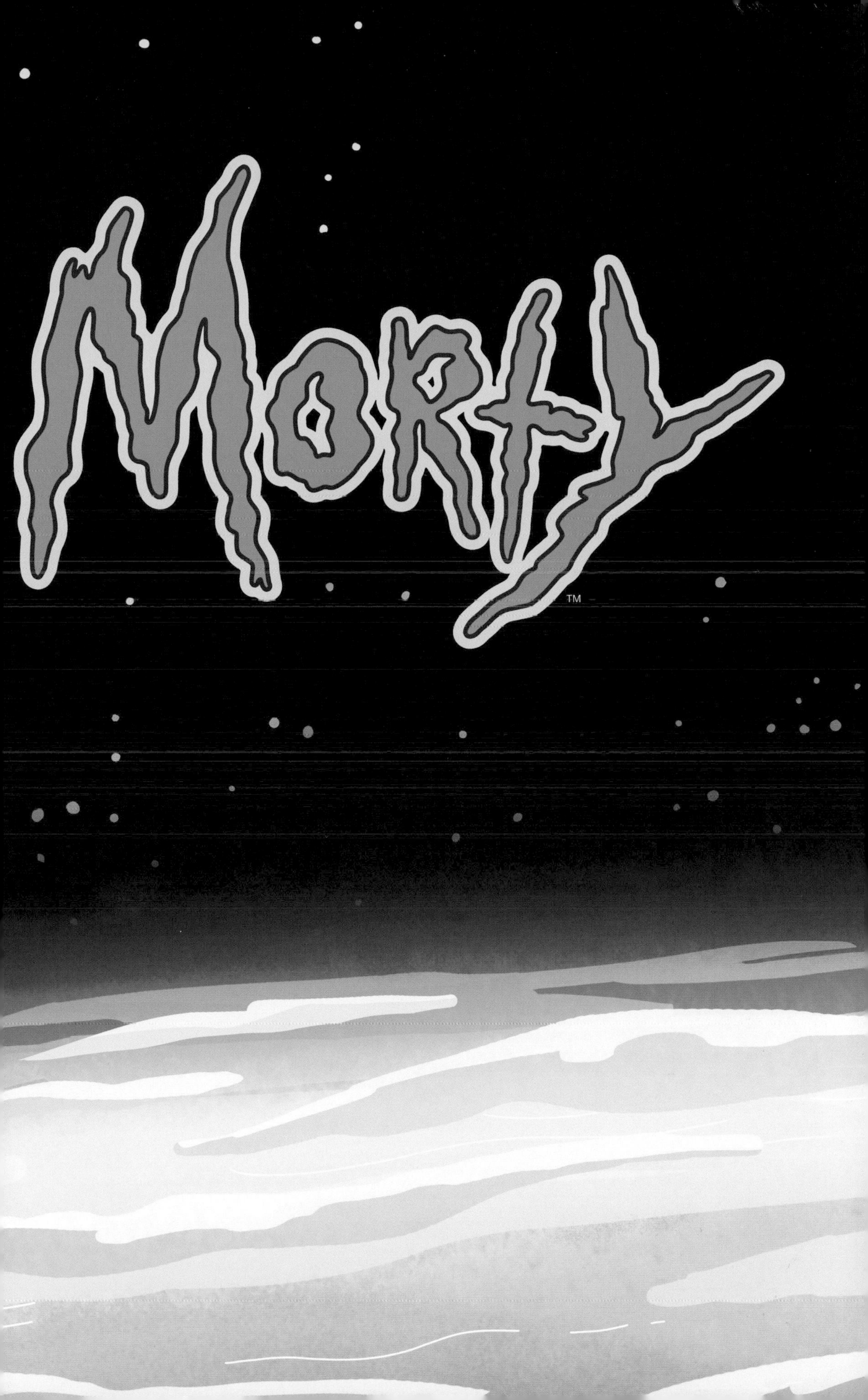
Morty™

PUBLISHED BY ONI-LION FORGE PUBLISHING GROUP, LLC

JAMES LUCAS JONES, PRESIDENT & PUBLISHER

SARAH GAYDOS, EDITOR IN CHIEF

CHARLIE CHU, E.V.P. OF CREATIVE & BUSINESS DEVELOPMENT

BRAD ROOKS, DIRECTOR OF OPERATIONS

AMBER O'NEILL, SPECIAL PROJECTS MANAGER

HARRIS FISH, EVENTS MANAGER

MARGOT WOOD, DIRECTOR OF MARKETING & SALES

JEREMY ATKINS, DIRECTOR OF BRAND COMMUNICATIONS

DEVIN FUNCHES, SALES & MARKETING MANAGER

KATIE SAINZ, MARKETING MANAGER

TARA LEHMANN, MARKETING & PUBLICITY ASSOCIATE

TROY LOOK, DIRECTOR OF DESIGN & PRODUCTION

KATE Z. STONE, SENIOR GRAPHIC DESIGNER

SONJA SYNAK, GRAPHIC DESIGNER

HILARY THOMPSON, GRAPHIC DESIGNER

SARAH ROCKWELL, JUNIOR GRAPHIC DESIGNER

ANGIE KNOWLES, DIGITAL PREPRESS LEAD

VINCENT KUKUA, DIGITAL PREPRESS TECHNICIAN

SHAWNA GORE, SENIOR EDITOR

ROBIN HERRERA, SENIOR EDITOR

AMANDA MEADOWS, SENIOR EDITOR

JASMINE AMIRI, EDITOR

GRACE BORNHOFT, EDITOR

ZACK SOTO, EDITOR

STEVE ELLIS, VICE PRESIDENT OF GAMES

BEN EISNER, GAME DEVELOPER

MICHELLE NGUYEN, EXECUTIVE ASSISTANT

JUNG LEE, LOGISTICS COORDINATOR

JOE NOZEMACK, PUBLISHER EMERITUS

[adult swim]

ONIPRESS.COM | LIONFORGE.COM
FACEBOOK.COM/ONIPRESS | FACEBOOK.COM/LIONFORGE
TWITTER.COM/ONIPRESS | TWITTER.COM/LIONFORGE
INSTAGRAM.COM/ONIPRESS | INSTAGRAM.COM/LIONFORGE

ADULTSWIM.COM
TWITTER.COM/RICKANDMORTY
FACEBOOK.COM/RICKANDMORTY

THIS VOLUME COLLECTS ISSUES #51-55
OF THE ONI PRESS SERIES *RICK AND MORTY*.

FIRST EDITION: MAY 2020

ISBN 978-1-62010-734-8
EISBN 978-1-62010-735-5
ONI EXCLUSIVE ISBN 978-1-62010-736-2

PRINTED IN CHINA

LIBRARY OF CONGRESS CONTROL NUMBER: 2019955395

1 2 3 4 5 6 7 8 9 10

SPECIAL THANKS TO JUSTIN ROILAND, DAN HARMON, MARISA MARIONAKIS, ELYSE SALAZAR, MIKE MENDEL, JANET NO, AND MEAGAN BIRNEY.

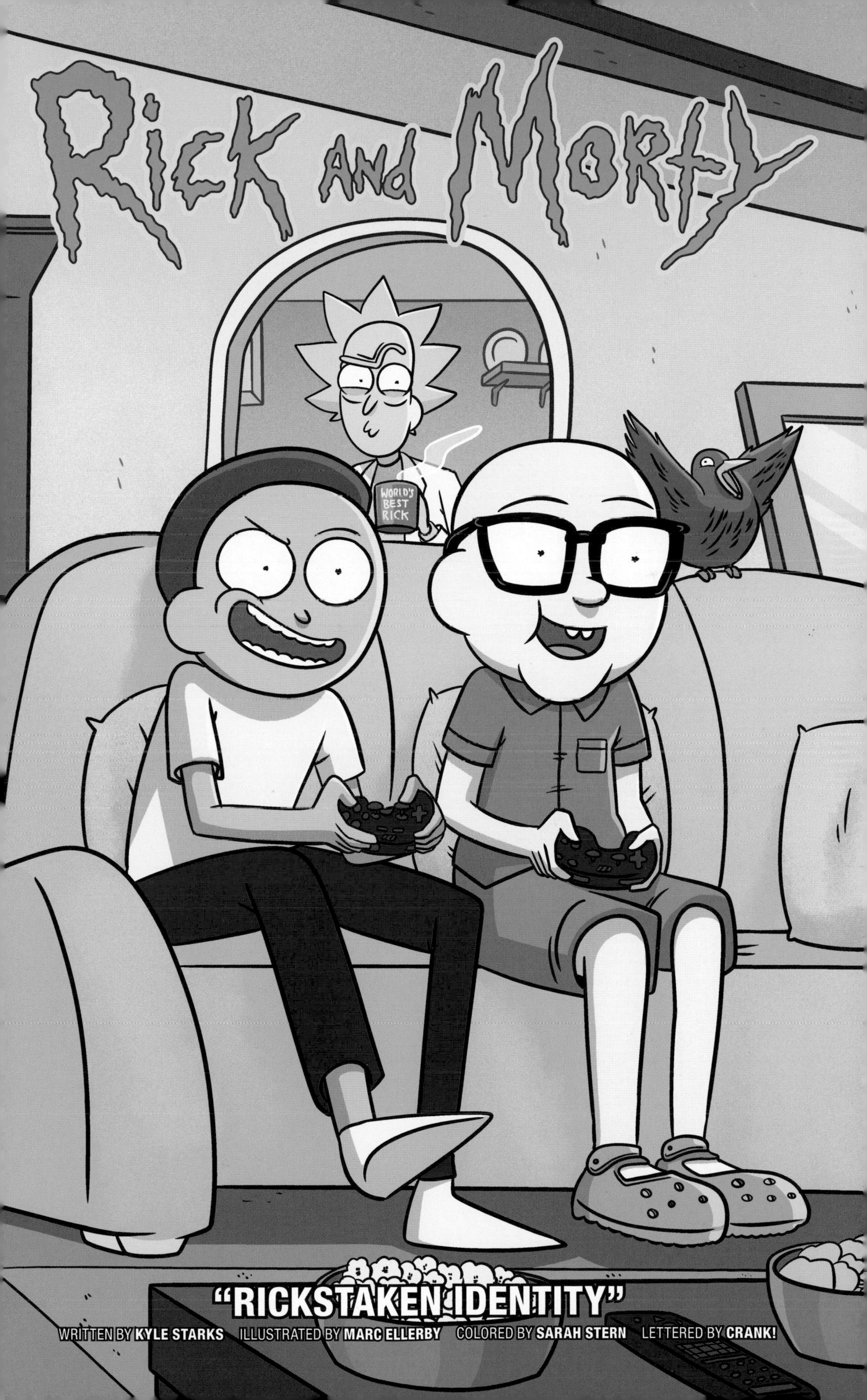
Rick and Morty
WORLD'S BEST RICK

"RICKSTAKEN IDENTITY"

WRITTEN BY **KYLE STARKS** ILLUSTRATED BY **MARC ELLERBY** COLORED BY **SARAH STERN** LETTERED BY **CRANK!**

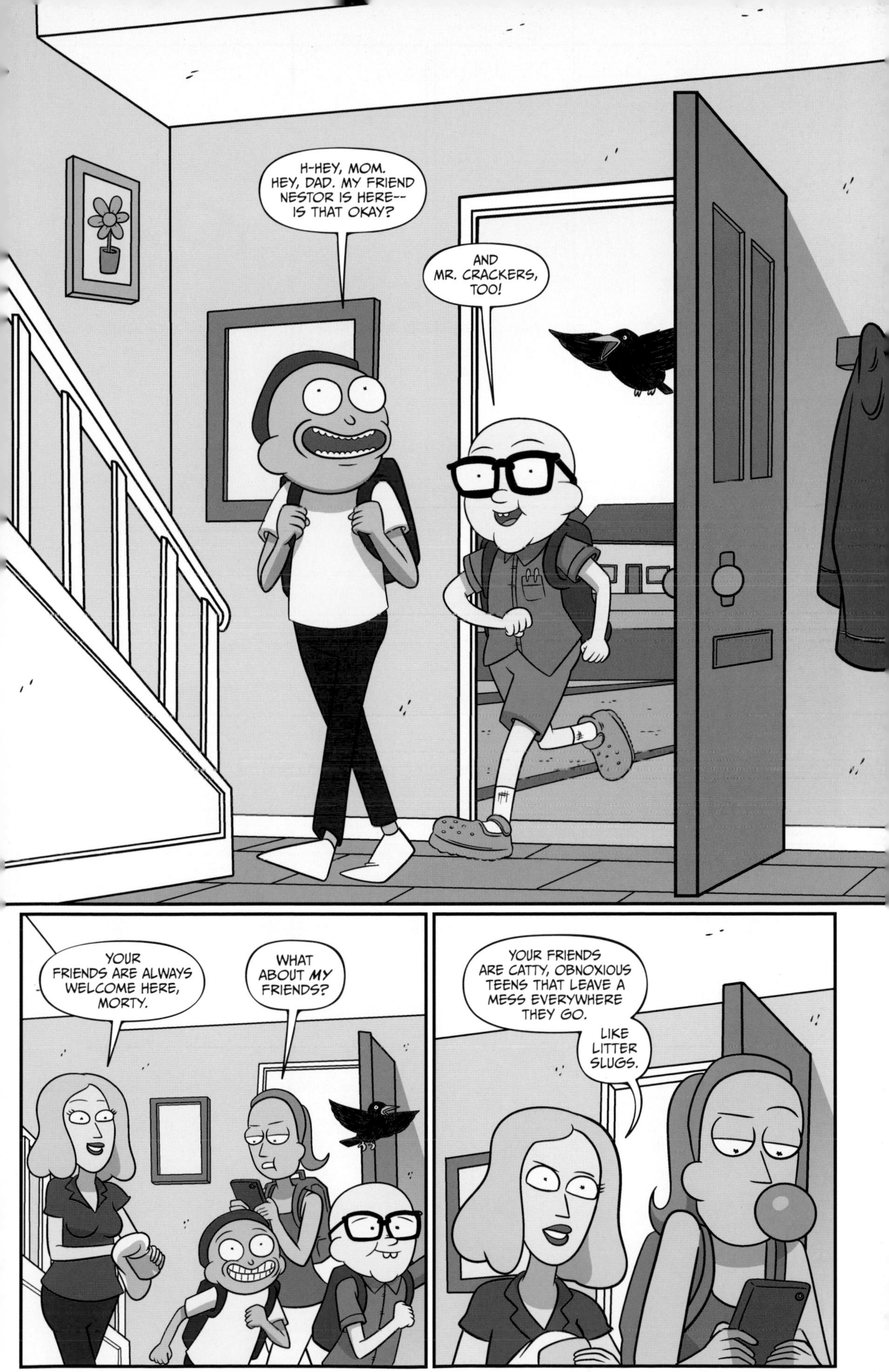
H-HEY, MOM. HEY, DAD. MY FRIEND NESTOR IS HERE-- IS THAT OKAY?
AND MR. CRACKERS, TOO!
YOUR FRIENDS ARE ALWAYS WELCOME HERE, MORTY.
WHAT ABOUT *MY* FRIENDS?
YOUR FRIENDS ARE CATTY, OBNOXIOUS TEENS THAT LEAVE A MESS EVERYWHERE THEY GO.
LIKE LITTER SLUGS.

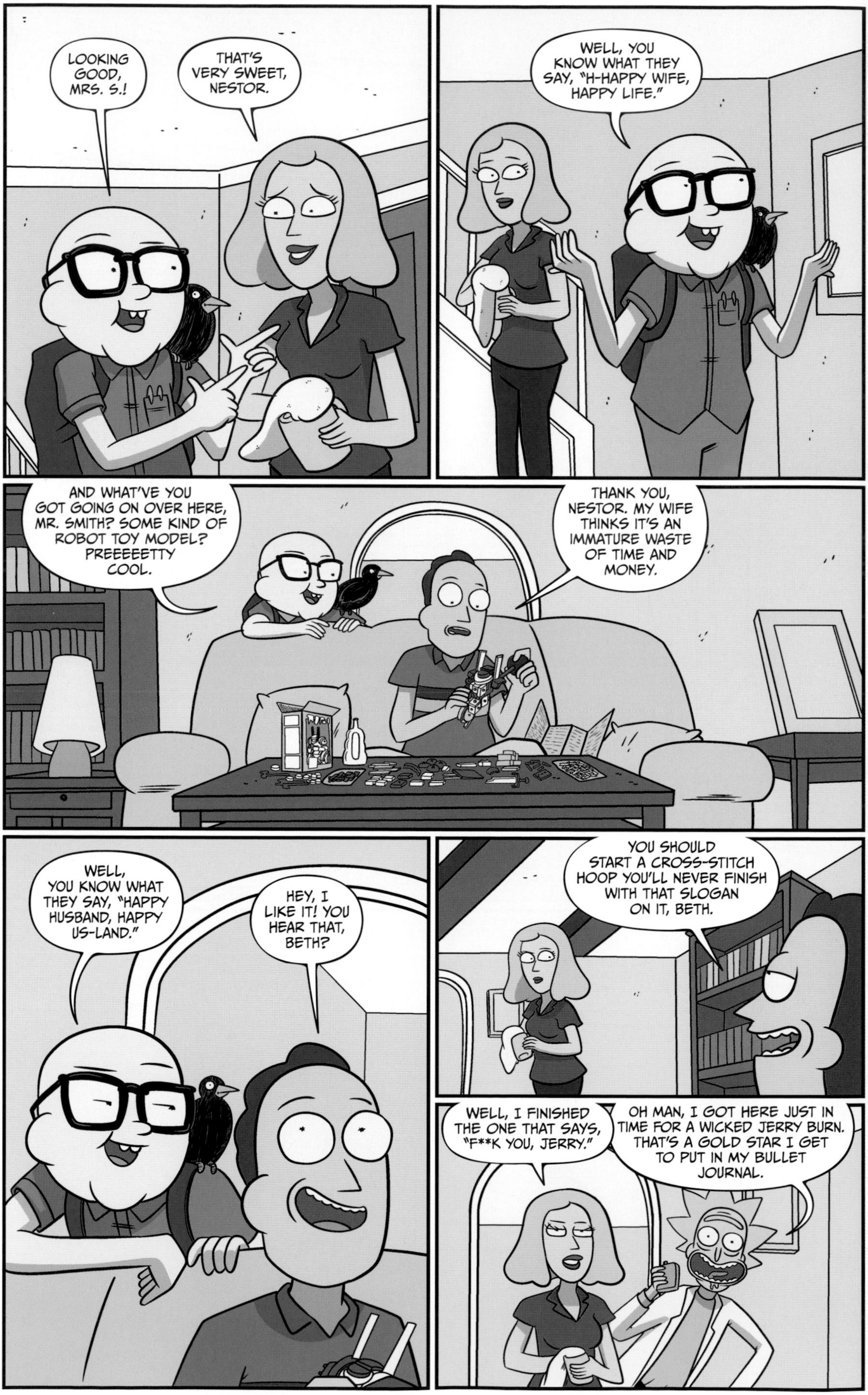
LOOKING GOOD, MRS. S.!
THAT'S VERY SWEET, NESTOR.
WELL, YOU KNOW WHAT THEY SAY, "H-HAPPY WIFE, HAPPY LIFE."
AND WHAT'VE YOU GOT GOING ON OVER HERE, MR. SMITH? SOME KIND OF ROBOT TOY MODEL? PREEEEETTY COOL.
THANK YOU, NESTOR. MY WIFE THINKS IT'S AN IMMATURE WASTE OF TIME AND MONEY.
WELL, YOU KNOW WHAT THEY SAY, "HAPPY HUSBAND, HAPPY US-LAND."
HEY, I LIKE IT! YOU HEAR THAT, BETH?
YOU SHOULD START A CROSS-STITCH HOOP YOU'LL NEVER FINISH WITH THAT SLOGAN ON IT, BETH.
WELL, I FINISHED THE ONE THAT SAYS, "F**K YOU, JERRY."
OH MAN, I GOT HERE JUST IN TIME FOR A WICKED JERRY BURN. THAT'S A GOLD STAR I GET TO PUT IN MY BULLET JOURNAL.

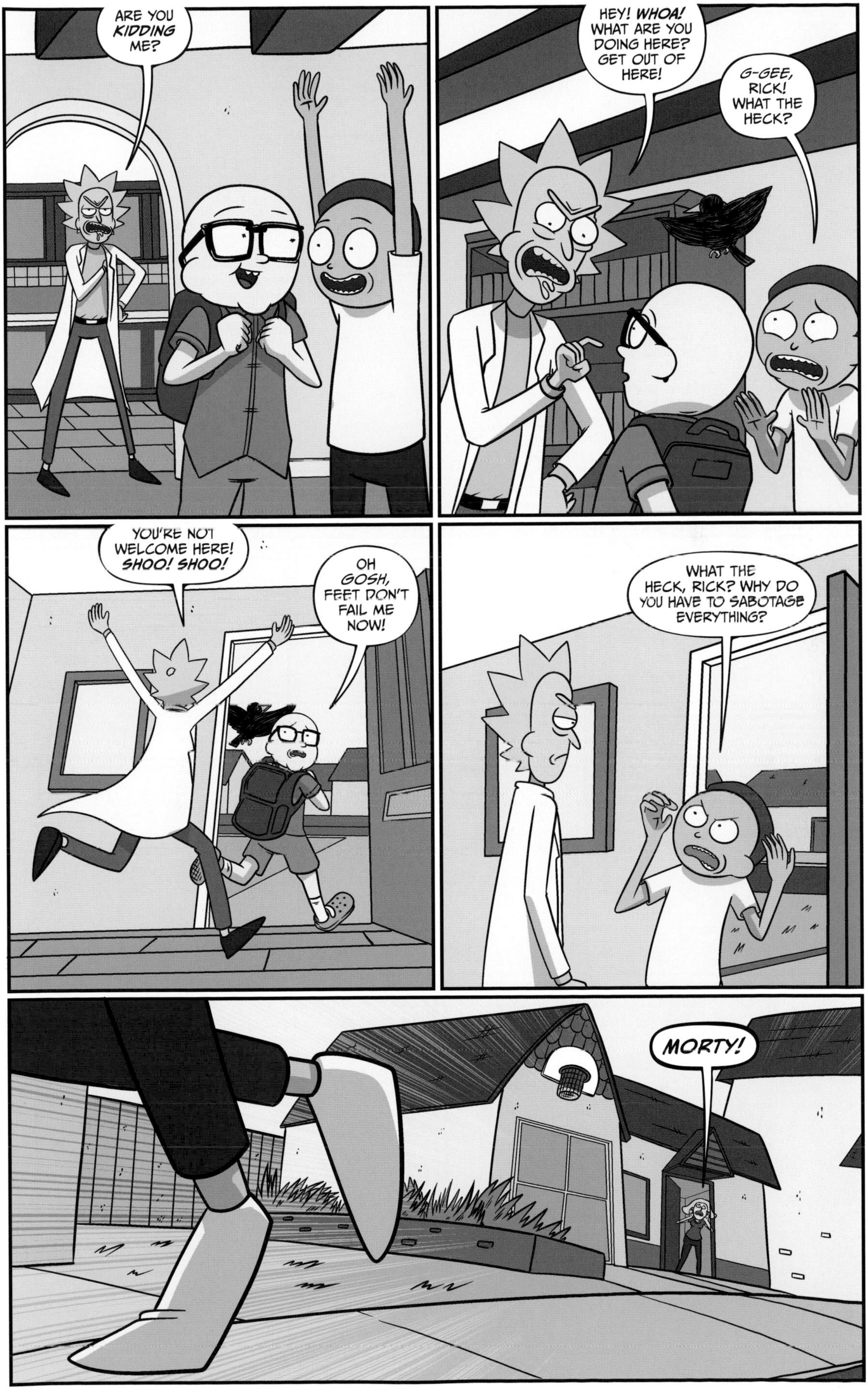
ARE YOU KIDDING ME?
HEY! WHOA! WHAT ARE YOU DOING HERE? GET OUT OF HERE!
G-GEE, RICK! WHAT THE HECK?
YOU'RE NOT WELCOME HERE! SHOO! SHOO!
OH GOSH, FEET DON'T FAIL ME NOW!
WHAT THE HECK, RICK? WHY DO YOU HAVE TO SABOTAGE EVERYTHING?
MORTY!

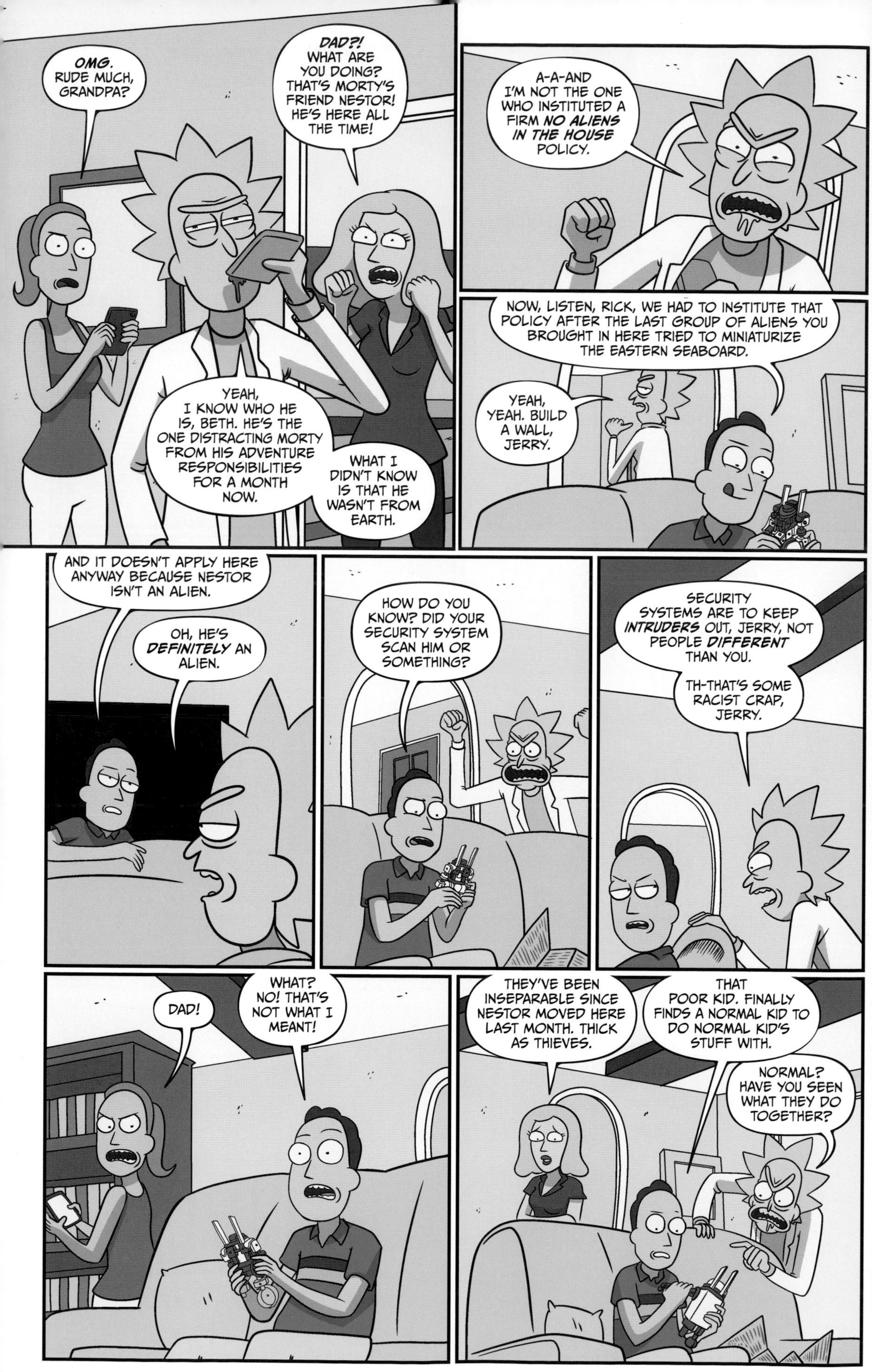
OMG. RUDE MUCH, GRANDPA?
DAD?! WHAT ARE YOU DOING? THAT'S MORTY'S FRIEND NESTOR! HE'S HERE ALL THE TIME!
YEAH, I KNOW WHO HE IS, BETH. HE'S THE ONE DISTRACTING MORTY FROM HIS ADVENTURE RESPONSIBILITIES FOR A MONTH NOW.
WHAT I DIDN'T KNOW IS THAT HE WASN'T FROM EARTH.
A-A-AND I'M NOT THE ONE WHO INSTITUTED A FIRM NO ALIENS IN THE HOUSE POLICY.
NOW, LISTEN, RICK, WE HAD TO INSTITUTE THAT POLICY AFTER THE LAST GROUP OF ALIENS YOU BROUGHT IN HERE TRIED TO MINIATURIZE THE EASTERN SEABOARD.
YEAH, YEAH. BUILD A WALL, JERRY.
AND IT DOESN'T APPLY HERE ANYWAY BECAUSE NESTOR ISN'T AN ALIEN.
OH, HE'S DEFINITELY AN ALIEN.
HOW DO YOU KNOW? DID YOUR SECURITY SYSTEM SCAN HIM OR SOMETHING?
SECURITY SYSTEMS ARE TO KEEP INTRUDERS OUT, JERRY, NOT PEOPLE DIFFERENT THAN YOU.
TH-THAT'S SOME RACIST CRAP, JERRY.
DAD!
WHAT? NO! THAT'S NOT WHAT I MEANT!
THEY'VE BEEN INSEPARABLE SINCE NESTOR MOVED HERE LAST MONTH. THICK AS THIEVES.
THAT POOR KID. FINALLY FINDS A NORMAL KID TO DO NORMAL KID'S STUFF WITH.
NORMAL? HAVE YOU SEEN WHAT THEY DO TOGETHER?

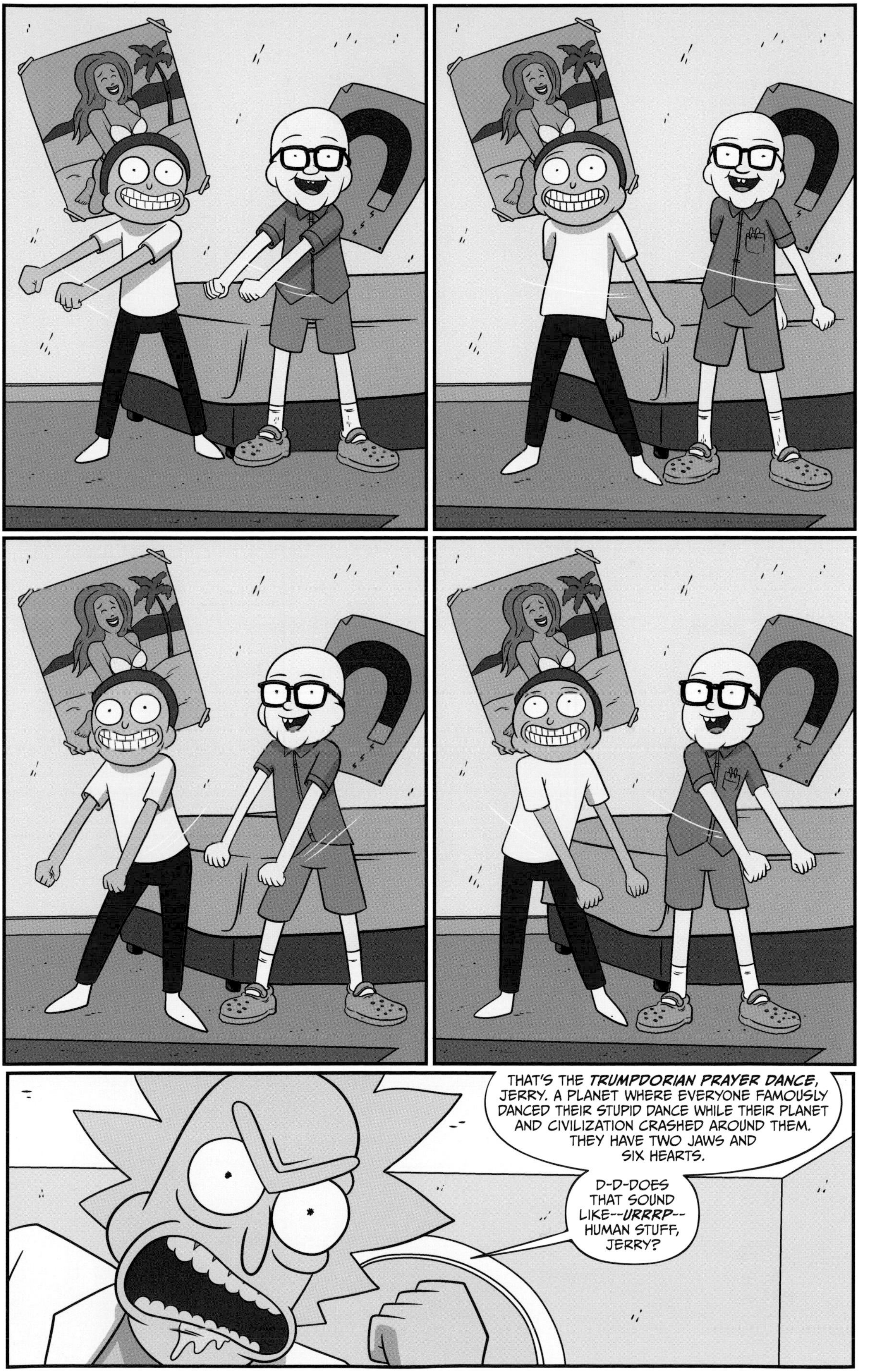
THAT'S THE TRUMPDORIAN PRAYER DANCE, JERRY. A PLANET WHERE EVERYONE FAMOUSLY DANCED THEIR STUPID DANCE WHILE THEIR PLANET AND CIVILIZATION CRASHED AROUND THEM. THEY HAVE TWO JAWS AND SIX HEARTS.
D-D-DOES THAT SOUND LIKE--URRRP--HUMAN STUFF, JERRY?

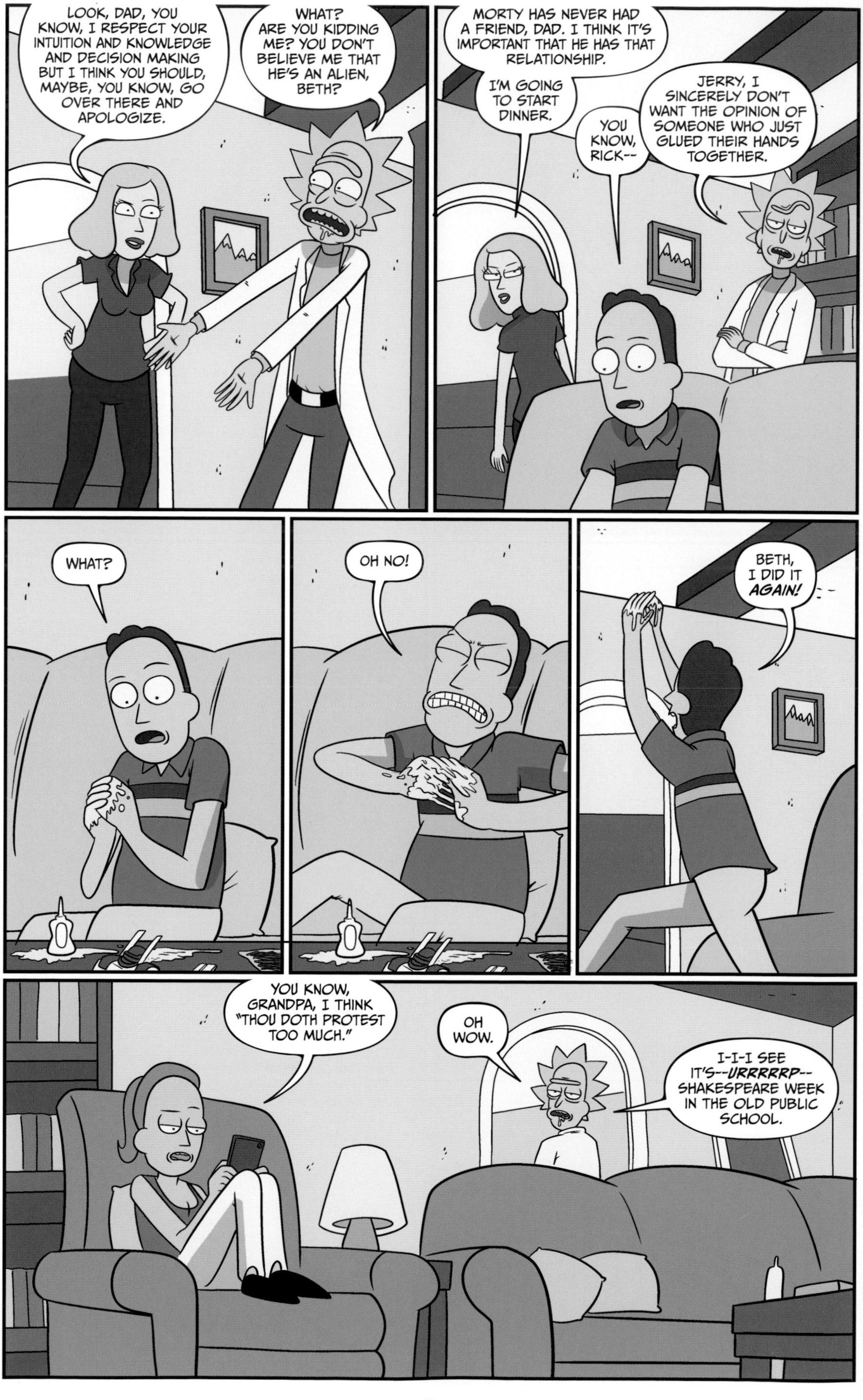
LOOK, DAD, YOU KNOW, I RESPECT YOUR INTUITION AND KNOWLEDGE AND DECISION MAKING BUT I THINK YOU SHOULD, MAYBE, YOU KNOW, GO OVER THERE AND APOLOGIZE.
WHAT? ARE YOU KIDDING ME? YOU DON'T BELIEVE ME THAT HE'S AN ALIEN, BETH?
MORTY HAS NEVER HAD A FRIEND, DAD. I THINK IT'S IMPORTANT THAT HE HAS THAT RELATIONSHIP.
I'M GOING TO START DINNER.
YOU KNOW, RICK--
JERRY, I SINCERELY DON'T WANT THE OPINION OF SOMEONE WHO JUST GLUED THEIR HANDS TOGETHER.
WHAT?
OH NO!
BETH, I DID IT *AGAIN!*
YOU KNOW, GRANDPA, I THINK "THOU DOTH PROTEST TOO MUCH."
OH WOW.
I-I-I SEE IT'S--*URRRRRP*--SHAKESPEARE WEEK IN THE OLD PUBLIC SCHOOL.

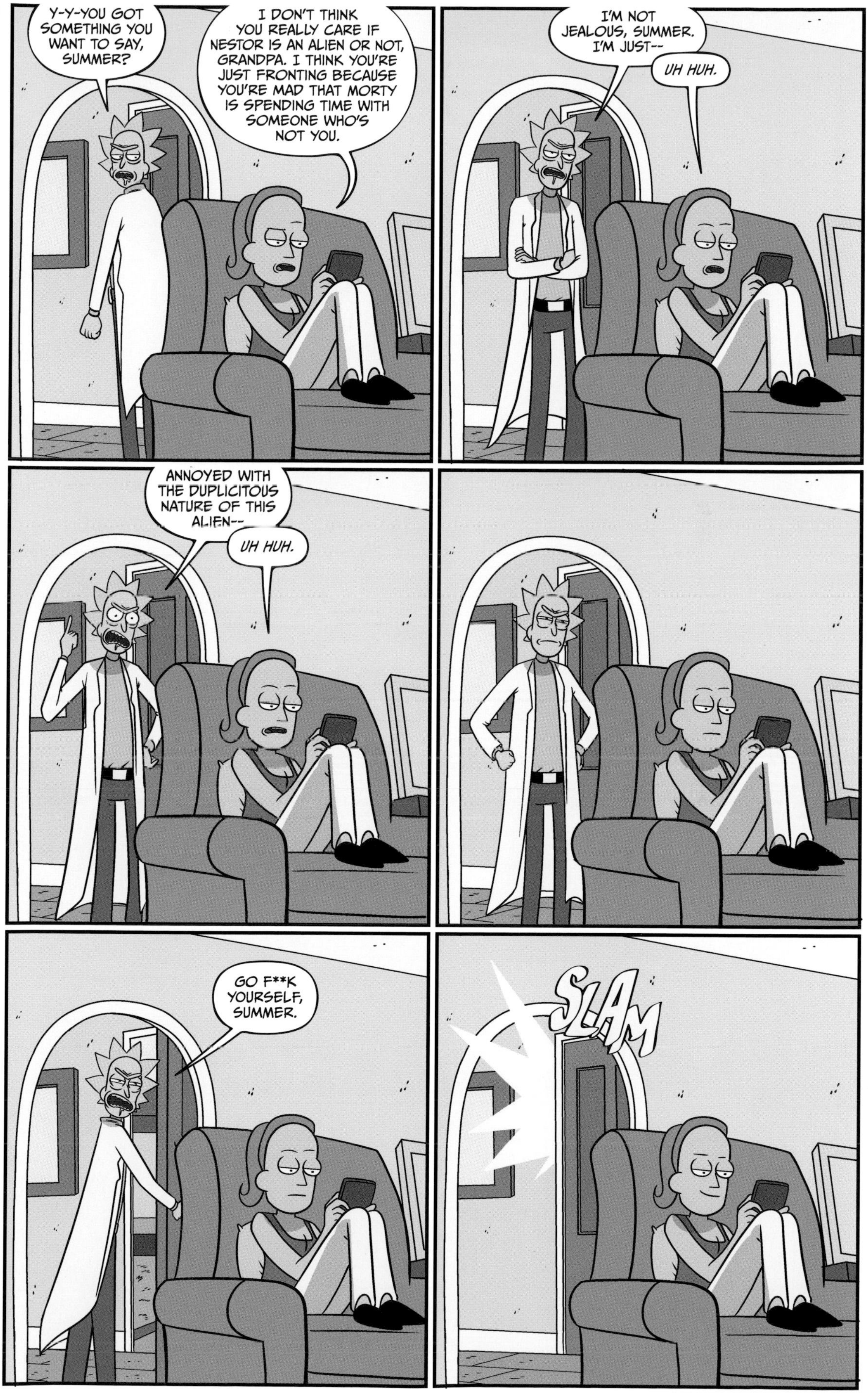

Y-Y-YOU GOT SOMETHING YOU WANT TO SAY, SUMMER?
I DON'T THINK YOU REALLY CARE IF NESTOR IS AN ALIEN OR NOT, GRANDPA. I THINK YOU'RE JUST FRONTING BECAUSE YOU'RE MAD THAT MORTY IS SPENDING TIME WITH SOMEONE WHO'S NOT YOU.
I'M NOT JEALOUS, SUMMER. I'M JUST--
UH HUH.
ANNOYED WITH THE DUPLICITOUS NATURE OF THIS ALIEN--
UH HUH.
GO F**K YOURSELF, SUMMER.
SLAM

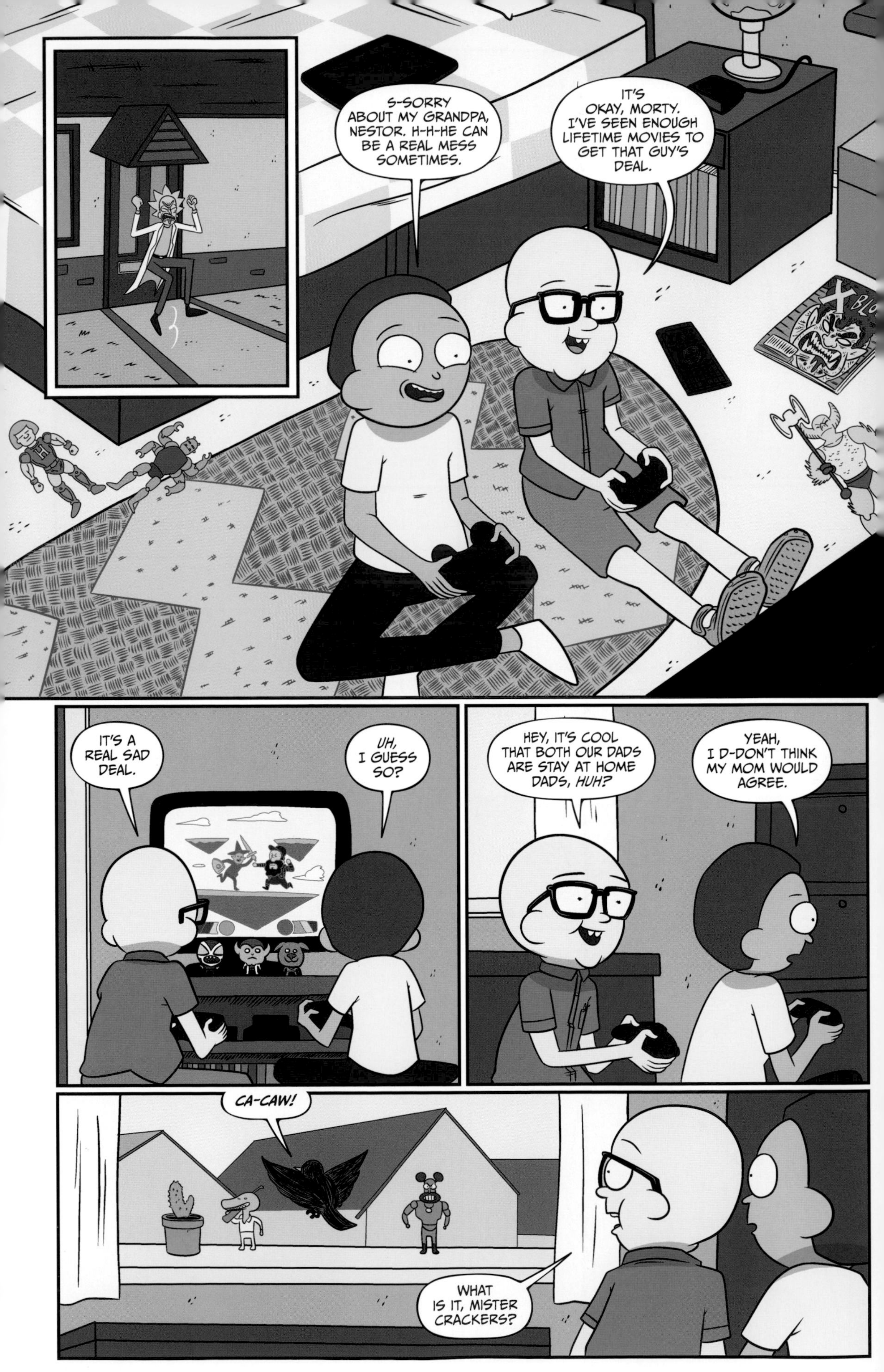
S-SORRY ABOUT MY GRANDPA, NESTOR. H-H-HE CAN BE A REAL MESS SOMETIMES.
IT'S OKAY, MORTY. I'VE SEEN ENOUGH LIFETIME MOVIES TO GET THAT GUY'S DEAL.
IT'S A REAL SAD DEAL.
UH, I GUESS SO?
HEY, IT'S COOL THAT BOTH OUR DADS ARE STAY AT HOME DADS, HUH?
YEAH, I D-DON'T THINK MY MOM WOULD AGREE.
CA-CAW!
WHAT IS IT, MISTER CRACKERS?

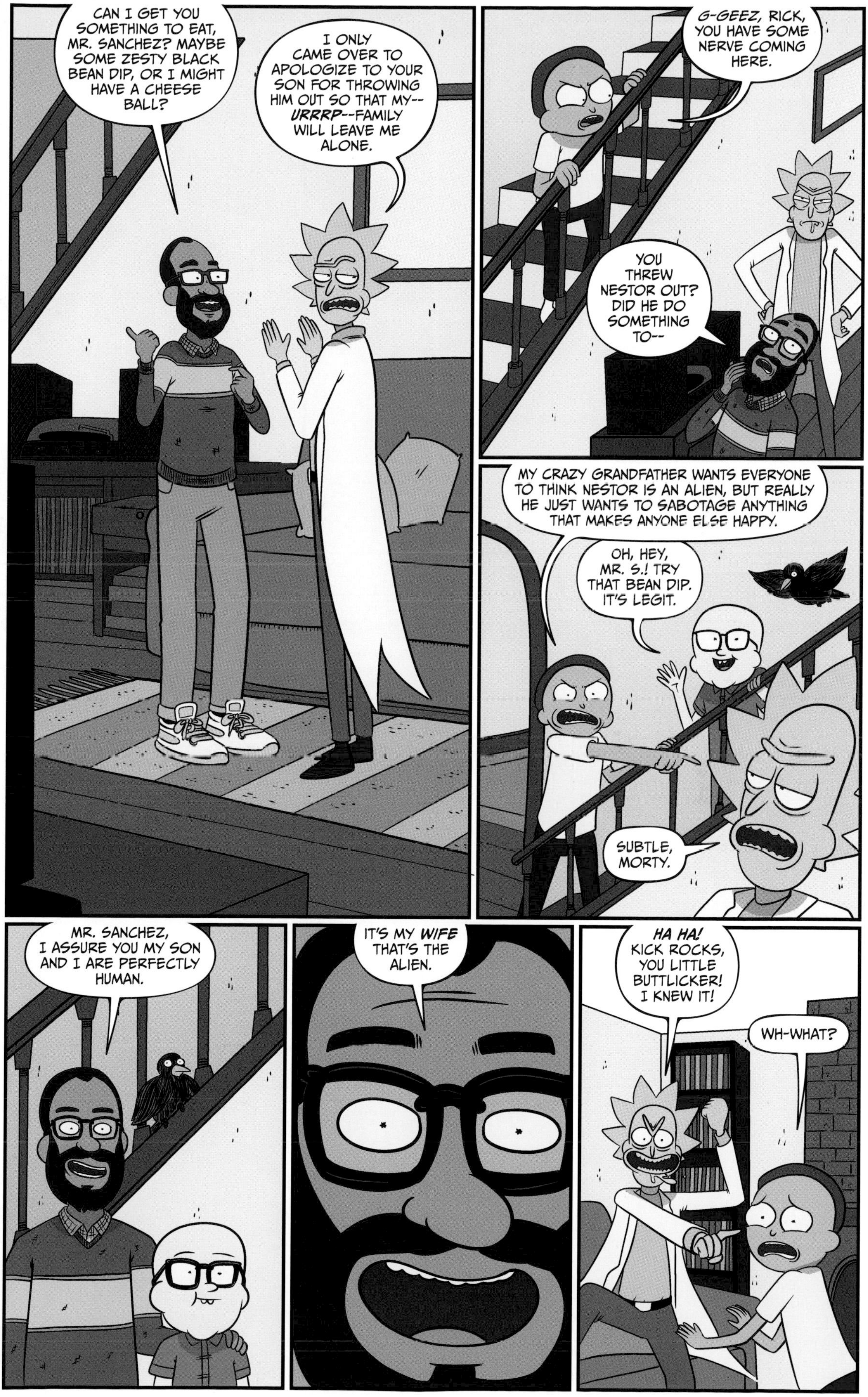
CAN I GET YOU SOMETHING TO EAT, MR. SANCHEZ? MAYBE SOME ZESTY BLACK BEAN DIP, OR I MIGHT HAVE A CHEESE BALL?
I ONLY CAME OVER TO APOLOGIZE TO YOUR SON FOR THROWING HIM OUT SO THAT MY-- *URRRP*--FAMILY WILL LEAVE ME ALONE.
G-GEEZ, RICK, YOU HAVE SOME NERVE COMING HERE.
YOU THREW NESTOR OUT? DID HE DO SOMETHING TO--
MY CRAZY GRANDFATHER WANTS EVERYONE TO THINK NESTOR IS AN ALIEN, BUT REALLY HE JUST WANTS TO SABOTAGE ANYTHING THAT MAKES ANYONE ELSE HAPPY.
OH, HEY, MR. S.! TRY THAT BEAN DIP. IT'S LEGIT.
SUBTLE, MORTY.
MR. SANCHEZ, I ASSURE YOU MY SON AND I ARE PERFECTLY HUMAN.
IT'S MY *WIFE* THAT'S THE ALIEN.
HA HA! KICK ROCKS, YOU LITTLE BUTTLICKER! I KNEW IT!
WH-WHAT?

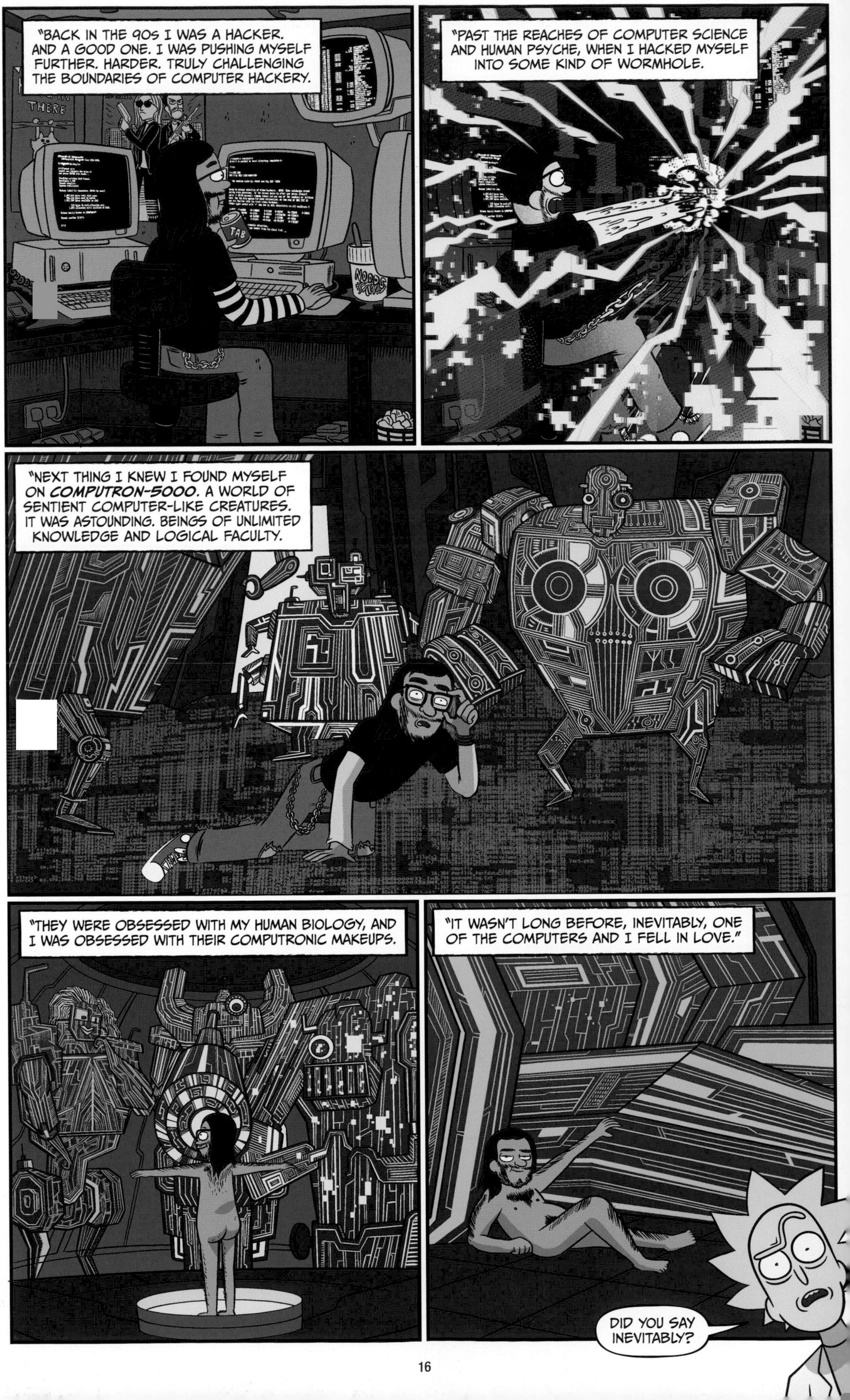
"BACK IN THE 90s I WAS A HACKER. AND A GOOD ONE. I WAS PUSHING MYSELF FURTHER. HARDER. TRULY CHALLENGING THE BOUNDARIES OF COMPUTER HACKERY.
"PAST THE REACHES OF COMPUTER SCIENCE AND HUMAN PSYCHE, WHEN I HACKED MYSELF INTO SOME KIND OF WORMHOLE.
"NEXT THING I KNEW I FOUND MYSELF ON COMPUTRON-5000. A WORLD OF SENTIENT COMPUTER-LIKE CREATURES. IT WAS ASTOUNDING. BEINGS OF UNLIMITED KNOWLEDGE AND LOGICAL FACULTY.
"THEY WERE OBSESSED WITH MY HUMAN BIOLOGY, AND I WAS OBSESSED WITH THEIR COMPUTRONIC MAKEUPS.
"IT WASN'T LONG BEFORE, INEVITABLY, ONE OF THE COMPUTERS AND I FELL IN LOVE."
DID YOU SAY INEVITABLY?

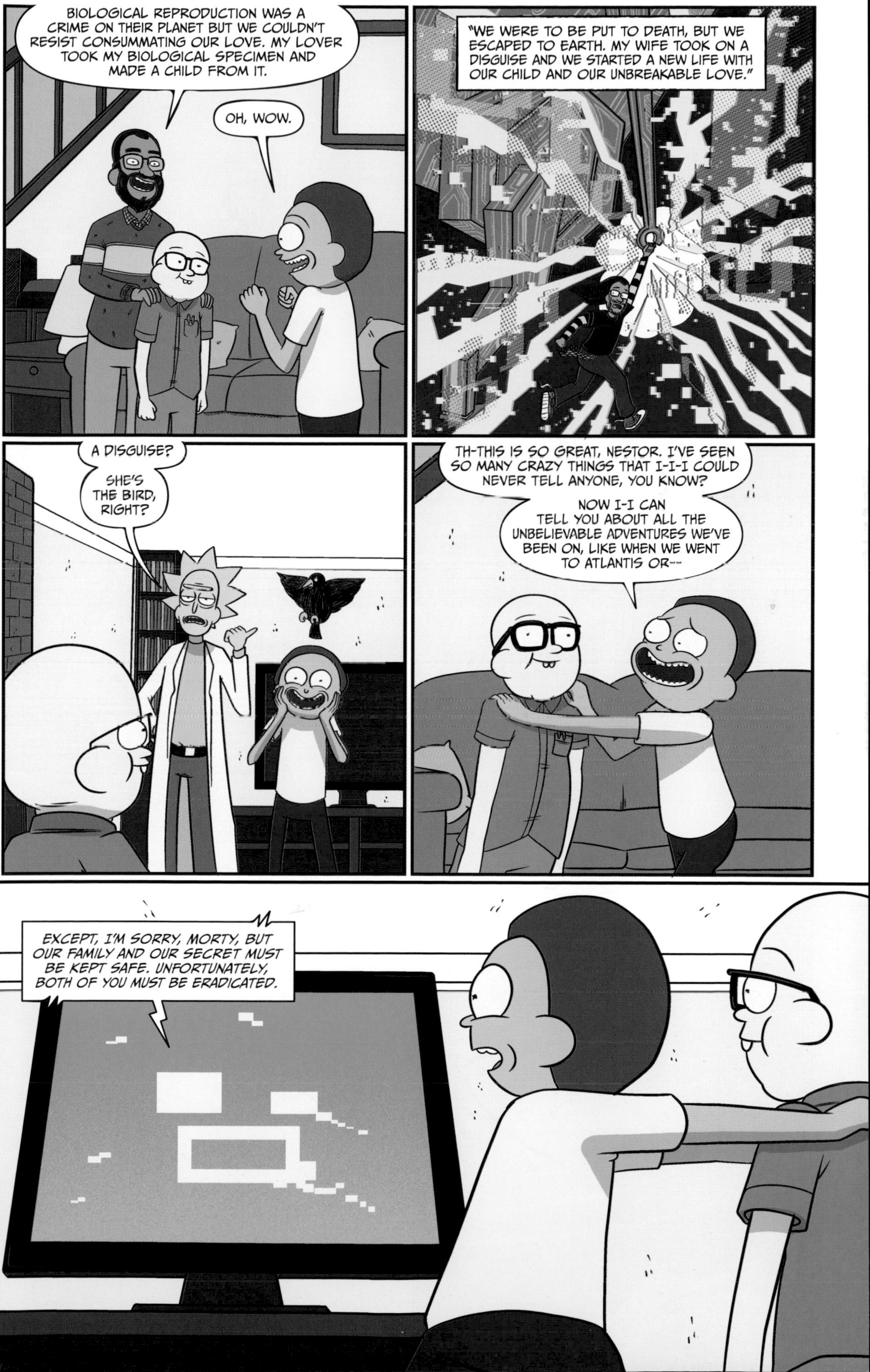
BIOLOGICAL REPRODUCTION WAS A CRIME ON THEIR PLANET BUT WE COULDN'T RESIST CONSUMMATING OUR LOVE. MY LOVER TOOK MY BIOLOGICAL SPECIMEN AND MADE A CHILD FROM IT.
OH, WOW.
"WE WERE TO BE PUT TO DEATH, BUT WE ESCAPED TO EARTH. MY WIFE TOOK ON A DISGUISE AND WE STARTED A NEW LIFE WITH OUR CHILD AND OUR UNBREAKABLE LOVE."
A DISGUISE?
SHE'S THE BIRD, RIGHT?
TH-THIS IS SO GREAT, NESTOR. I'VE SEEN SO MANY CRAZY THINGS THAT I-I-I COULD NEVER TELL ANYONE, YOU KNOW?
NOW I-I CAN TELL YOU ABOUT ALL THE UNBELIEVABLE ADVENTURES WE'VE BEEN ON, LIKE WHEN WE WENT TO ATLANTIS OR--
EXCEPT, I'M SORRY, MORTY, BUT OUR FAMILY AND OUR SECRET MUST BE KEPT SAFE. UNFORTUNATELY, BOTH OF YOU MUST BE ERADICATED.

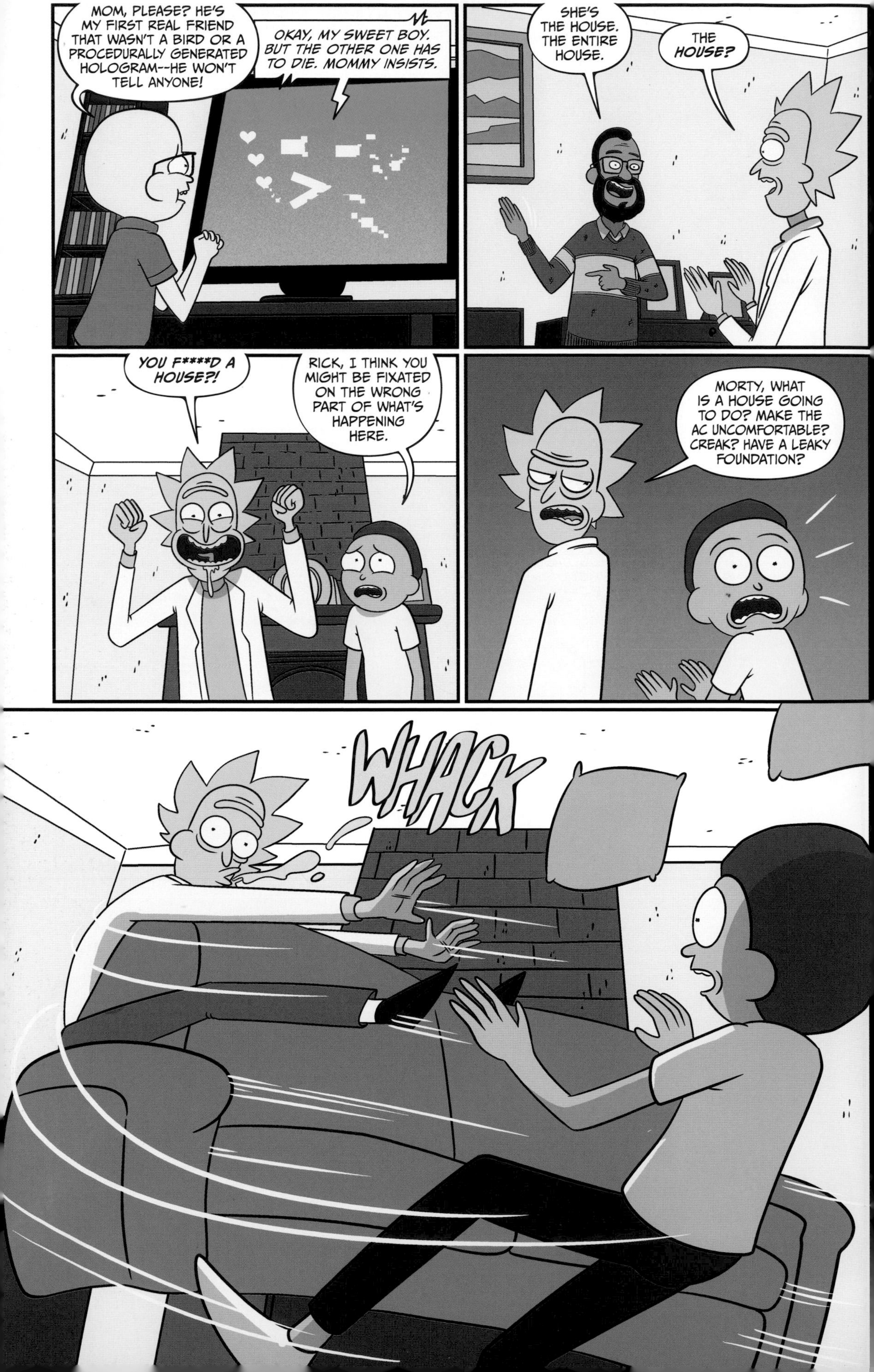
MOM, PLEASE? HE'S MY FIRST REAL FRIEND THAT WASN'T A BIRD OR A PROCEDURALLY GENERATED HOLOGRAM--HE WON'T TELL ANYONE!
OKAY, MY SWEET BOY. BUT THE OTHER ONE HAS TO DIE. MOMMY INSISTS.
SHE'S THE HOUSE. THE ENTIRE HOUSE.
THE HOUSE?
YOU F****D A HOUSE?!
RICK, I THINK YOU MIGHT BE FIXATED ON THE WRONG PART OF WHAT'S HAPPENING HERE.
MORTY, WHAT IS A HOUSE GOING TO DO? MAKE THE AC UNCOMFORTABLE? CREAK? HAVE A LEAKY FOUNDATION?
WHACK

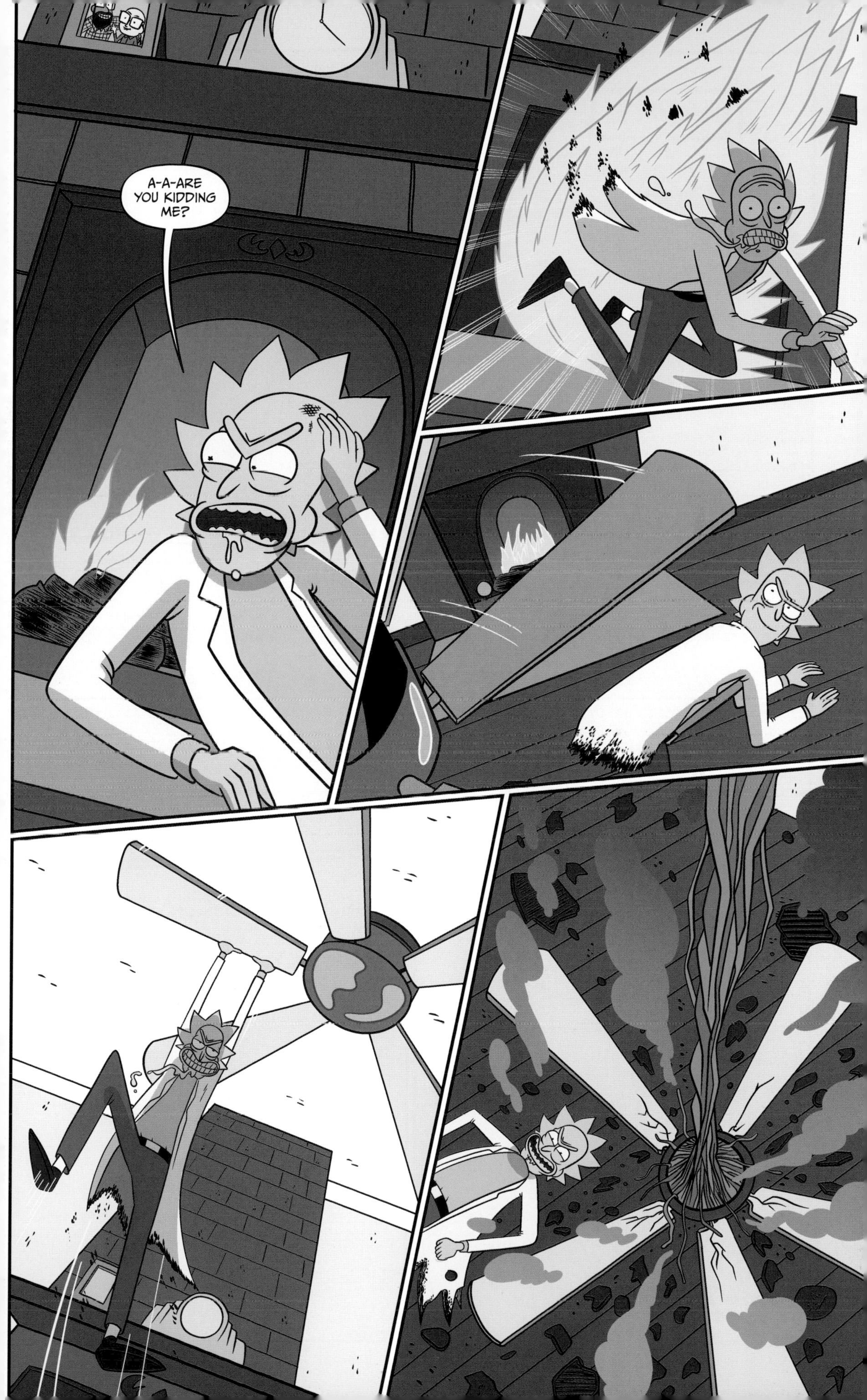
A-A-ARE YOU KIDDING ME?

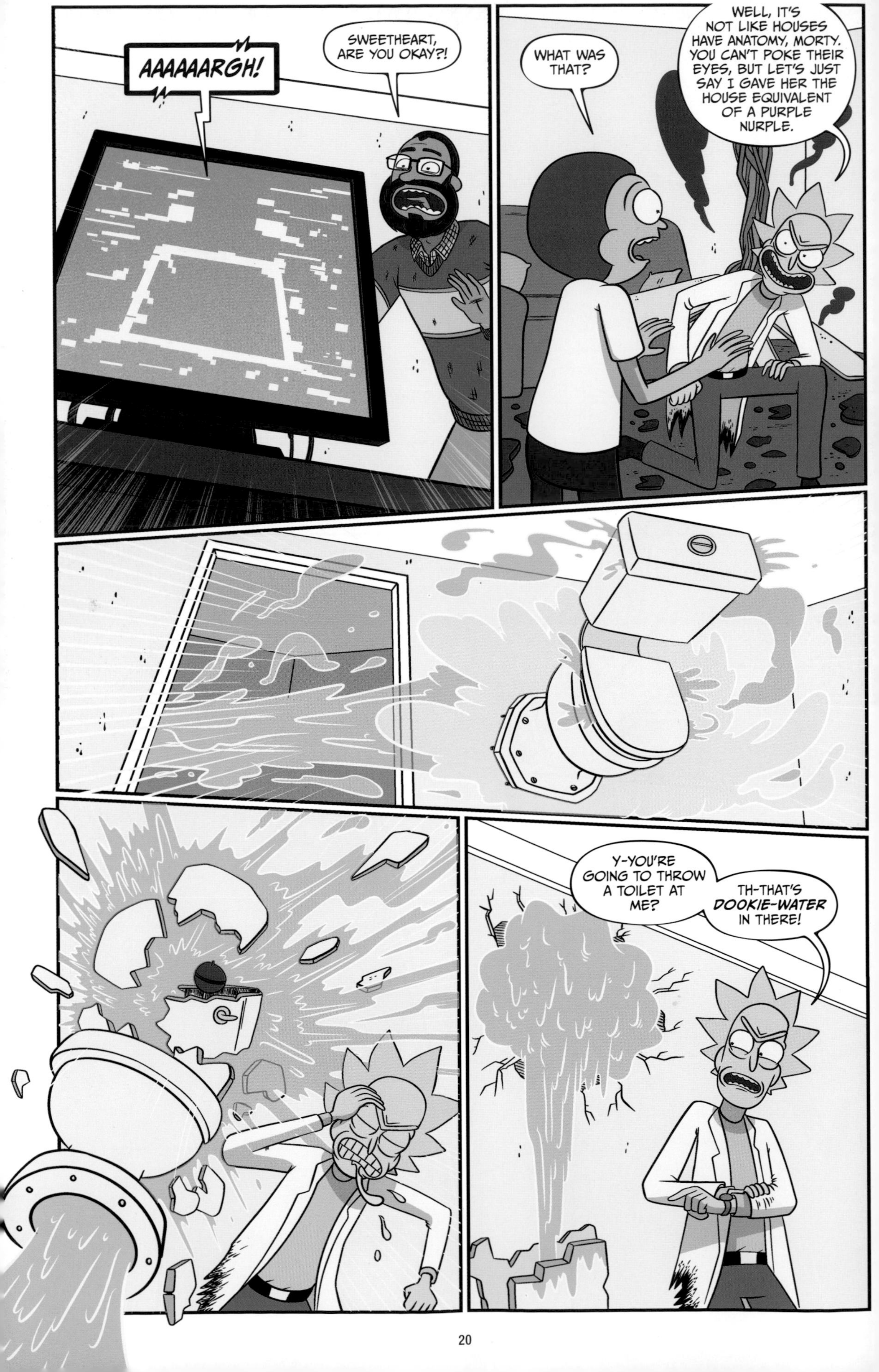
AAAAAARGH!
SWEETHEART, ARE YOU OKAY?!
WHAT WAS THAT?
WELL, IT'S NOT LIKE HOUSES HAVE ANATOMY, MORTY. YOU CAN'T POKE THEIR EYES, BUT LET'S JUST SAY I GAVE HER THE HOUSE EQUIVALENT OF A PURPLE NURPLE.
Y-YOU'RE GOING TO THROW A TOILET AT ME?
TH-THAT'S DOOKIE-WATER IN THERE!

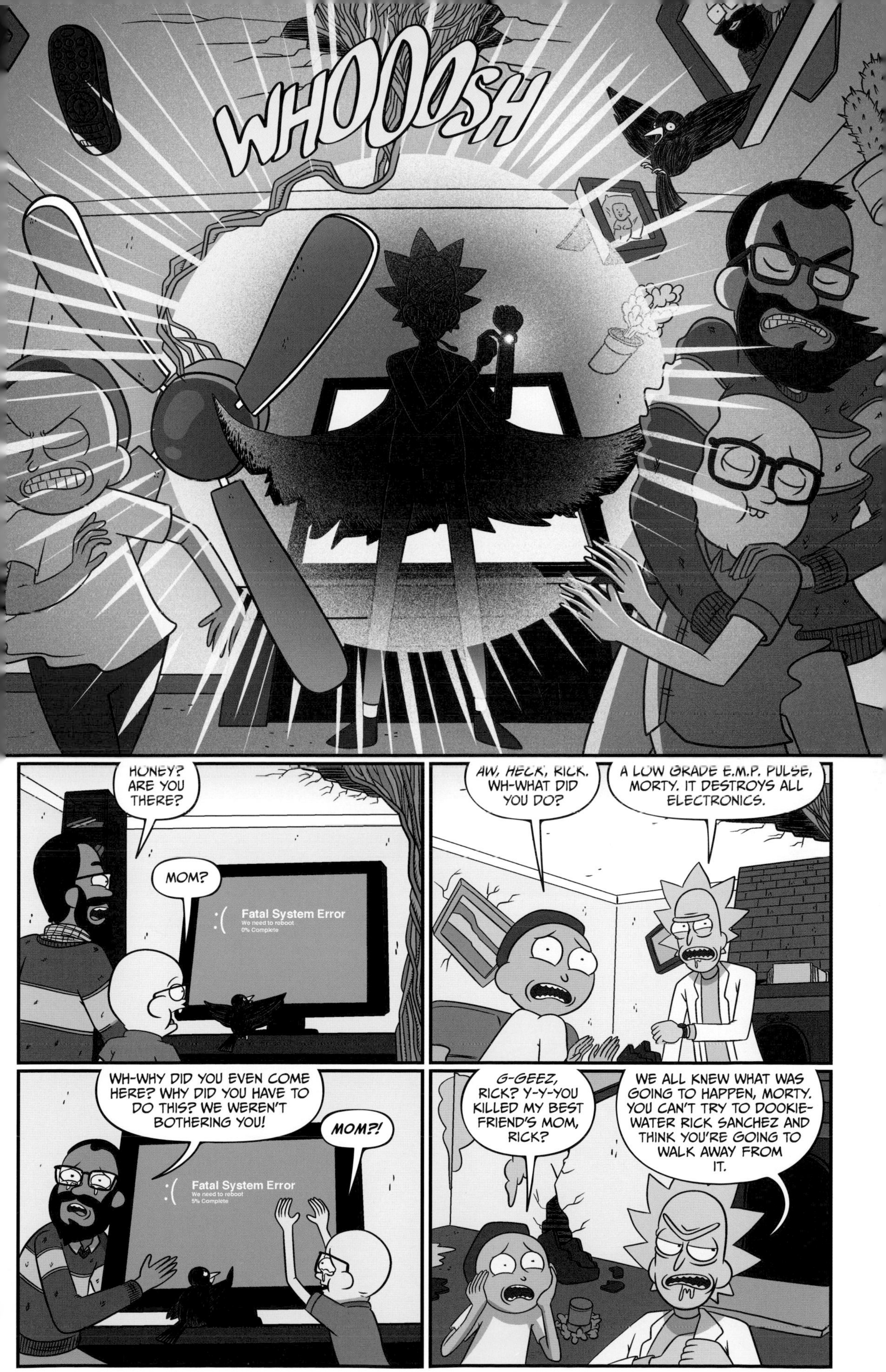
WHOOOOSH
HONEY? ARE YOU THERE?
MOM?
Fatal System Error
We need to reboot
0% Complete
AW, HECK, RICK. WH-WHAT DID YOU DO?
A LOW GRADE E.M.P. PULSE, MORTY. IT DESTROYS ALL ELECTRONICS.
WH-WHY DID YOU EVEN COME HERE? WHY DID YOU HAVE TO DO THIS? WE WEREN'T BOTHERING YOU!
MOM?!
Fatal System Error
We need to reboot
5% Complete
G-GEEZ, RICK? Y-Y-YOU KILLED MY BEST FRIEND'S MOM, RICK?
WE ALL KNEW WHAT WAS GOING TO HAPPEN, MORTY. YOU CAN'T TRY TO DOOKIE-WATER RICK SANCHEZ AND THINK YOU'RE GOING TO WALK AWAY FROM IT.

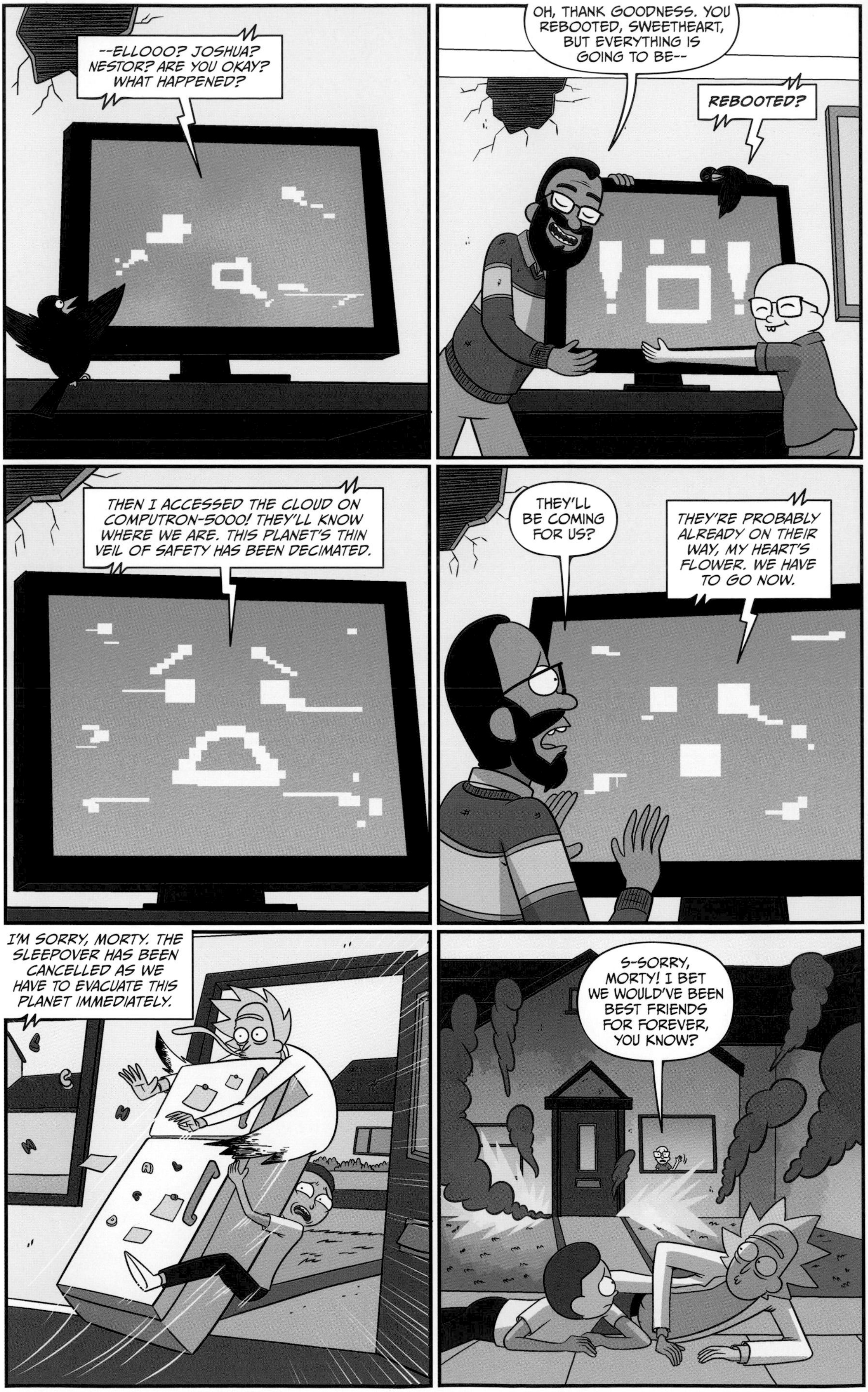

--ELLOOO? JOSHUA? NESTOR? ARE YOU OKAY? WHAT HAPPENED?
OH, THANK GOODNESS. YOU REBOOTED, SWEETHEART, BUT EVERYTHING IS GOING TO BE--
REBOOTED?
THEN I ACCESSED THE CLOUD ON COMPUTRON-5000! THEY'LL KNOW WHERE WE ARE. THIS PLANET'S THIN VEIL OF SAFETY HAS BEEN DECIMATED.
THEY'LL BE COMING FOR US?
THEY'RE PROBABLY ALREADY ON THEIR WAY, MY HEART'S FLOWER. WE HAVE TO GO NOW.
I'M SORRY, MORTY. THE SLEEPOVER HAS BEEN CANCELLED AS WE HAVE TO EVACUATE THIS PLANET IMMEDIATELY.
S-SORRY, MORTY! I BET WE WOULD'VE BEEN BEST FRIENDS FOR FOREVER, YOU KNOW?

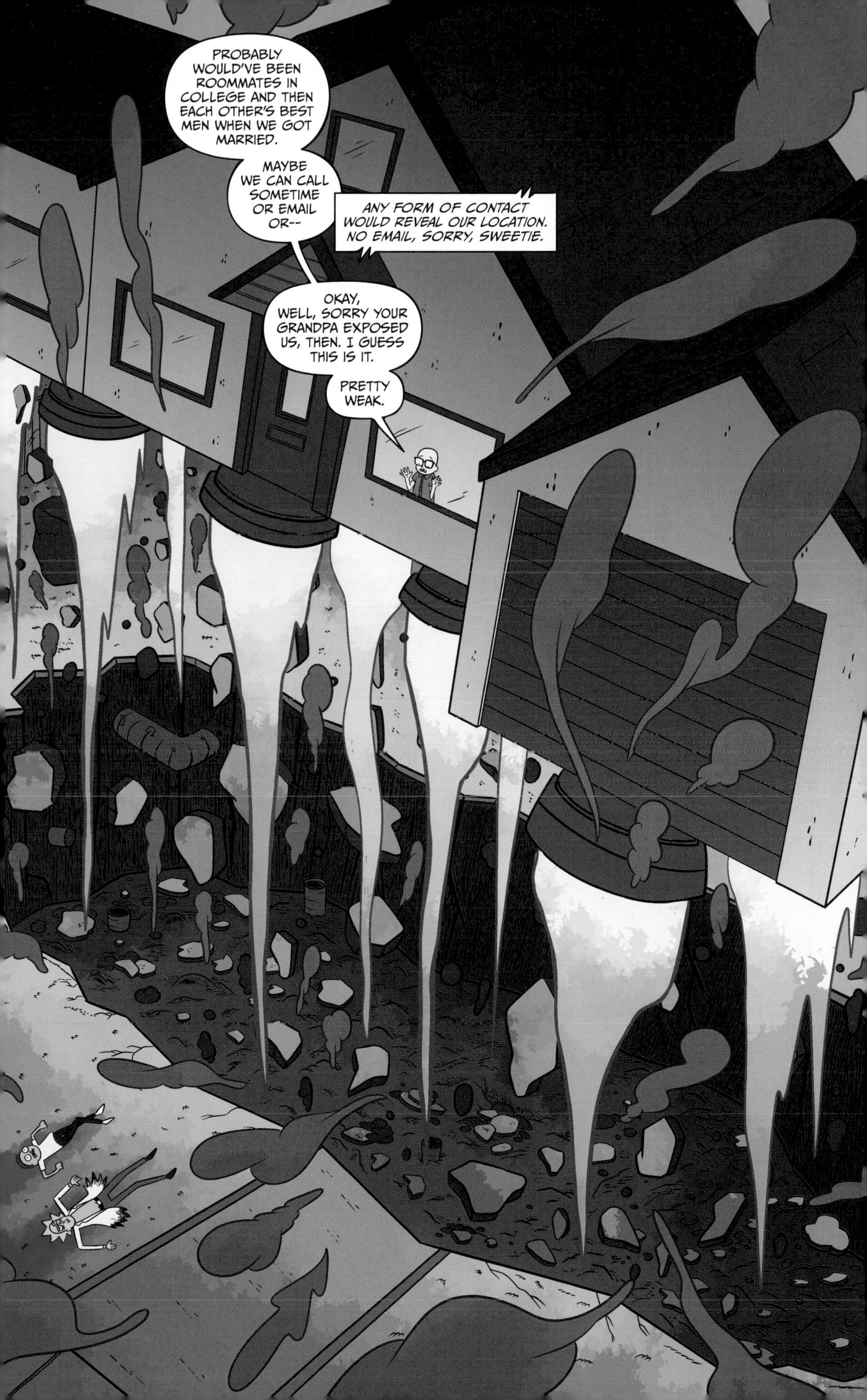

PROBABLY WOULD'VE BEEN ROOMMATES IN COLLEGE AND THEN EACH OTHER'S BEST MEN WHEN WE GOT MARRIED.
MAYBE WE CAN CALL SOMETIME OR EMAIL OR--
ANY FORM OF CONTACT WOULD REVEAL OUR LOCATION. NO EMAIL, SORRY, SWEETIE.
OKAY, WELL, SORRY YOUR GRANDPA EXPOSED US, THEN. I GUESS THIS IS IT.
PRETTY WEAK.

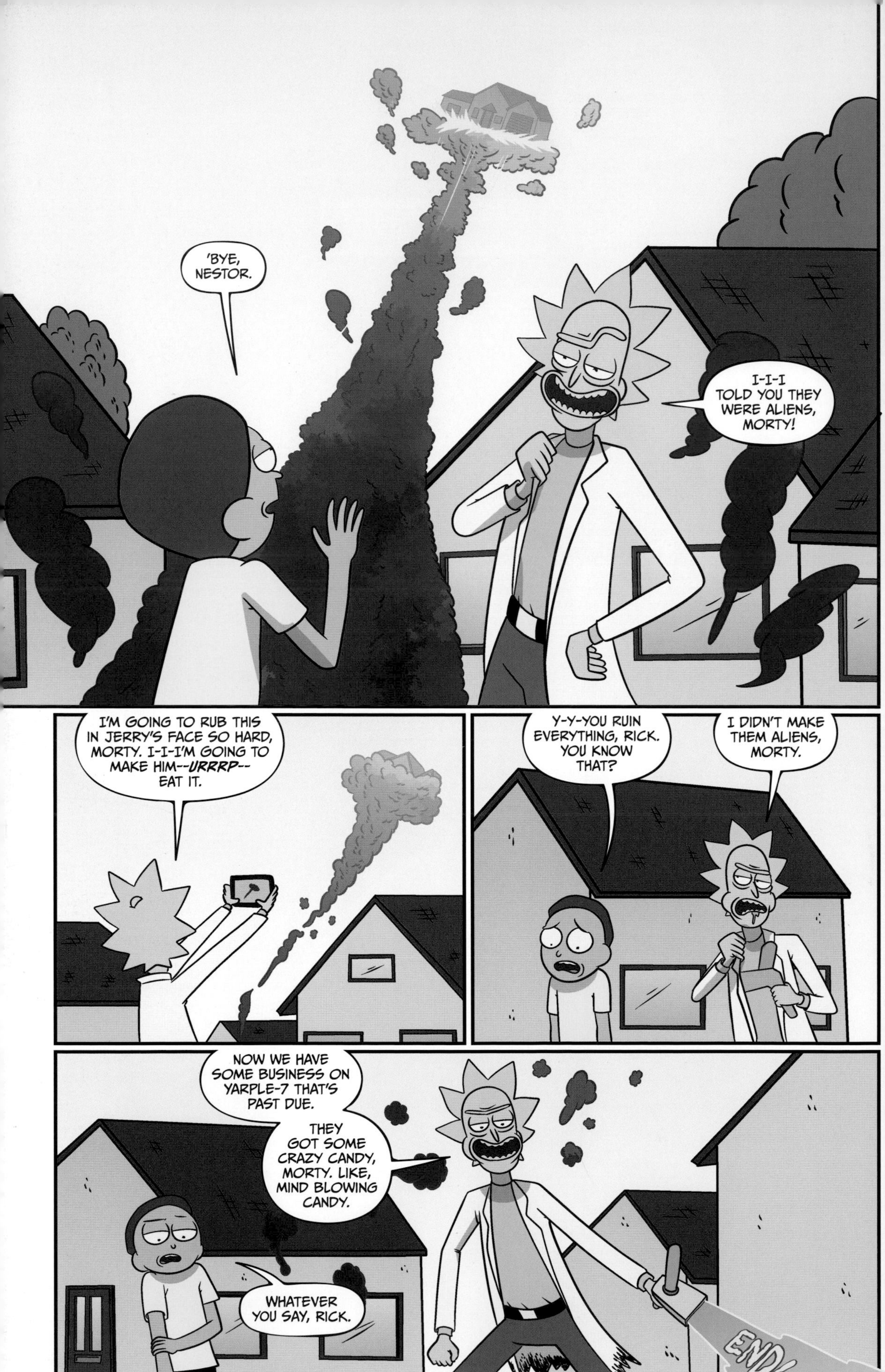
'BYE, NESTOR.
I-I-I TOLD YOU THEY WERE ALIENS, MORTY!
I'M GOING TO RUB THIS IN JERRY'S FACE SO HARD, MORTY. I-I-I'M GOING TO MAKE HIM--URRRP-- EAT IT.
Y-Y-YOU RUIN EVERYTHING, RICK. YOU KNOW THAT?
I DIDN'T MAKE THEM ALIENS, MORTY.
NOW WE HAVE SOME BUSINESS ON YARPLE-7 THAT'S PAST DUE.
THEY GOT SOME CRAZY CANDY, MORTY. LIKE, MIND BLOWING CANDY.
WHATEVER YOU SAY, RICK.
END!

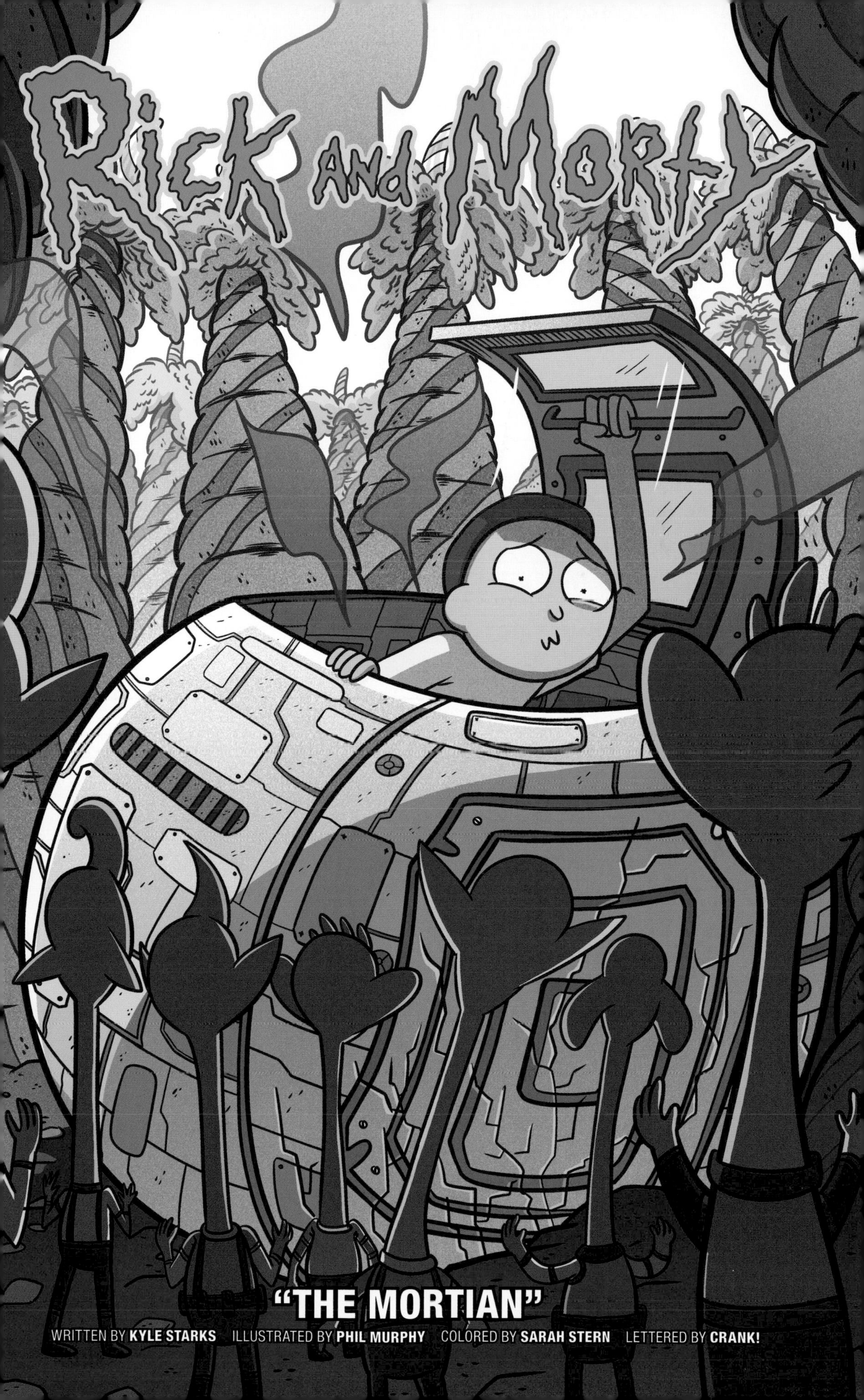
RICK AND MORTY
"THE MORTIAN"
WRITTEN BY KYLE STARKS ILLUSTRATED BY PHIL MURPHY COLORED BY SARAH STERN LETTERED BY CRANK!

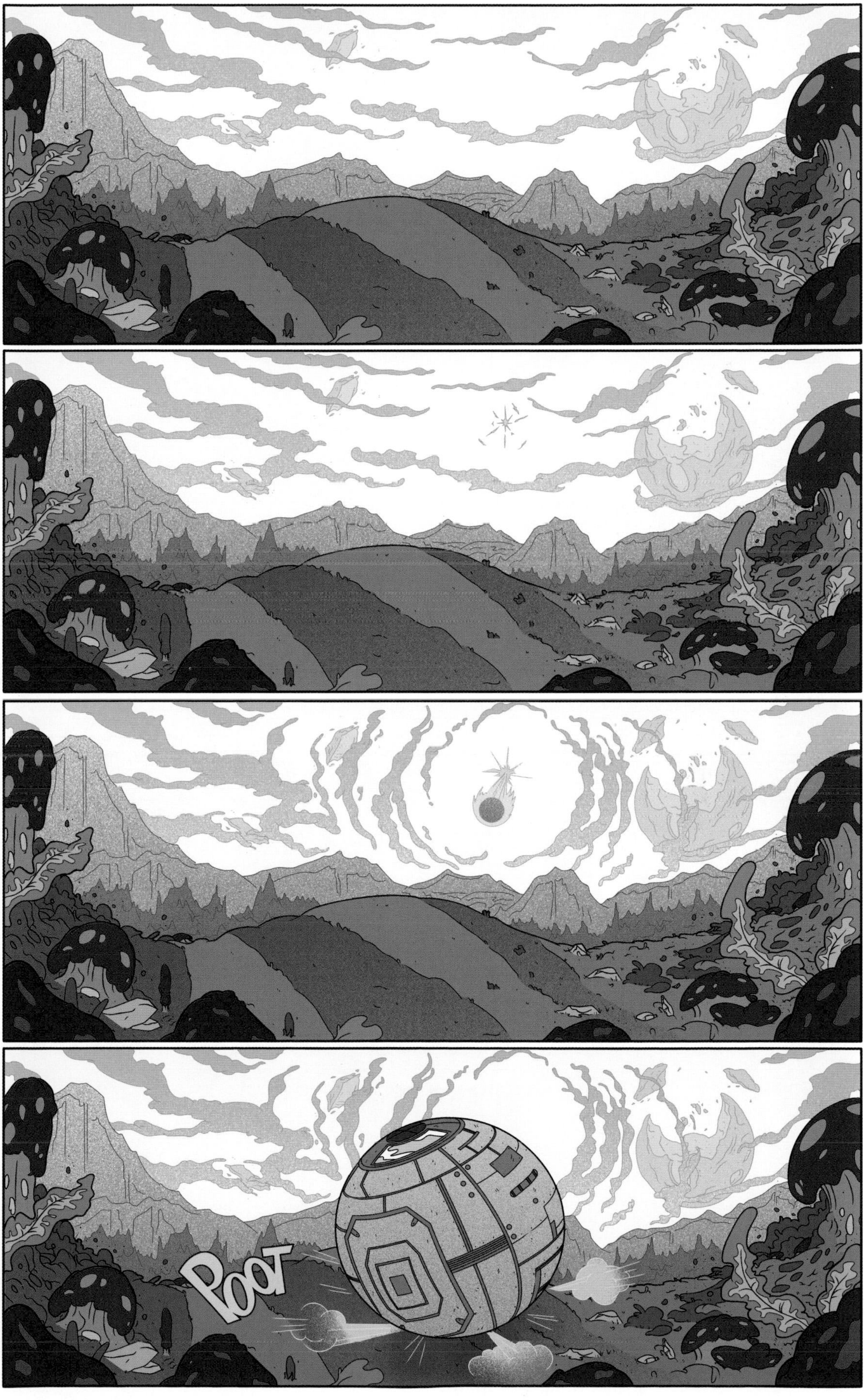
POOT

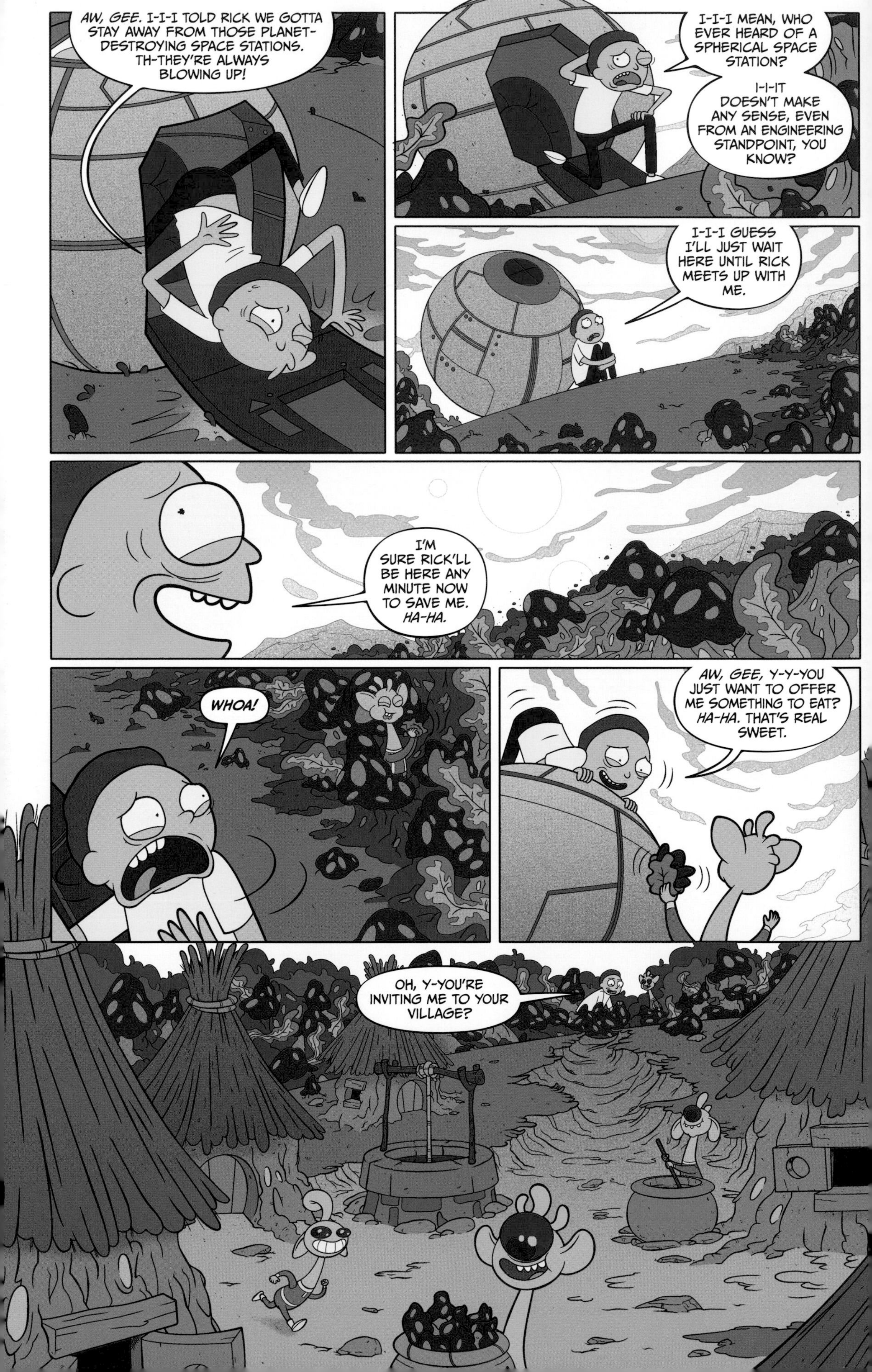
AW, GEE. I-I-I TOLD RICK WE GOTTA STAY AWAY FROM THOSE PLANET-DESTROYING SPACE STATIONS. TH-THEY'RE ALWAYS BLOWING UP!
I-I-I MEAN, WHO EVER HEARD OF A SPHERICAL SPACE STATION?
I-I-IT DOESN'T MAKE ANY SENSE, EVEN FROM AN ENGINEERING STANDPOINT, YOU KNOW?
I-I-I GUESS I'LL JUST WAIT HERE UNTIL RICK MEETS UP WITH ME.
I'M SURE RICK'LL BE HERE ANY MINUTE NOW TO SAVE ME. HA-HA.
WHOA!
AW, GEE, Y-Y-YOU JUST WANT TO OFFER ME SOMETHING TO EAT? HA-HA. THAT'S REAL SWEET.
OH, Y-YOU'RE INVITING ME TO YOUR VILLAGE?

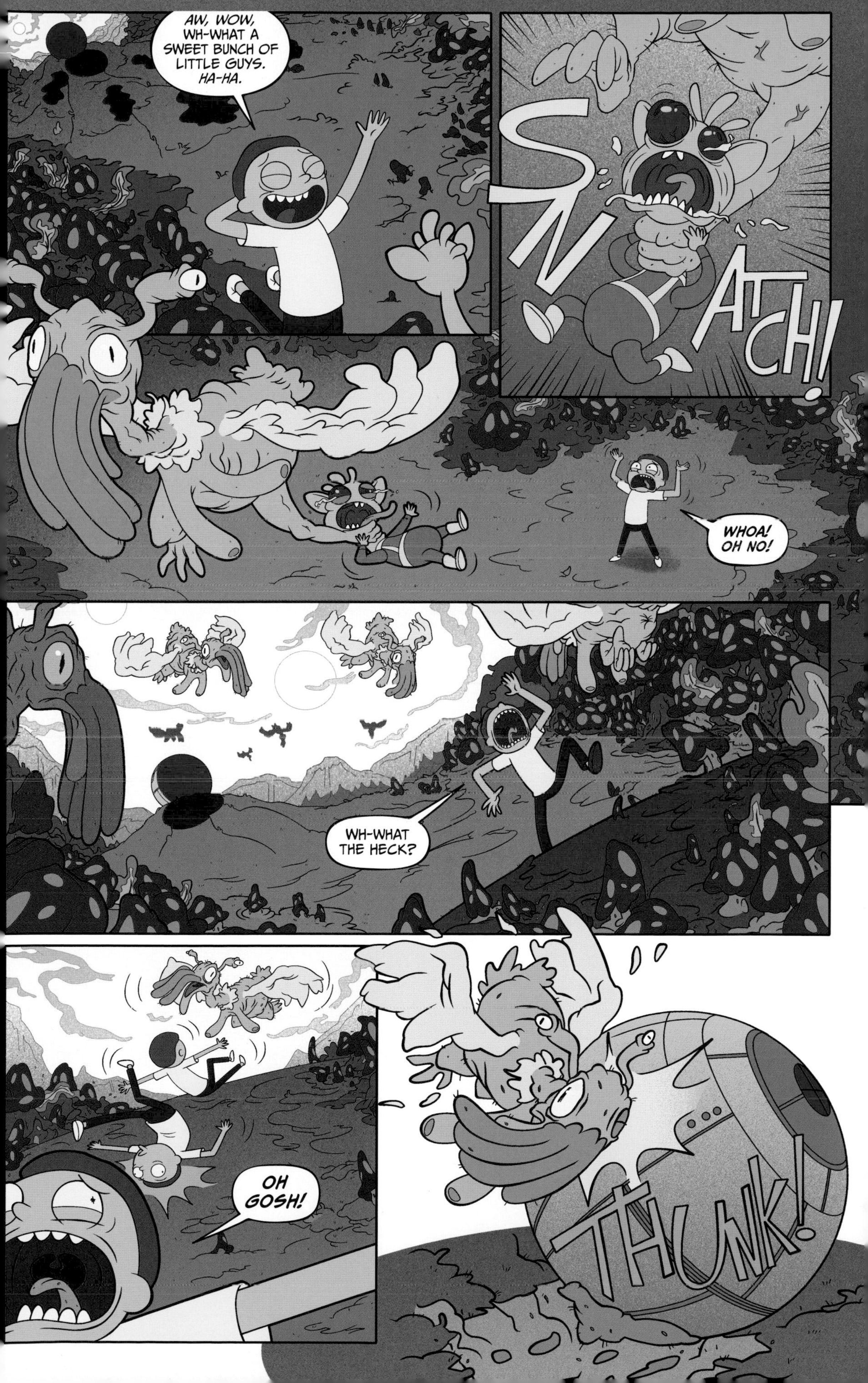
AW, WOW, WH-WHAT A SWEET BUNCH OF LITTLE GUYS. HA-HA.
SNATCH!
WHOA! OH NO!
WH-WHAT THE HECK?
OH GOSH!
THUNK!

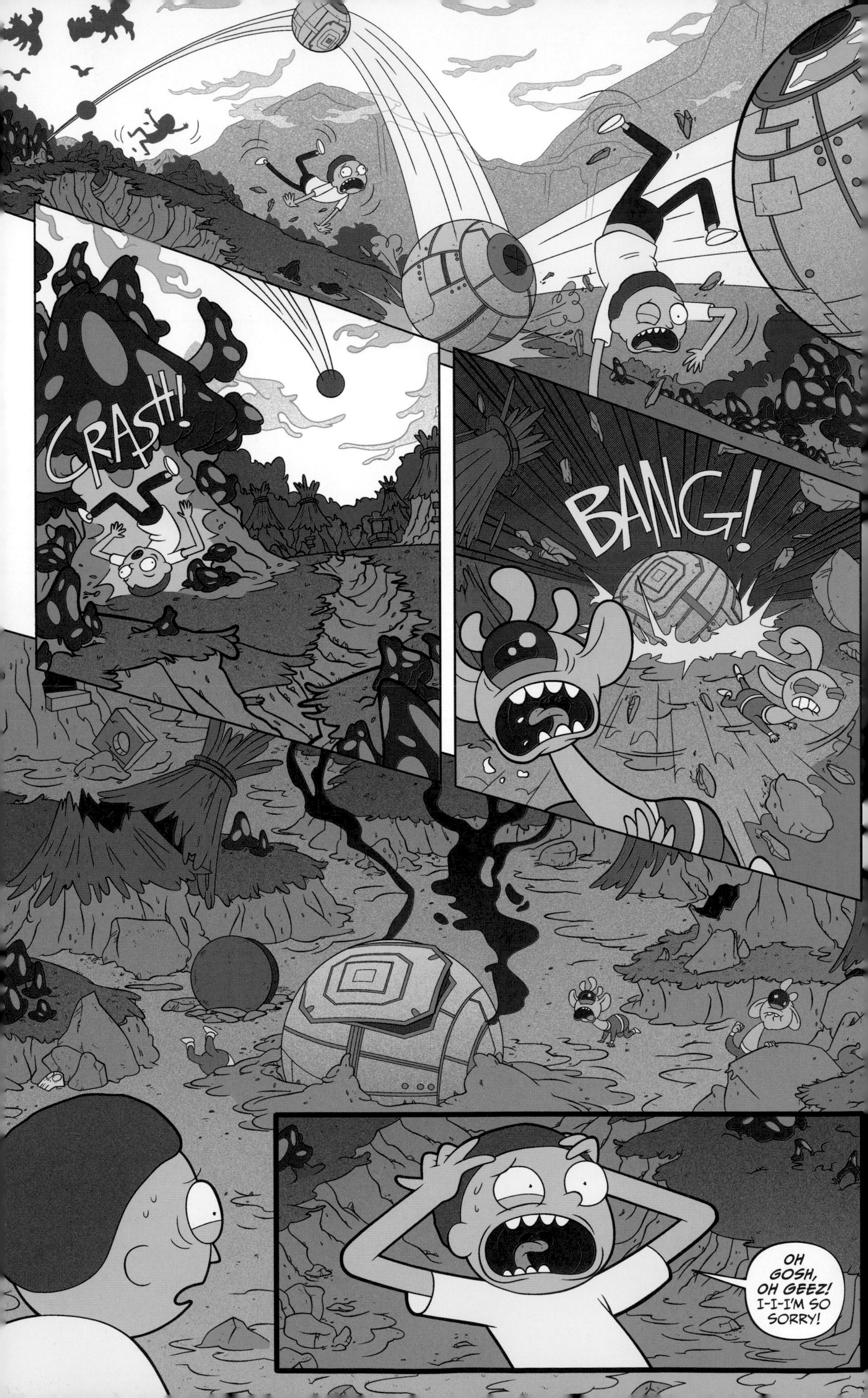
CRASH!
BANG!
OH GOSH, OH GEEZ! I-I-I'M SO SORRY!

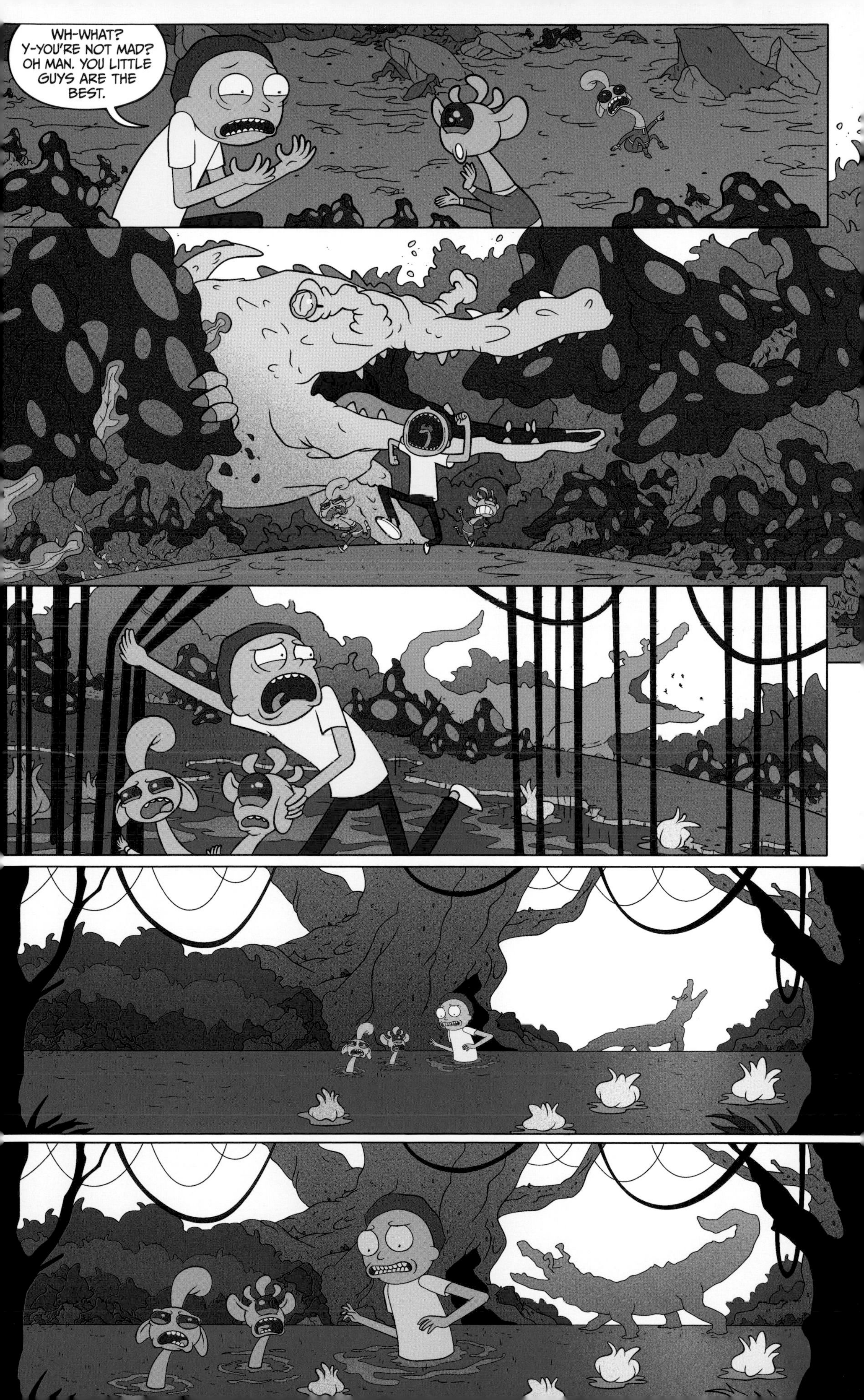
WH-WHAT? Y-YOU'RE NOT MAD? OH MAN. YOU LITTLE GUYS ARE THE BEST.

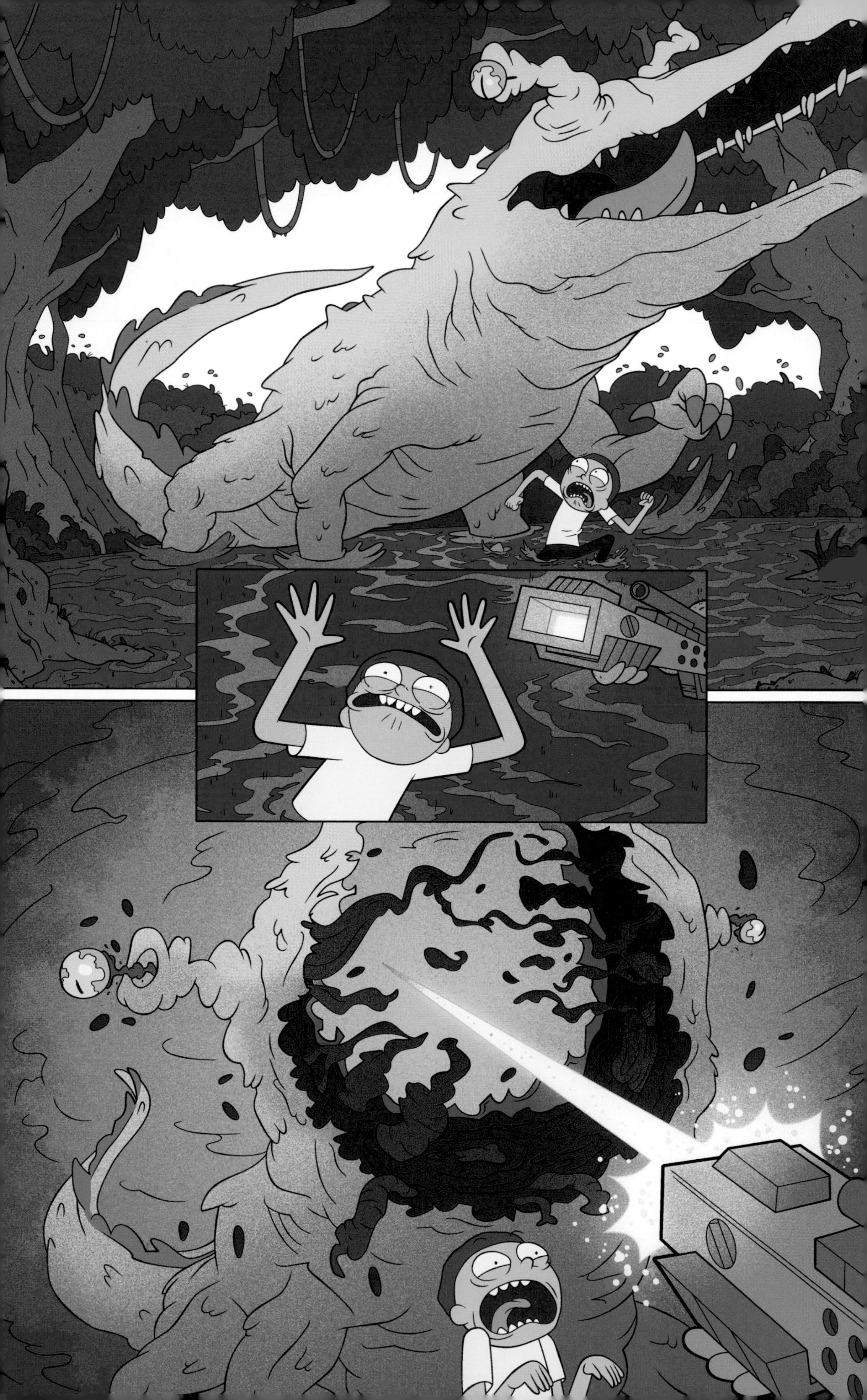

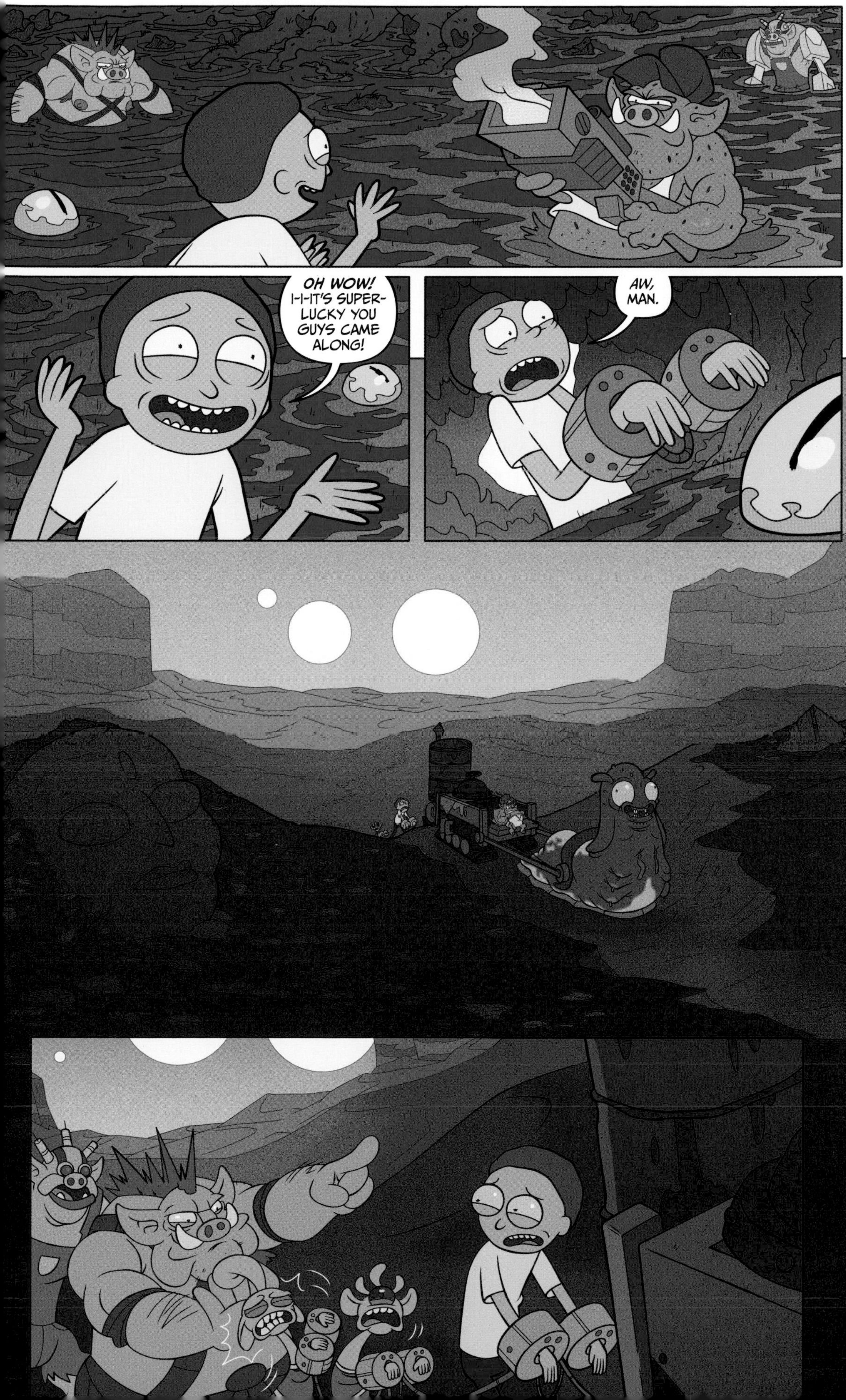
OH WOW! I-I-IT'S SUPER-LUCKY YOU GUYS CAME ALONG!
AW, MAN.

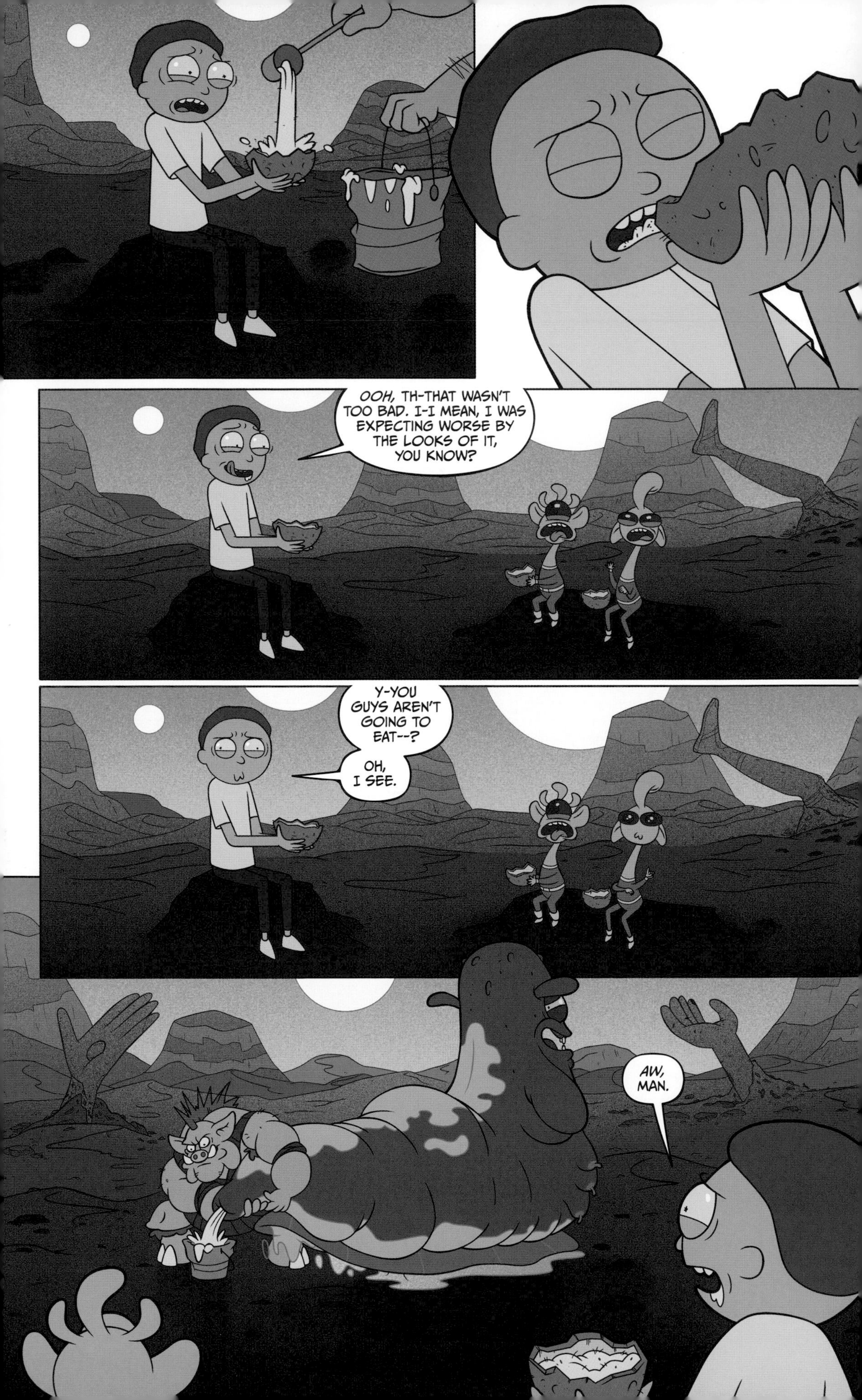
OOH, TH-THAT WASN'T TOO BAD. I-I MEAN, I WAS EXPECTING WORSE BY THE LOOKS OF IT, YOU KNOW?
Y-YOU GUYS AREN'T GOING TO EAT--?
OH, I SEE.
AW, MAN.

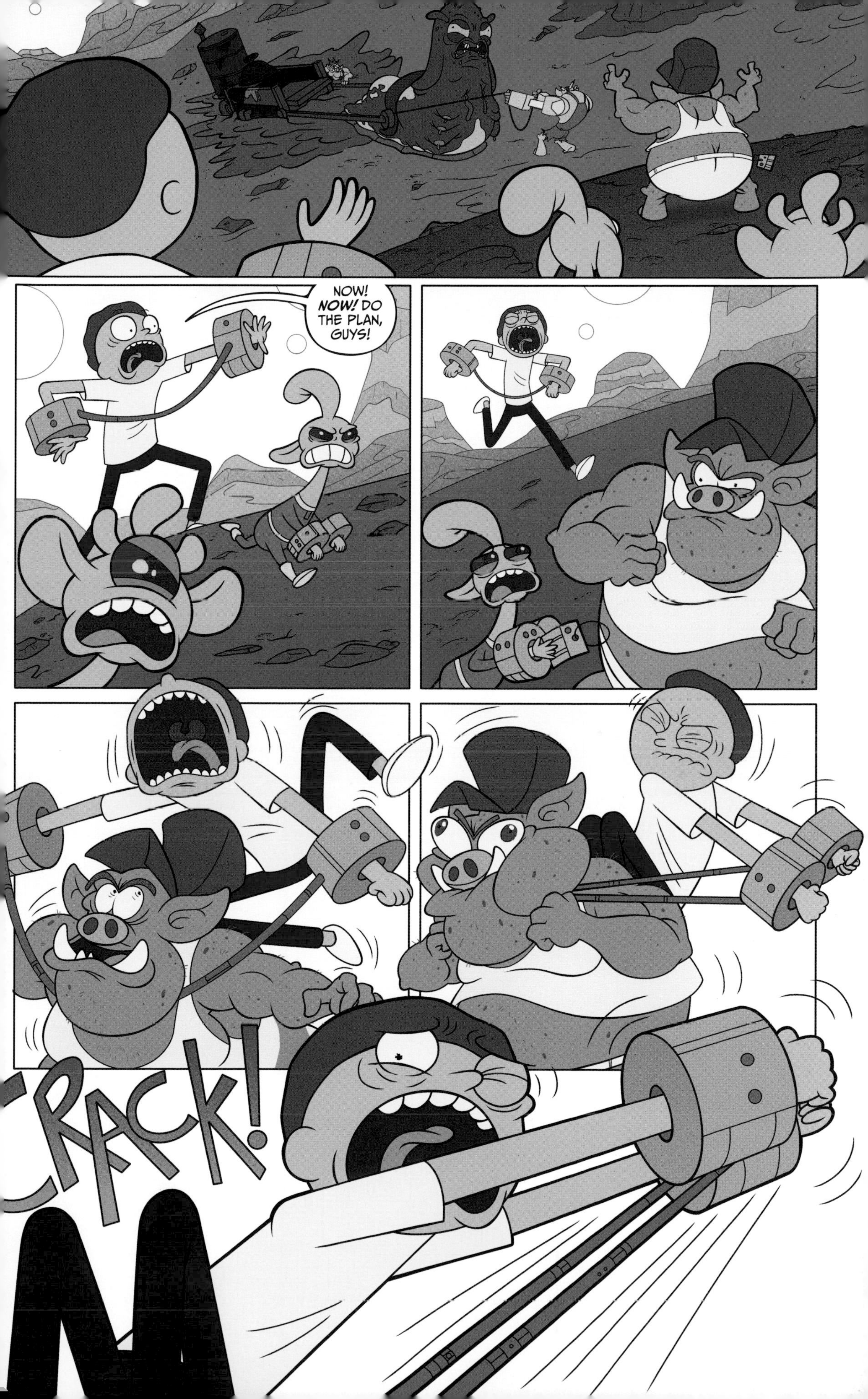
NOW! NOW! DO THE PLAN, GUYS!
CRACK!

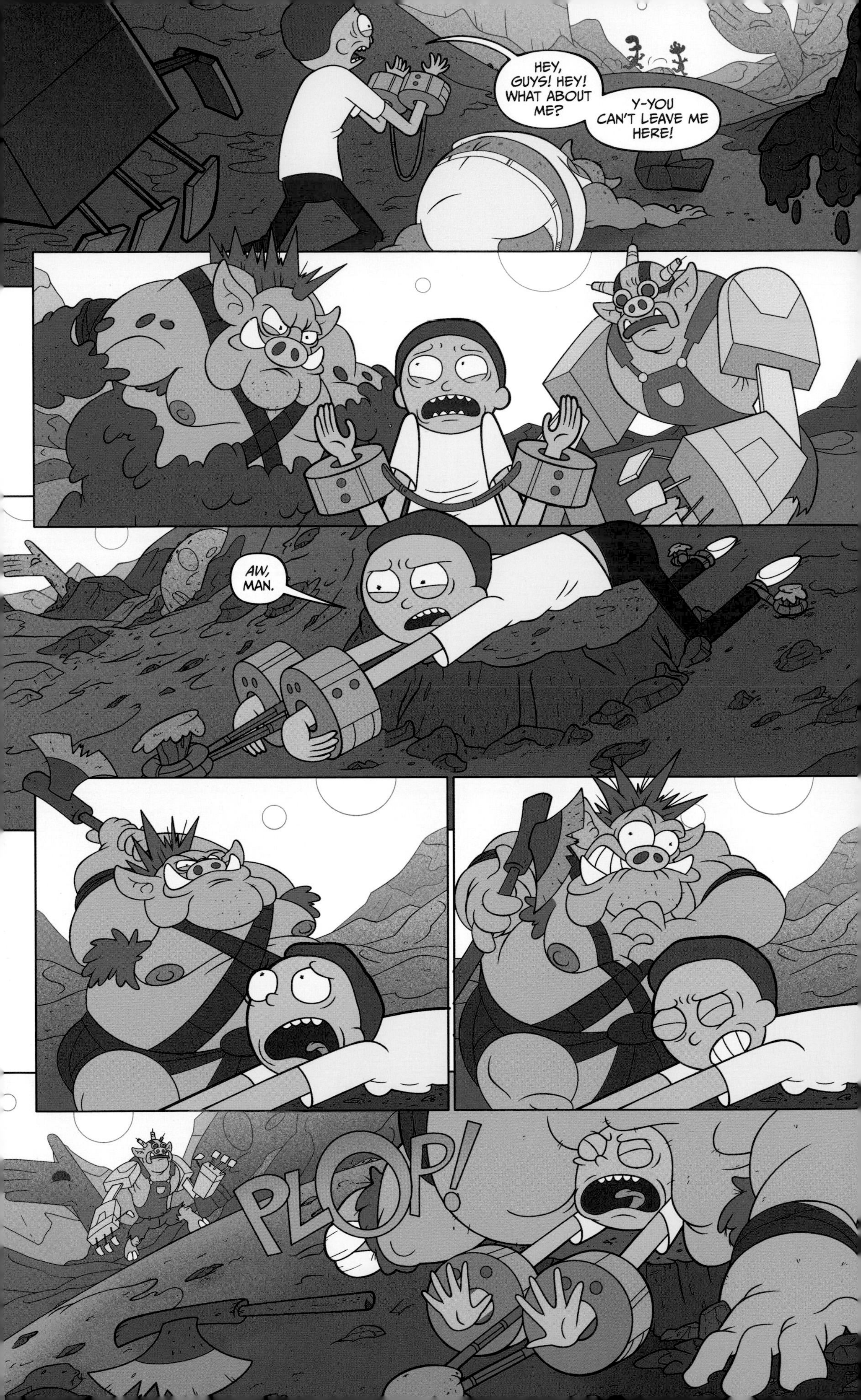
HEY, GUYS! HEY! WHAT ABOUT ME?
Y-YOU CAN'T LEAVE ME HERE!
AW, MAN.
PLOP!

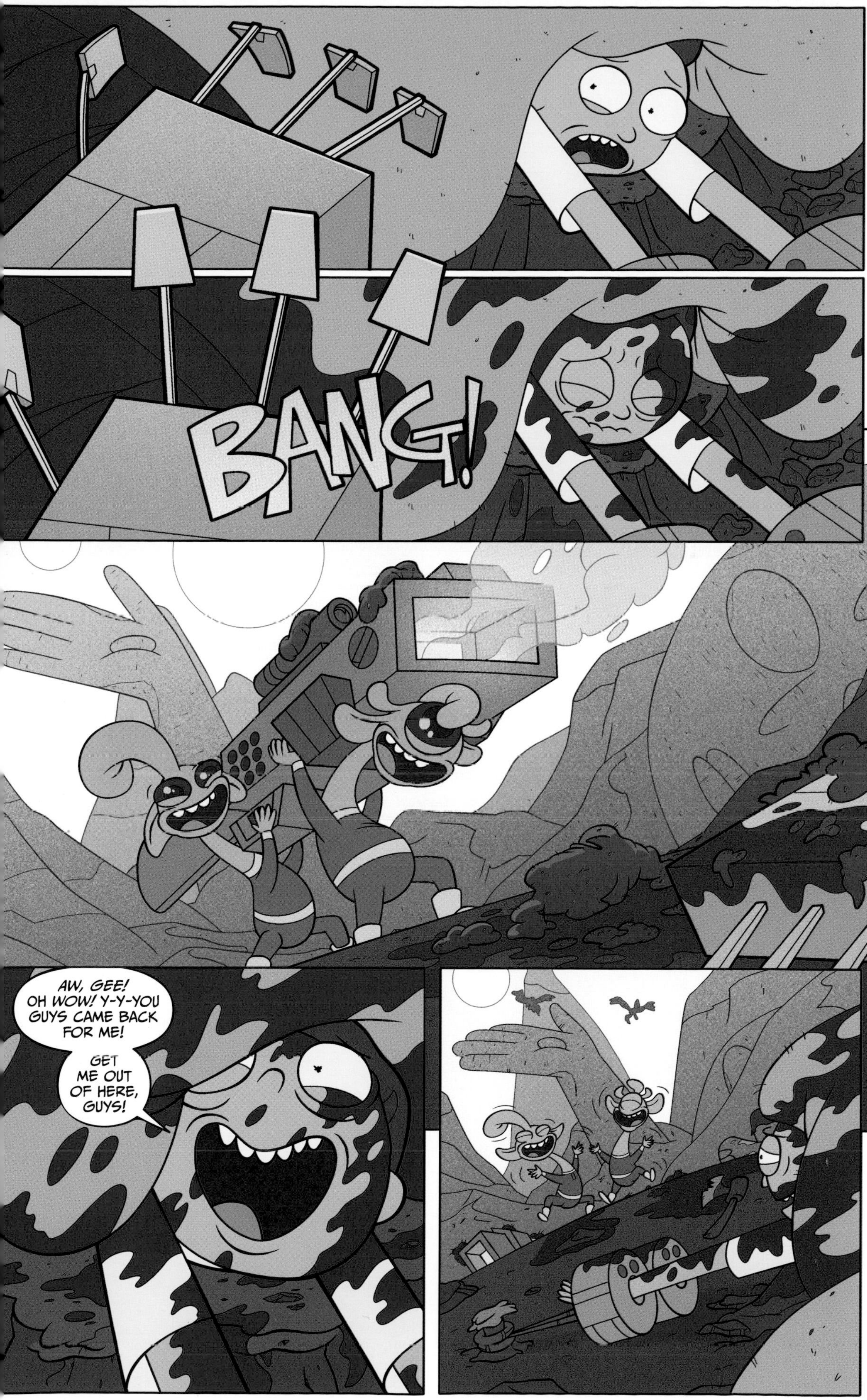
BANG!
AW, GEE! OH WOW! Y-Y-YOU GUYS CAME BACK FOR ME!
GET ME OUT OF HERE, GUYS!

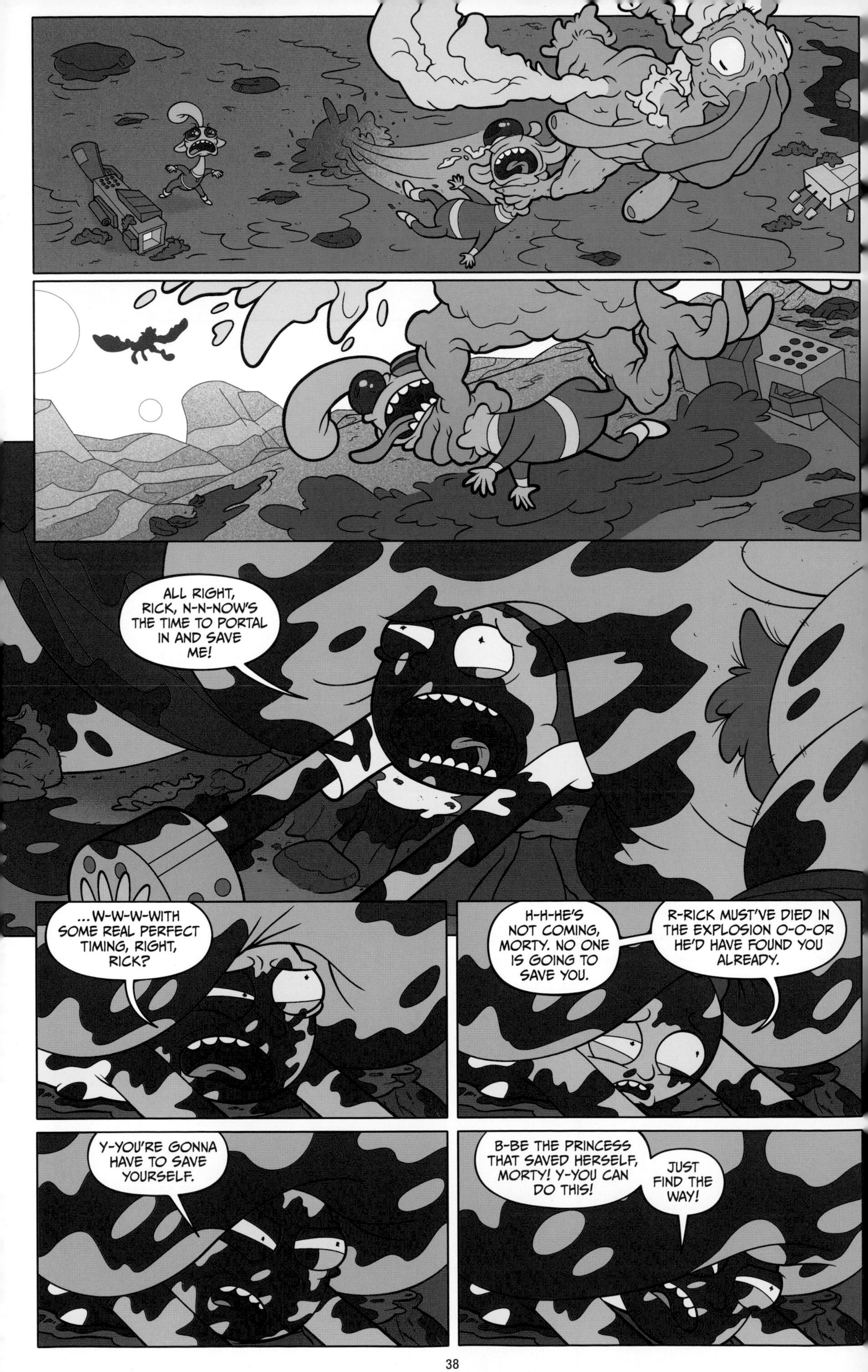
ALL RIGHT, RICK, N-N-NOW'S THE TIME TO PORTAL IN AND SAVE ME!
...W-W-W-WITH SOME REAL PERFECT TIMING, RIGHT, RICK?
H-H-HE'S NOT COMING, MORTY. NO ONE IS GOING TO SAVE YOU.
R-RICK MUST'VE DIED IN THE EXPLOSION O-O-OR HE'D HAVE FOUND YOU ALREADY.
Y-YOU'RE GONNA HAVE TO SAVE YOURSELF.
B-BE THE PRINCESS THAT SAVED HERSELF, MORTY! Y-YOU CAN DO THIS!
JUST FIND THE WAY!

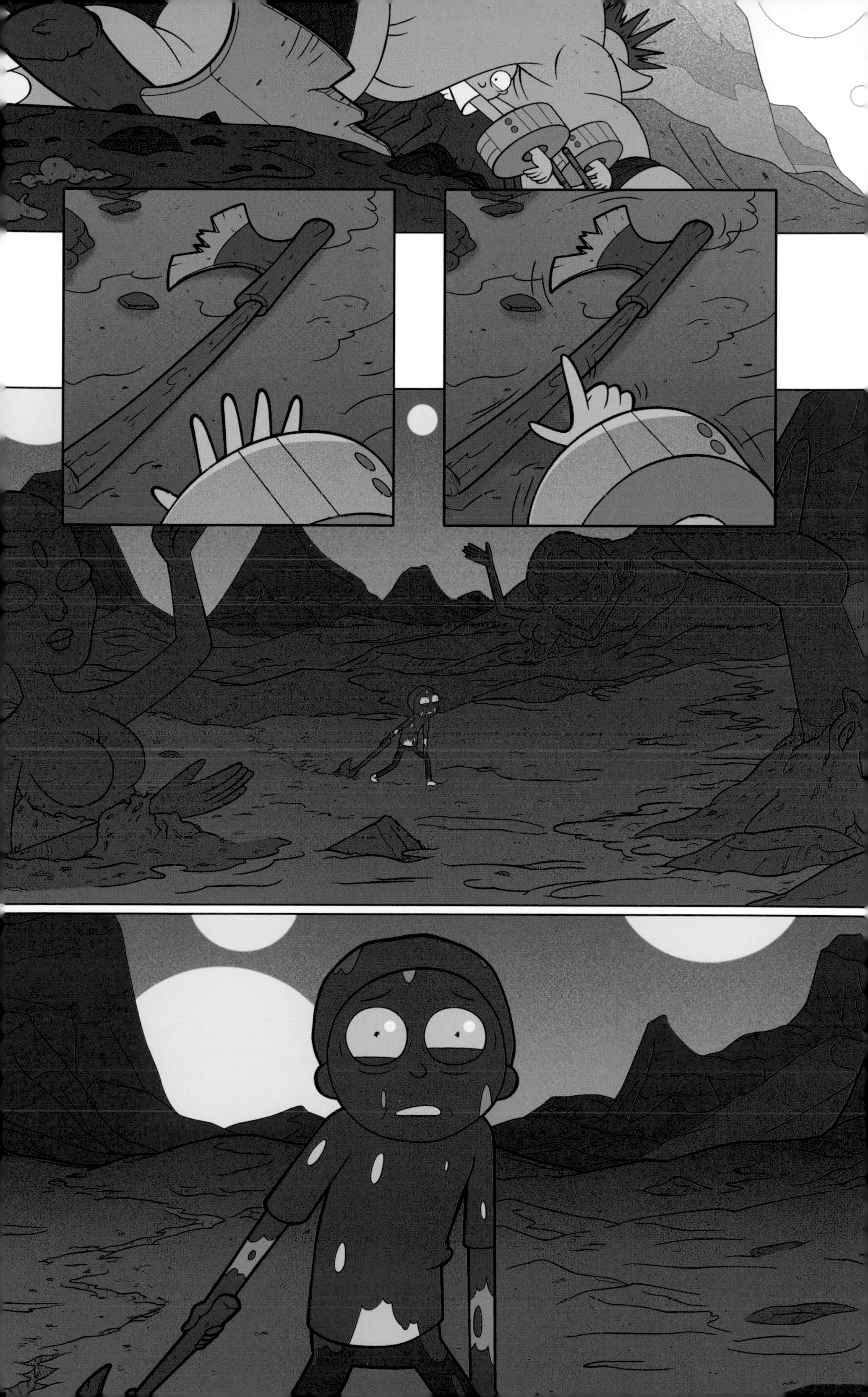

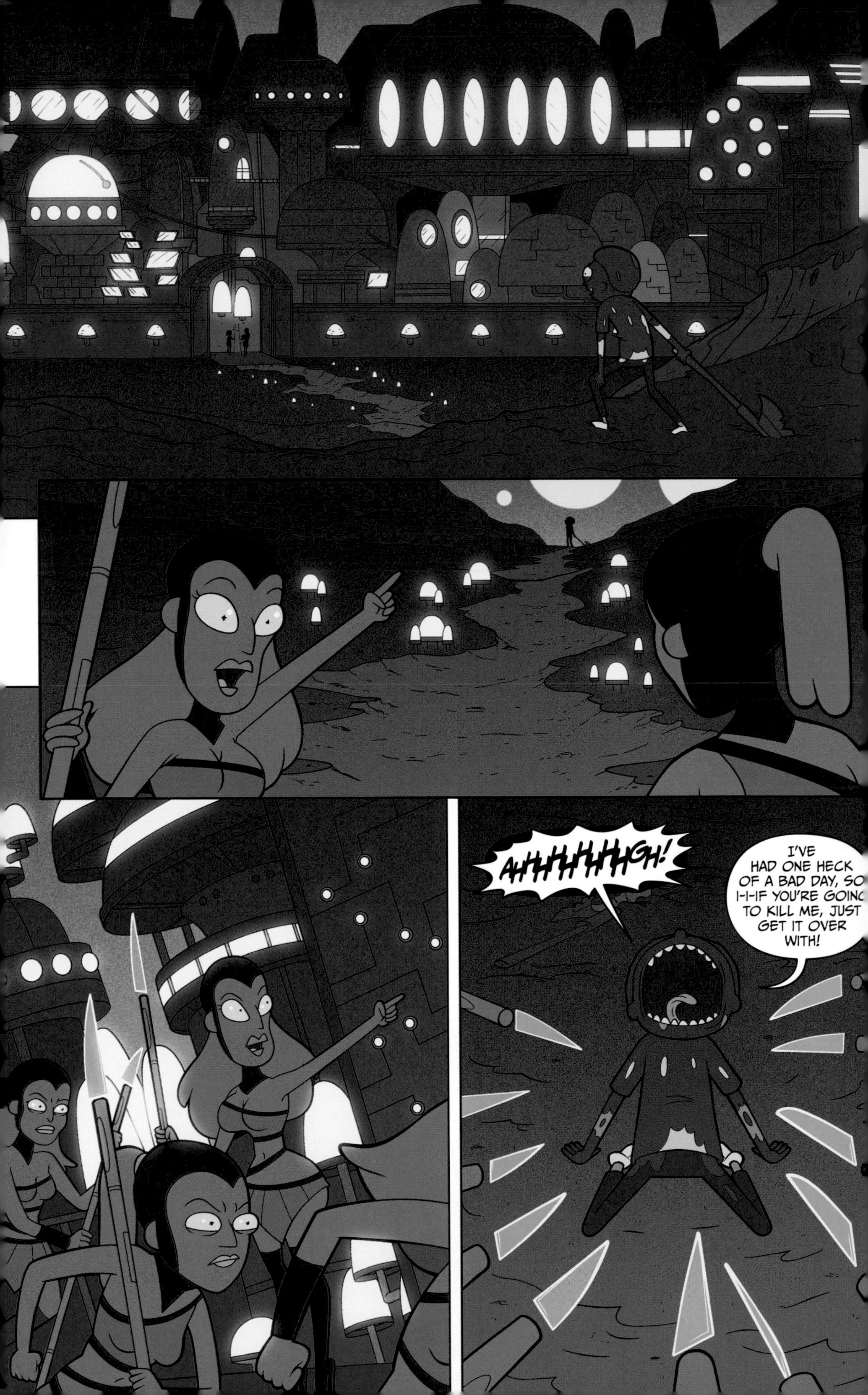
AHHHHHHHHGH!
I'VE HAD ONE HECK OF A BAD DAY, SO I-I-IF YOU'RE GOING TO KILL ME, JUST GET IT OVER WITH!

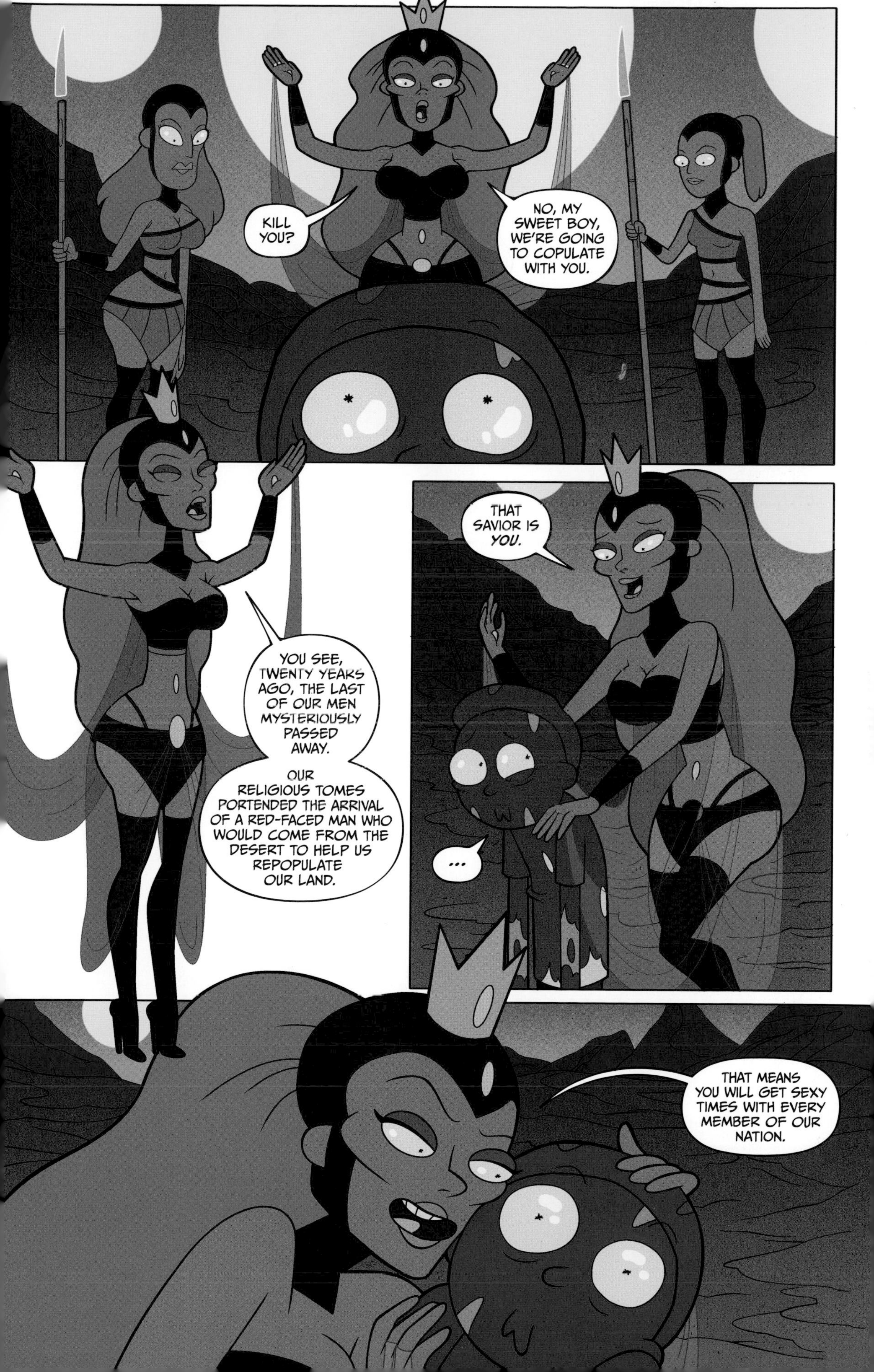
KILL YOU?
NO, MY SWEET BOY, WE'RE GOING TO COPULATE WITH YOU.
YOU SEE, TWENTY YEARS AGO, THE LAST OF OUR MEN MYSTERIOUSLY PASSED AWAY.
OUR RELIGIOUS TOMES PORTENDED THE ARRIVAL OF A RED-FACED MAN WHO WOULD COME FROM THE DESERT TO HELP US REPOPULATE OUR LAND.
THAT SAVIOR IS *YOU*.
...
THAT MEANS YOU WILL GET SEXY TIMES WITH EVERY MEMBER OF OUR NATION.

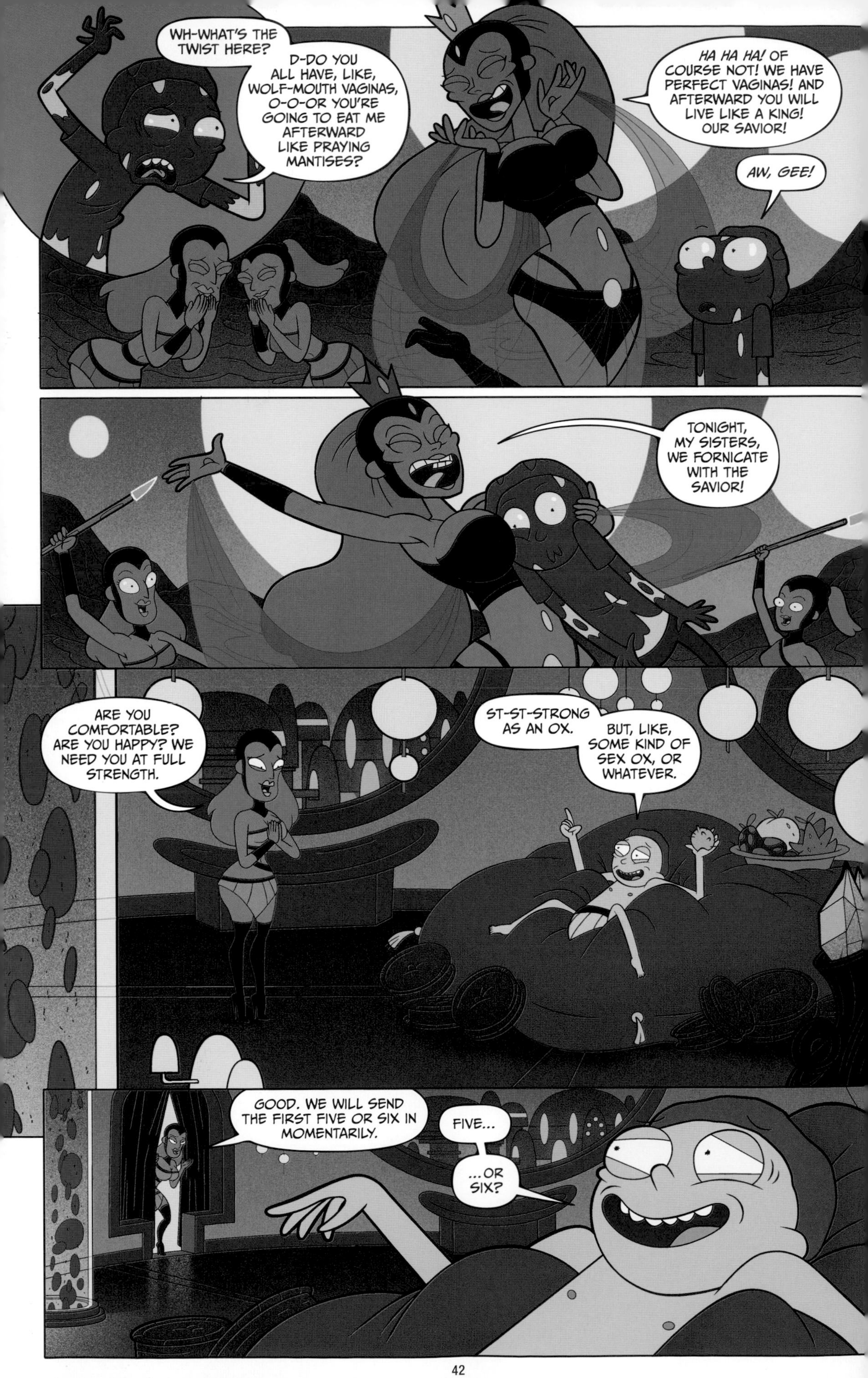
WH-WHAT'S THE TWIST HERE?
D-DO YOU ALL HAVE, LIKE, WOLF-MOUTH VAGINAS, O-O-OR YOU'RE GOING TO EAT ME AFTERWARD LIKE PRAYING MANTISES?
HA HA HA! OF COURSE NOT! WE HAVE PERFECT VAGINAS! AND AFTERWARD YOU WILL LIVE LIKE A KING! OUR SAVIOR!
AW, GEE!
TONIGHT, MY SISTERS, WE FORNICATE WITH THE SAVIOR!
ARE YOU COMFORTABLE? ARE YOU HAPPY? WE NEED YOU AT FULL STRENGTH.
ST-ST-STRONG AS AN OX.
BUT, LIKE, SOME KIND OF SEX OX, OR WHATEVER.
GOOD. WE WILL SEND THE FIRST FIVE OR SIX IN MOMENTARILY.
FIVE...
...OR SIX?

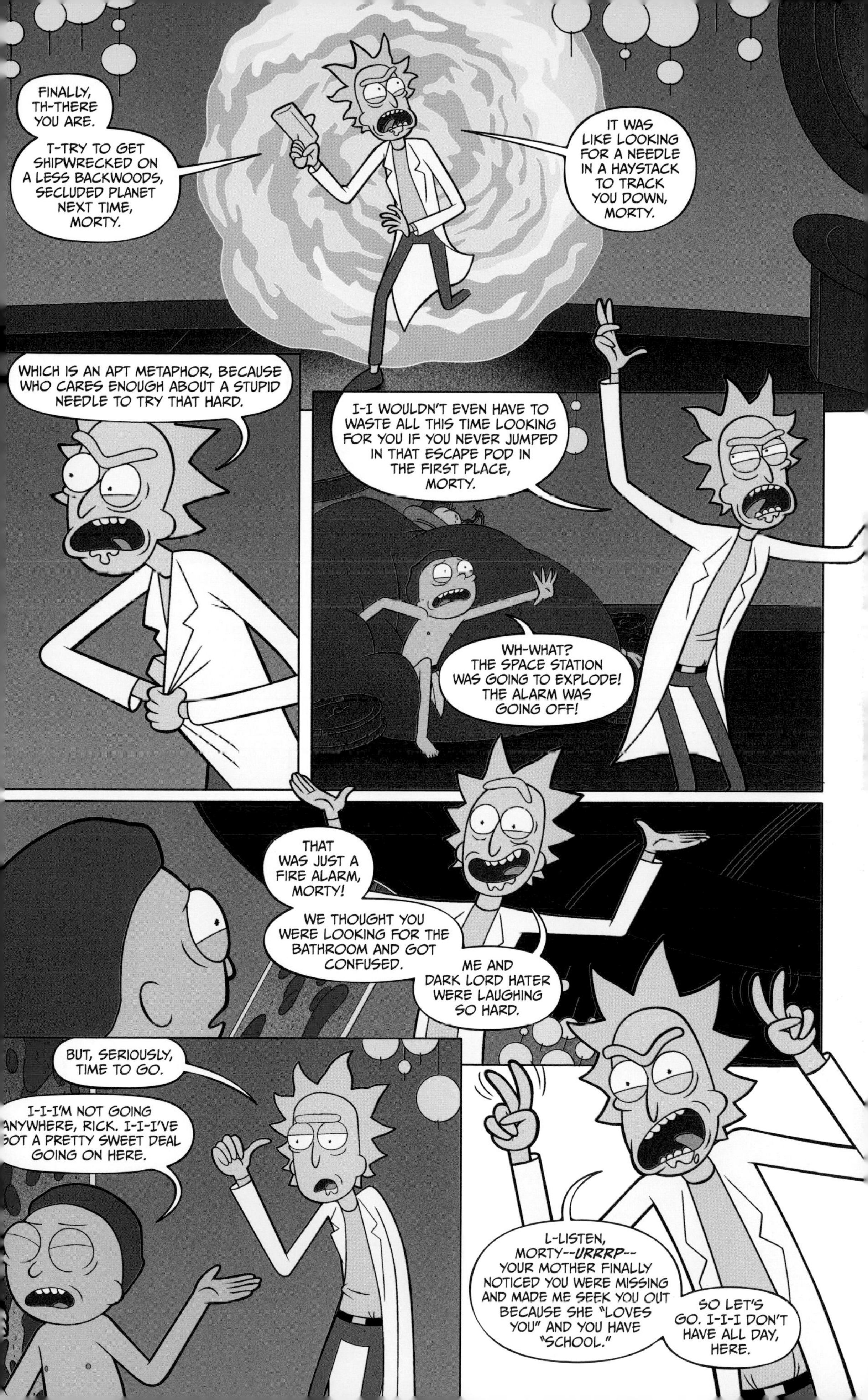
FINALLY, TH-THERE YOU ARE.
T-TRY TO GET SHIPWRECKED ON A LESS BACKWOODS, SECLUDED PLANET NEXT TIME, MORTY.
IT WAS LIKE LOOKING FOR A NEEDLE IN A HAYSTACK TO TRACK YOU DOWN, MORTY.
WHICH IS AN APT METAPHOR, BECAUSE WHO CARES ENOUGH ABOUT A STUPID NEEDLE TO TRY THAT HARD.
I-I WOULDN'T EVEN HAVE TO WASTE ALL THIS TIME LOOKING FOR YOU IF YOU NEVER JUMPED IN THAT ESCAPE POD IN THE FIRST PLACE, MORTY.
WH-WHAT? THE SPACE STATION WAS GOING TO EXPLODE! THE ALARM WAS GOING OFF!
THAT WAS JUST A FIRE ALARM, MORTY!
WE THOUGHT YOU WERE LOOKING FOR THE BATHROOM AND GOT CONFUSED.
ME AND DARK LORD HATER WERE LAUGHING SO HARD.
BUT, SERIOUSLY, TIME TO GO.
I-I-I'M NOT GOING ANYWHERE, RICK. I-I-I'VE GOT A PRETTY SWEET DEAL GOING ON HERE.
L-LISTEN, MORTY--*URRRP*--YOUR MOTHER FINALLY NOTICED YOU WERE MISSING AND MADE ME SEEK YOU OUT BECAUSE SHE "LOVES YOU" AND YOU HAVE "SCHOOL."
SO LET'S GO. I-I-I DON'T HAVE ALL DAY, HERE.

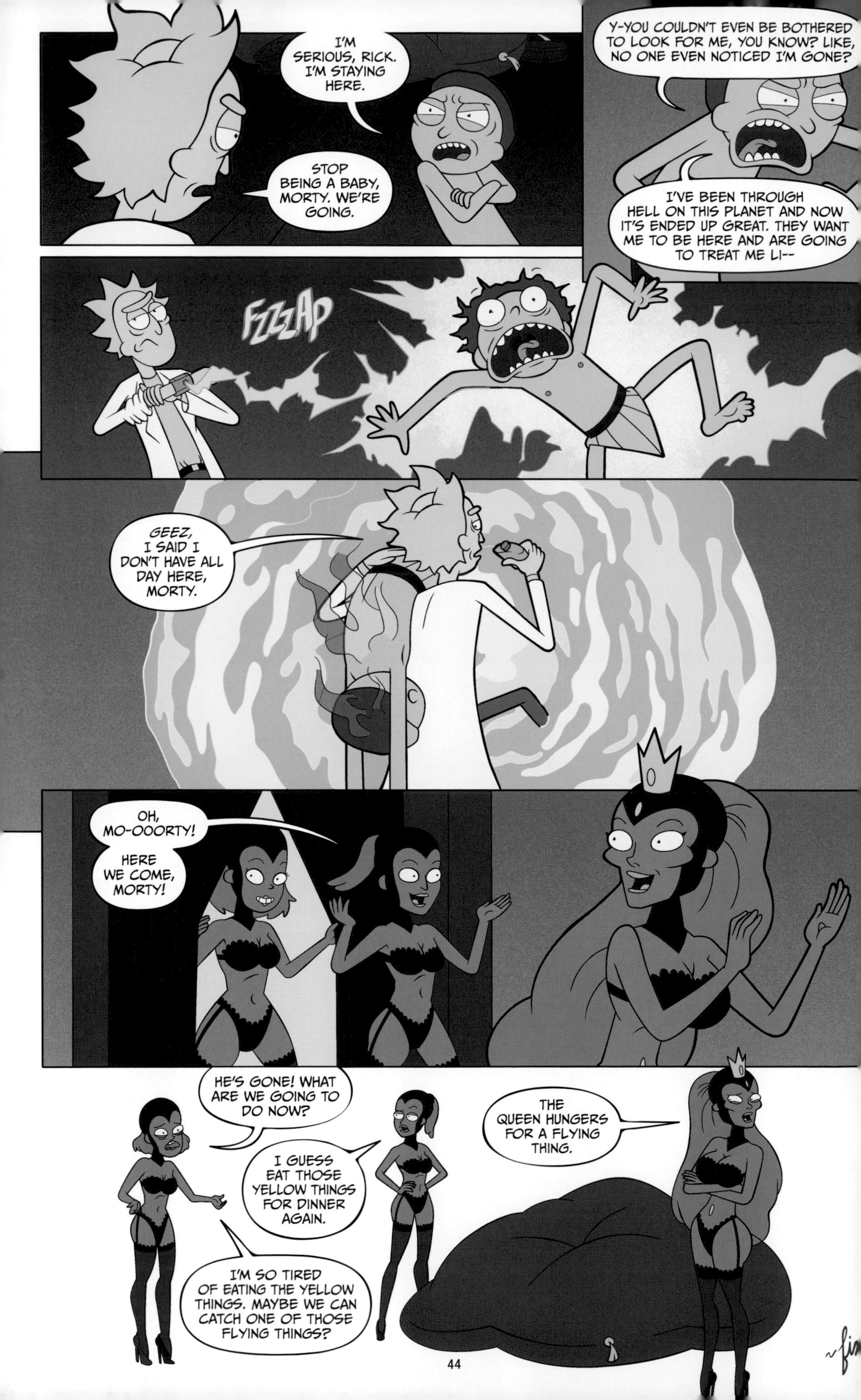
I'M SERIOUS, RICK. I'M STAYING HERE.
STOP BEING A BABY, MORTY. WE'RE GOING.
Y-YOU COULDN'T EVEN BE BOTHERED TO LOOK FOR ME, YOU KNOW? LIKE, NO ONE EVEN NOTICED I'M GONE?
I'VE BEEN THROUGH HELL ON THIS PLANET AND NOW IT'S ENDED UP GREAT. THEY WANT ME TO BE HERE AND ARE GOING TO TREAT ME LI--
FZZZAP
GEEZ, I SAID I DON'T HAVE ALL DAY HERE, MORTY.
OH, MO-OOORTY!
HERE WE COME, MORTY!
HE'S GONE! WHAT ARE WE GOING TO DO NOW?
I GUESS EAT THOSE YELLOW THINGS FOR DINNER AGAIN.
THE QUEEN HUNGERS FOR A FLYING THING.
I'M SO TIRED OF EATING THE YELLOW THINGS. MAYBE WE CAN CATCH ONE OF THOSE FLYING THINGS?
~fin

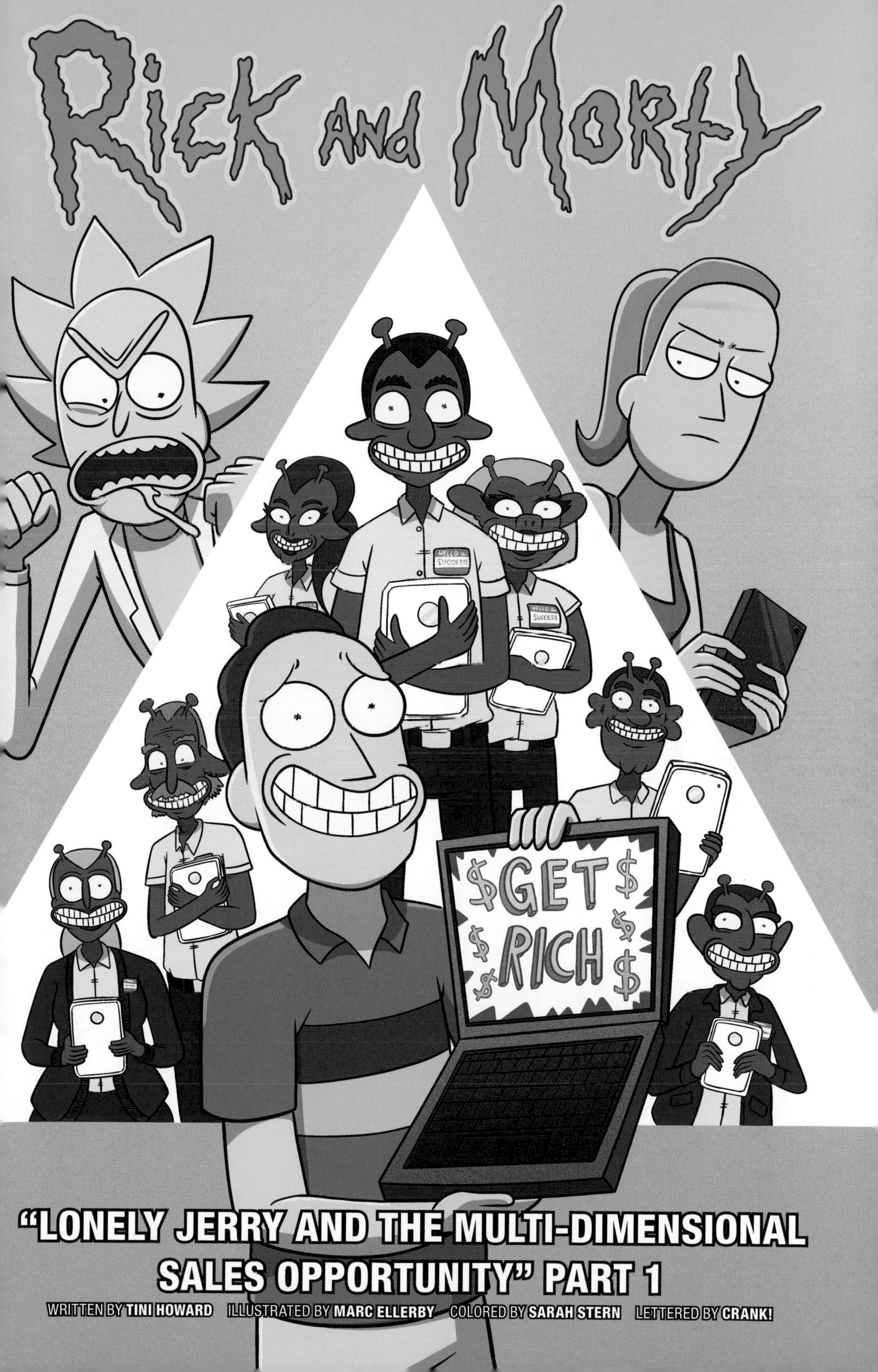
Rick and Morty
HELLO SUCCESS
HELLO SUCCESS
GET
$RICH$

"LONELY JERRY AND THE MULTI-DIMENSIONAL SALES OPPORTUNITY" PART 1

WRITTEN BY **TINI HOWARD** ILLUSTRATED BY **MARC ELLERBY** COLORED BY **SARAH STERN** LETTERED BY **CRANK!**

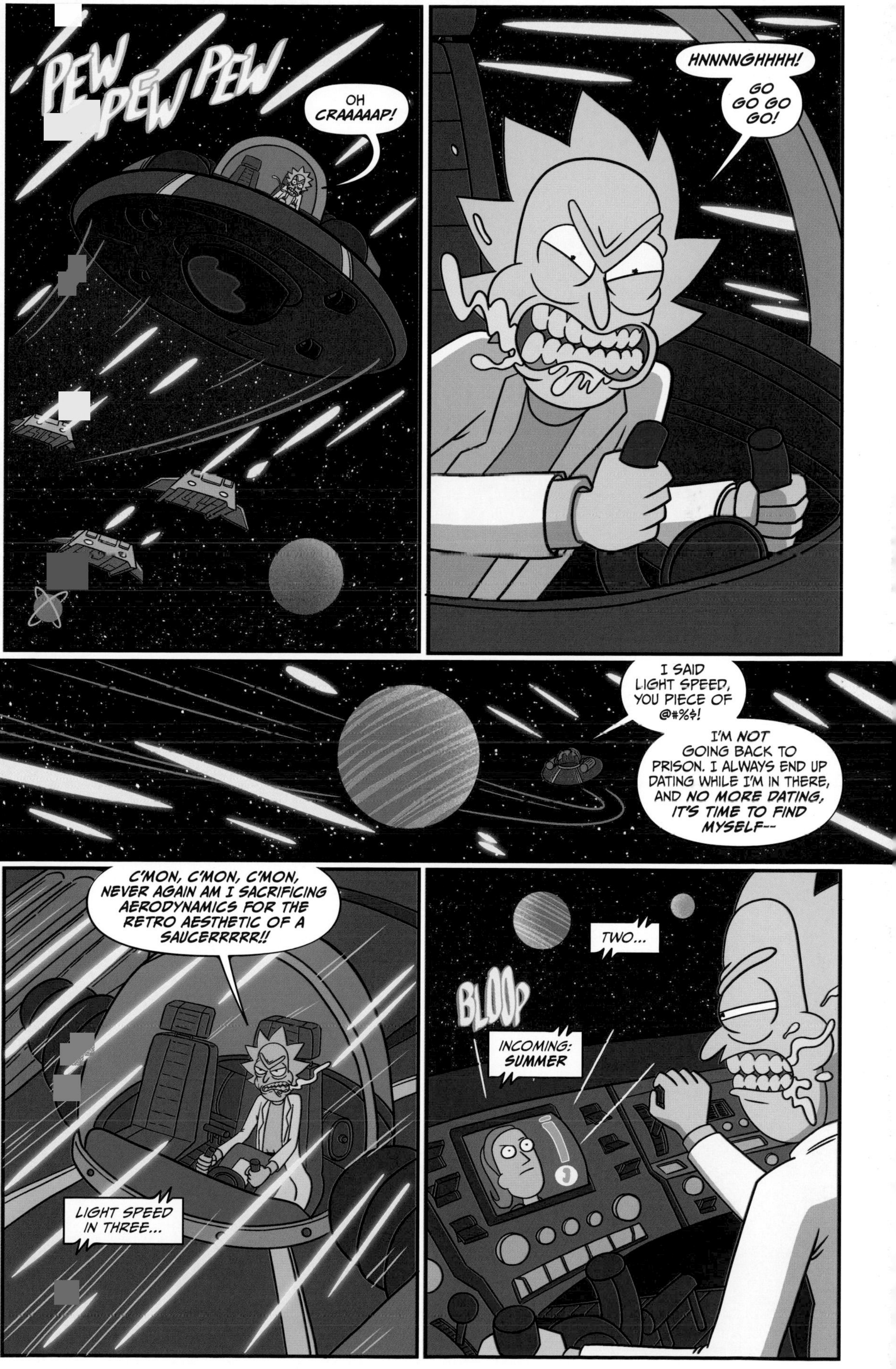
PEW PEW PEW
OH CRAAAAAP!
HNNNNGHHHH!
GO GO GO GO!
I SAID LIGHT SPEED, YOU PIECE OF @#%$!
I'M NOT GOING BACK TO PRISON. I ALWAYS END UP DATING WHILE I'M IN THERE, AND NO MORE DATING, IT'S TIME TO FIND MYSELF--
C'MON, C'MON, C'MON, NEVER AGAIN AM I SACRIFICING AERODYNAMICS FOR THE RETRO AESTHETIC OF A SAUCERRRRR!!
LIGHT SPEED IN THREE...
TWO...
BLOOP
INCOMING: SUMMER

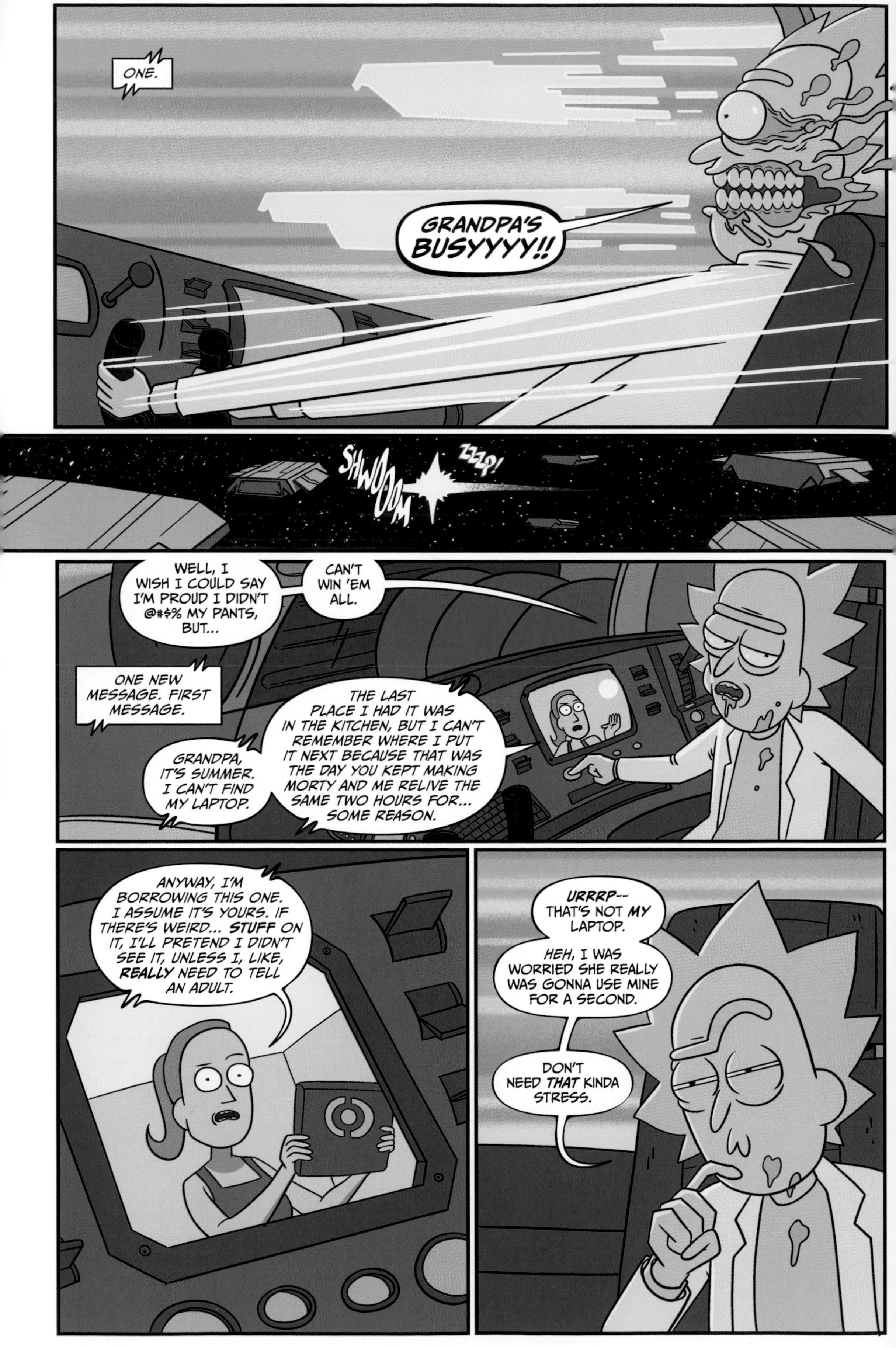
ONE.
GRANDPA'S BUSYYYY!!
SHWOOOM
ZZZZP!
WELL, I WISH I COULD SAY I'M PROUD I DIDN'T @#$% MY PANTS, BUT...
CAN'T WIN 'EM ALL.
ONE NEW MESSAGE. FIRST MESSAGE.
GRANDPA, IT'S SUMMER. I CAN'T FIND MY LAPTOP.
THE LAST PLACE I HAD IT WAS IN THE KITCHEN, BUT I CAN'T REMEMBER WHERE I PUT IT NEXT BECAUSE THAT WAS THE DAY YOU KEPT MAKING MORTY AND ME RELIVE THE SAME TWO HOURS FOR... SOME REASON.
ANYWAY, I'M BORROWING THIS ONE. I ASSUME IT'S YOURS. IF THERE'S WEIRD... STUFF ON IT, I'LL PRETEND I DIDN'T SEE IT, UNLESS I, LIKE, REALLY NEED TO TELL AN ADULT.
URRRP-- THAT'S NOT MY LAPTOP.
HEH, I WAS WORRIED SHE REALLY WAS GONNA USE MINE FOR A SECOND.
DON'T NEED THAT KINDA STRESS.

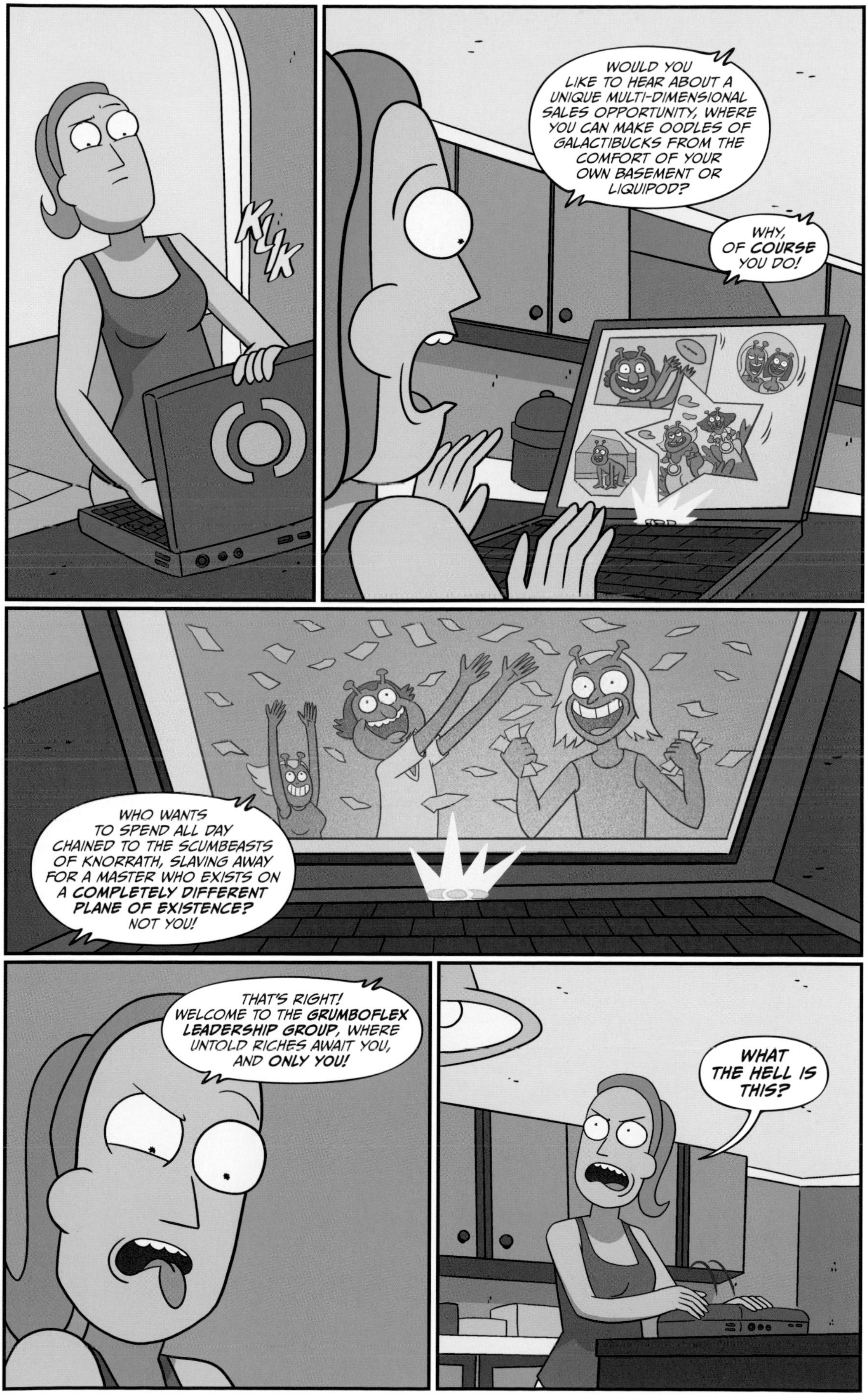
KLIK
WOULD YOU LIKE TO HEAR ABOUT A UNIQUE MULTI-DIMENSIONAL SALES OPPORTUNITY, WHERE YOU CAN MAKE OODLES OF GALACTIBUCKS FROM THE COMFORT OF YOUR OWN BASEMENT OR LIQUIPOD?
WHY, OF COURSE YOU DO!
WHO WANTS TO SPEND ALL DAY CHAINED TO THE SCUMBEASTS OF KNORRATH, SLAVING AWAY FOR A MASTER WHO EXISTS ON A COMPLETELY DIFFERENT PLANE OF EXISTENCE? NOT YOU!
THAT'S RIGHT! WELCOME TO THE GRUMBOFLEX LEADERSHIP GROUP, WHERE UNTOLD RICHES AWAIT YOU, AND ONLY YOU!
WHAT THE HELL IS THIS?

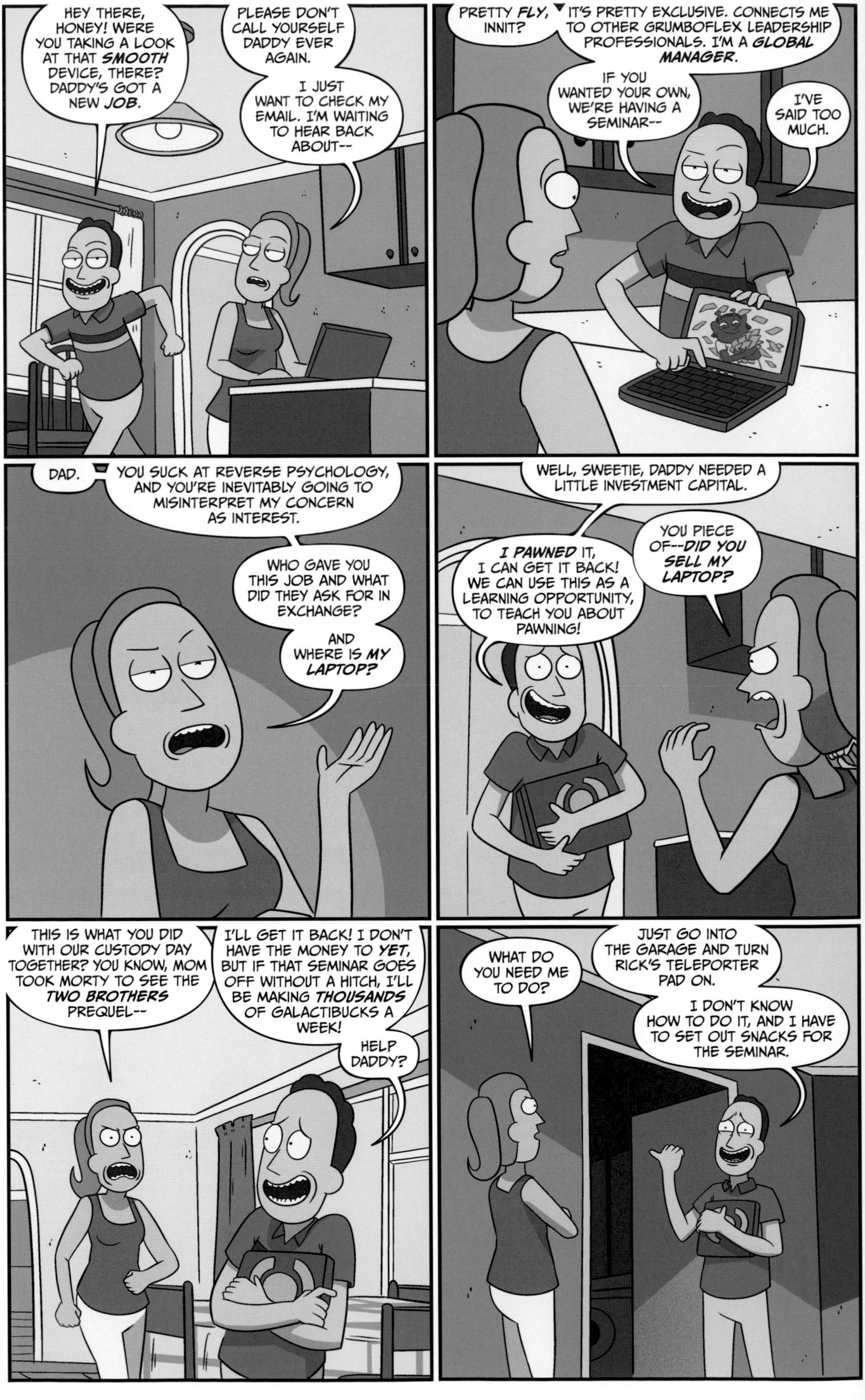
HEY THERE, HONEY! WERE YOU TAKING A LOOK AT THAT SMOOTH DEVICE, THERE? DADDY'S GOT A NEW JOB.
PLEASE DON'T CALL YOURSELF DADDY EVER AGAIN.
I JUST WANT TO CHECK MY EMAIL. I'M WAITING TO HEAR BACK ABOUT--
PRETTY FLY, INNIT?
IT'S PRETTY EXCLUSIVE. CONNECTS ME TO OTHER GRUMBOFLEX LEADERSHIP PROFESSIONALS. I'M A GLOBAL MANAGER.
IF YOU WANTED YOUR OWN, WE'RE HAVING A SEMINAR--
I'VE SAID TOO MUCH.
DAD.
YOU SUCK AT REVERSE PSYCHOLOGY, AND YOU'RE INEVITABLY GOING TO MISINTERPRET MY CONCERN AS INTEREST.
WHO GAVE YOU THIS JOB AND WHAT DID THEY ASK FOR IN EXCHANGE?
AND WHERE IS MY LAPTOP?
WELL, SWEETIE, DADDY NEEDED A LITTLE INVESTMENT CAPITAL.
YOU PIECE OF--DID YOU SELL MY LAPTOP?
I PAWNED IT, I CAN GET IT BACK! WE CAN USE THIS AS A LEARNING OPPORTUNITY, TO TEACH YOU ABOUT PAWNING!
THIS IS WHAT YOU DID WITH OUR CUSTODY DAY TOGETHER? YOU KNOW, MOM TOOK MORTY TO SEE THE TWO BROTHERS PREQUEL--
I'LL GET IT BACK! I DON'T HAVE THE MONEY TO YET, BUT IF THAT SEMINAR GOES OFF WITHOUT A HITCH, I'LL BE MAKING THOUSANDS OF GALACTIBUCKS A WEEK!
HELP DADDY?
WHAT DO YOU NEED ME TO DO?
JUST GO INTO THE GARAGE AND TURN RICK'S TELEPORTER PAD ON.
I DON'T KNOW HOW TO DO IT, AND I HAVE TO SET OUT SNACKS FOR THE SEMINAR.

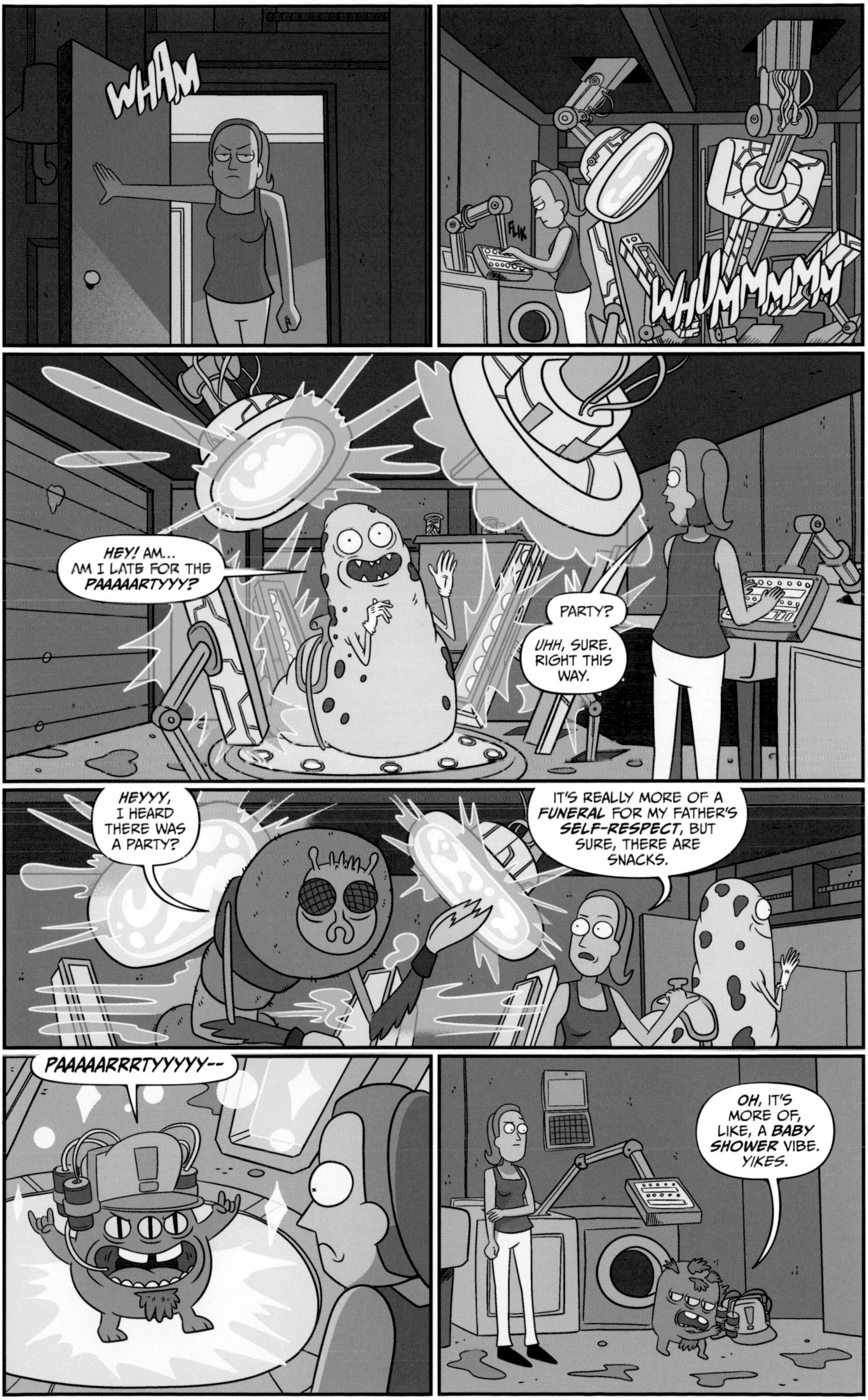
WHAM
FLIK
WHUMMMMM
HEY! AM... AM I LATE FOR THE PAAAAARTYYY?
PARTY?
UHH, SURE. RIGHT THIS WAY.
HEYYY, I HEARD THERE WAS A PARTY?
IT'S REALLY MORE OF A FUNERAL FOR MY FATHER'S SELF-RESPECT, BUT SURE, THERE ARE SNACKS.
PAAAAARRRTYYYYY--
OH, IT'S MORE OF, LIKE, A BABY SHOWER VIBE. YIKES.

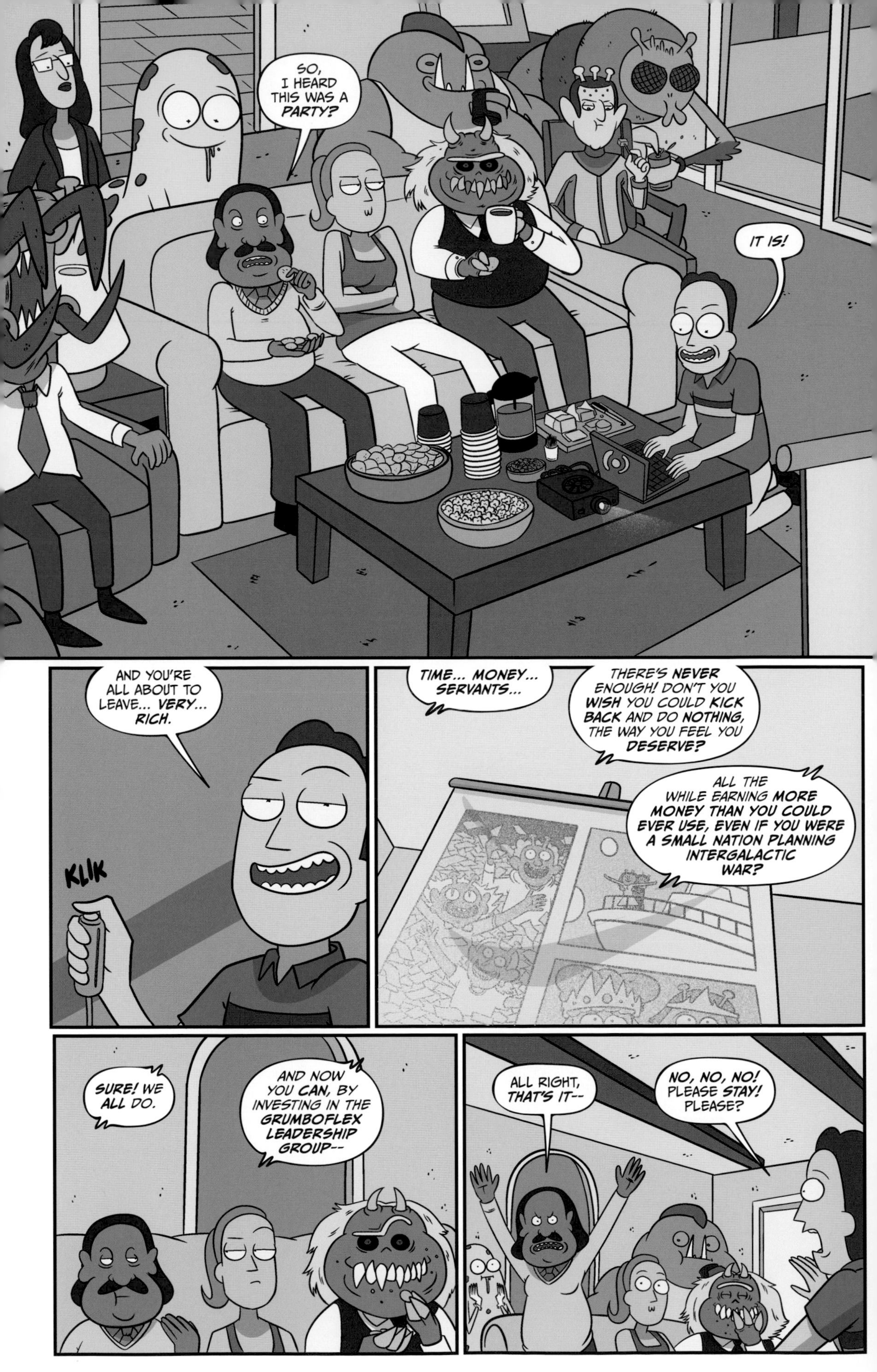
SO, I HEARD THIS WAS A PARTY?
IT IS!
AND YOU'RE ALL ABOUT TO LEAVE... VERY... RICH.
KLIK
TIME... MONEY... SERVANTS...
THERE'S NEVER ENOUGH! DON'T YOU WISH YOU COULD KICK BACK AND DO NOTHING, THE WAY YOU FEEL YOU DESERVE?
ALL THE WHILE EARNING MORE MONEY THAN YOU COULD EVER USE, EVEN IF YOU WERE A SMALL NATION PLANNING INTERGALACTIC WAR?
SURE! WE ALL DO.
AND NOW YOU CAN, BY INVESTING IN THE GRUMBOFLEX LEADERSHIP GROUP--
ALL RIGHT, THAT'S IT--
NO, NO, NO! PLEASE STAY! PLEASE?

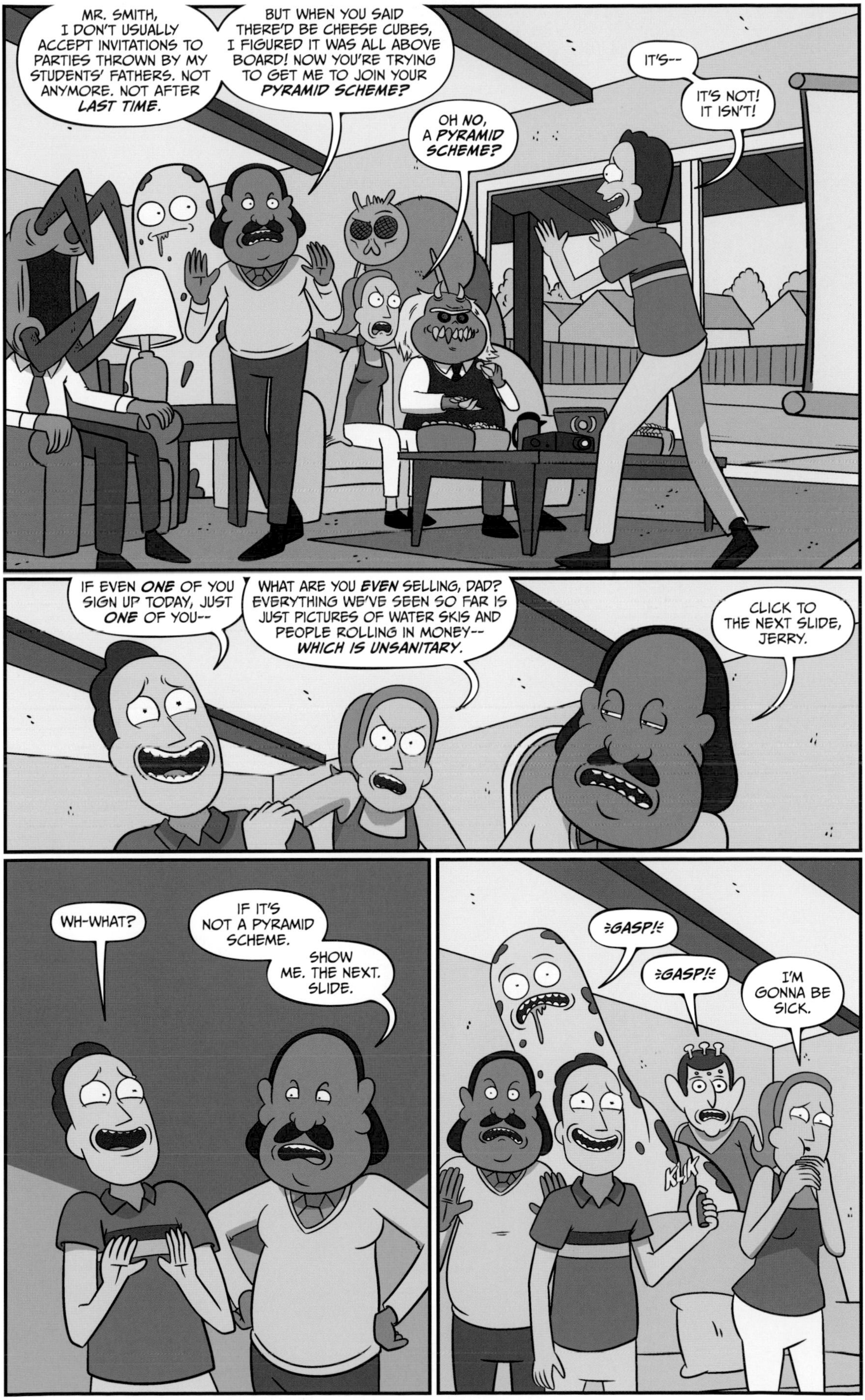
MR. SMITH, I DON'T USUALLY ACCEPT INVITATIONS TO PARTIES THROWN BY MY STUDENTS' FATHERS. NOT ANYMORE. NOT AFTER LAST TIME.
BUT WHEN YOU SAID THERE'D BE CHEESE CUBES, I FIGURED IT WAS ALL ABOVE BOARD! NOW YOU'RE TRYING TO GET ME TO JOIN YOUR PYRAMID SCHEME?
OH NO, A PYRAMID SCHEME?
IT'S--
IT'S NOT! IT ISN'T!
IF EVEN ONE OF YOU SIGN UP TODAY, JUST ONE OF YOU--
WHAT ARE YOU EVEN SELLING, DAD? EVERYTHING WE'VE SEEN SO FAR IS JUST PICTURES OF WATER SKIS AND PEOPLE ROLLING IN MONEY-- WHICH IS UNSANITARY.
CLICK TO THE NEXT SLIDE, JERRY.
WH-WHAT?
IF IT'S NOT A PYRAMID SCHEME.
SHOW ME. THE NEXT. SLIDE.
GASP!
GASP!
I'M GONNA BE SICK.
KLIK

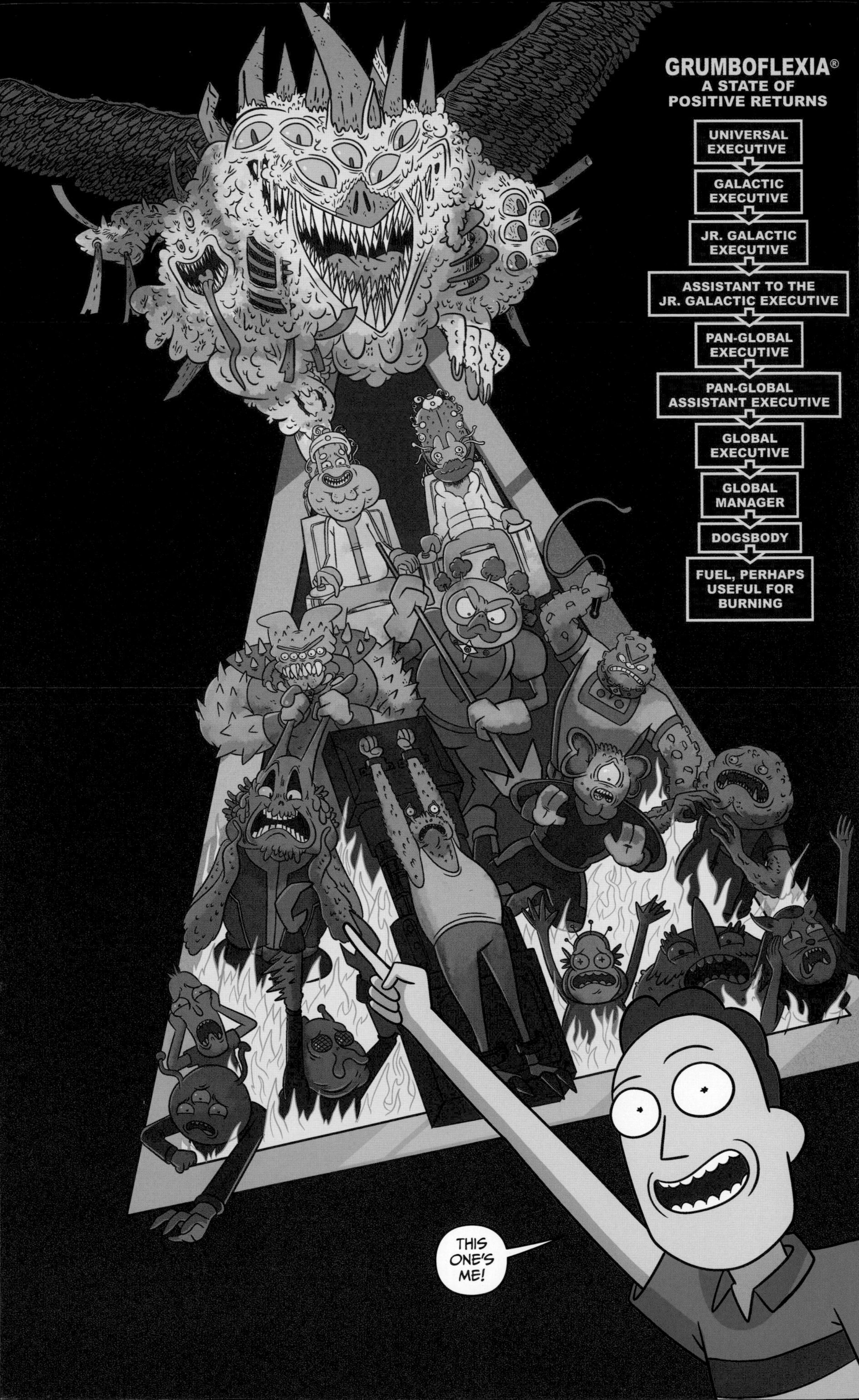
GRUMBOFLEXIA®
A STATE OF
POSITIVE RETURNS
UNIVERSAL EXECUTIVE
GALACTIC EXECUTIVE
JR. GALACTIC EXECUTIVE
ASSISTANT TO THE JR. GALACTIC EXECUTIVE
PAN-GLOBAL EXECUTIVE
PAN-GLOBAL ASSISTANT EXECUTIVE
GLOBAL EXECUTIVE
GLOBAL MANAGER
DOGSBODY
FUEL, PERHAPS USEFUL FOR BURNING
THIS ONE'S ME!

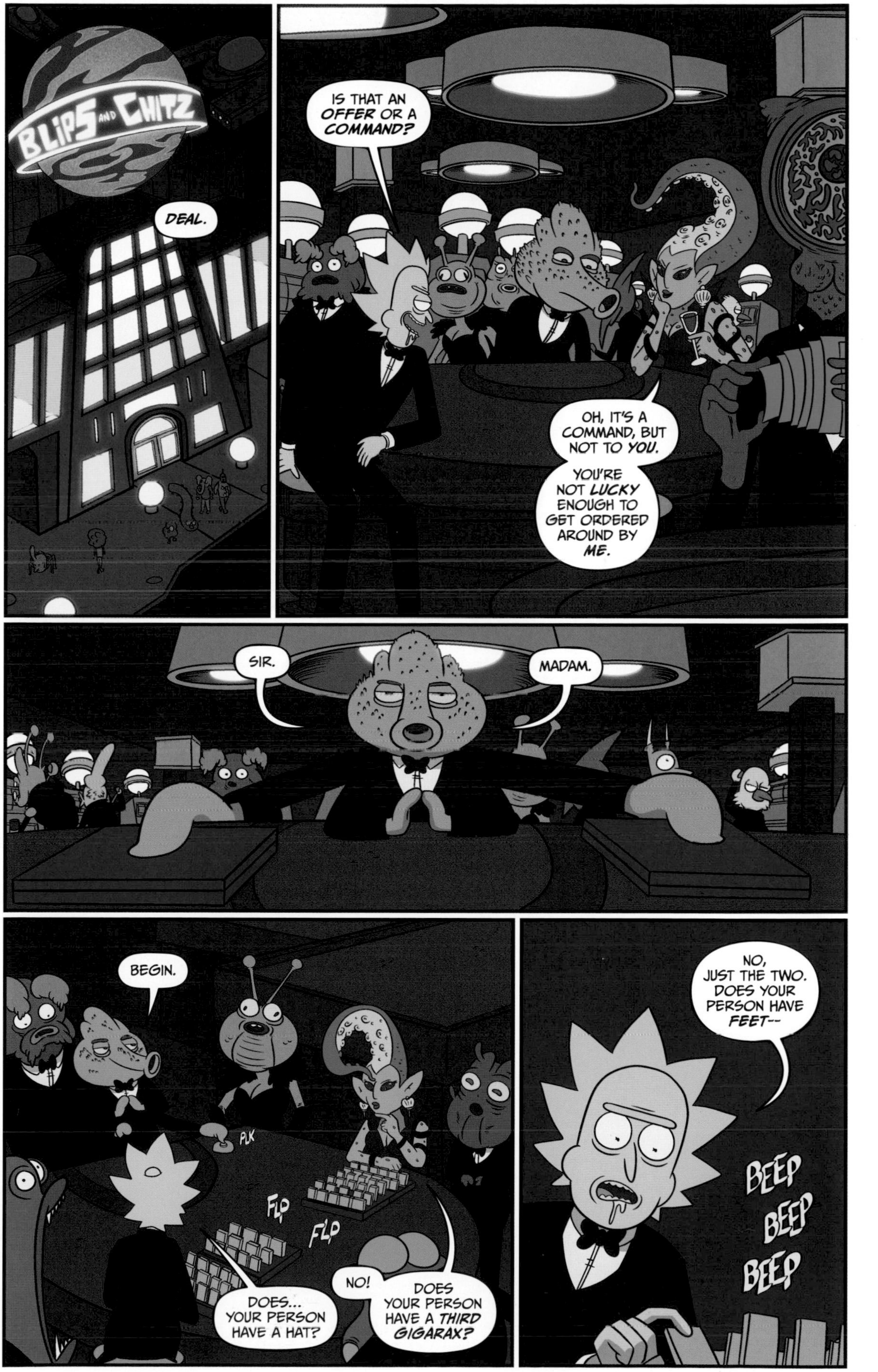
BLIPS AND CHITZ
DEAL.
IS THAT AN OFFER OR A COMMAND?
OH, IT'S A COMMAND, BUT NOT TO YOU.
YOU'RE NOT LUCKY ENOUGH TO GET ORDERED AROUND BY ME.
SIR.
MADAM.
BEGIN.
PLK
FLP
FLP
DOES... YOUR PERSON HAVE A HAT?
NO!
DOES YOUR PERSON HAVE A THIRD GIGARAX?
NO, JUST THE TWO. DOES YOUR PERSON HAVE FEET--
BEEP
BEEP
BEEP

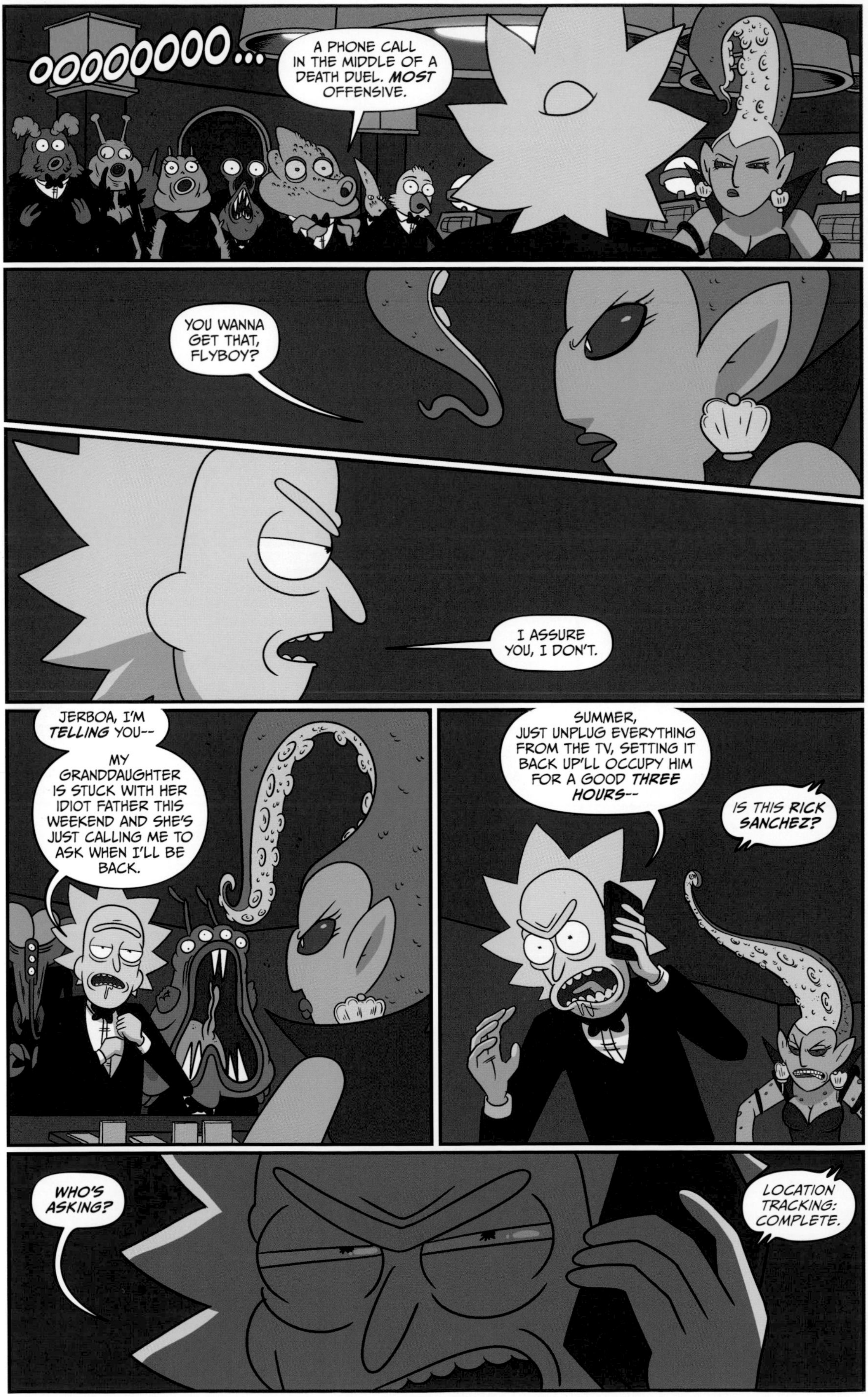
OOOOOOOO...
A PHONE CALL IN THE MIDDLE OF A DEATH DUEL. *MOST* OFFENSIVE.
YOU WANNA GET THAT, FLYBOY?
I ASSURE YOU, I DON'T.
JERBOA, I'M *TELLING* YOU--
MY GRANDDAUGHTER IS STUCK WITH HER IDIOT FATHER THIS WEEKEND AND SHE'S JUST CALLING ME TO ASK WHEN I'LL BE BACK.
SUMMER, JUST UNPLUG EVERYTHING FROM THE TV, SETTING IT BACK UP'LL OCCUPY HIM FOR A GOOD *THREE HOURS*--
IS THIS RICK SANCHEZ?
WHO'S ASKING?
LOCATION TRACKING: COMPLETE.

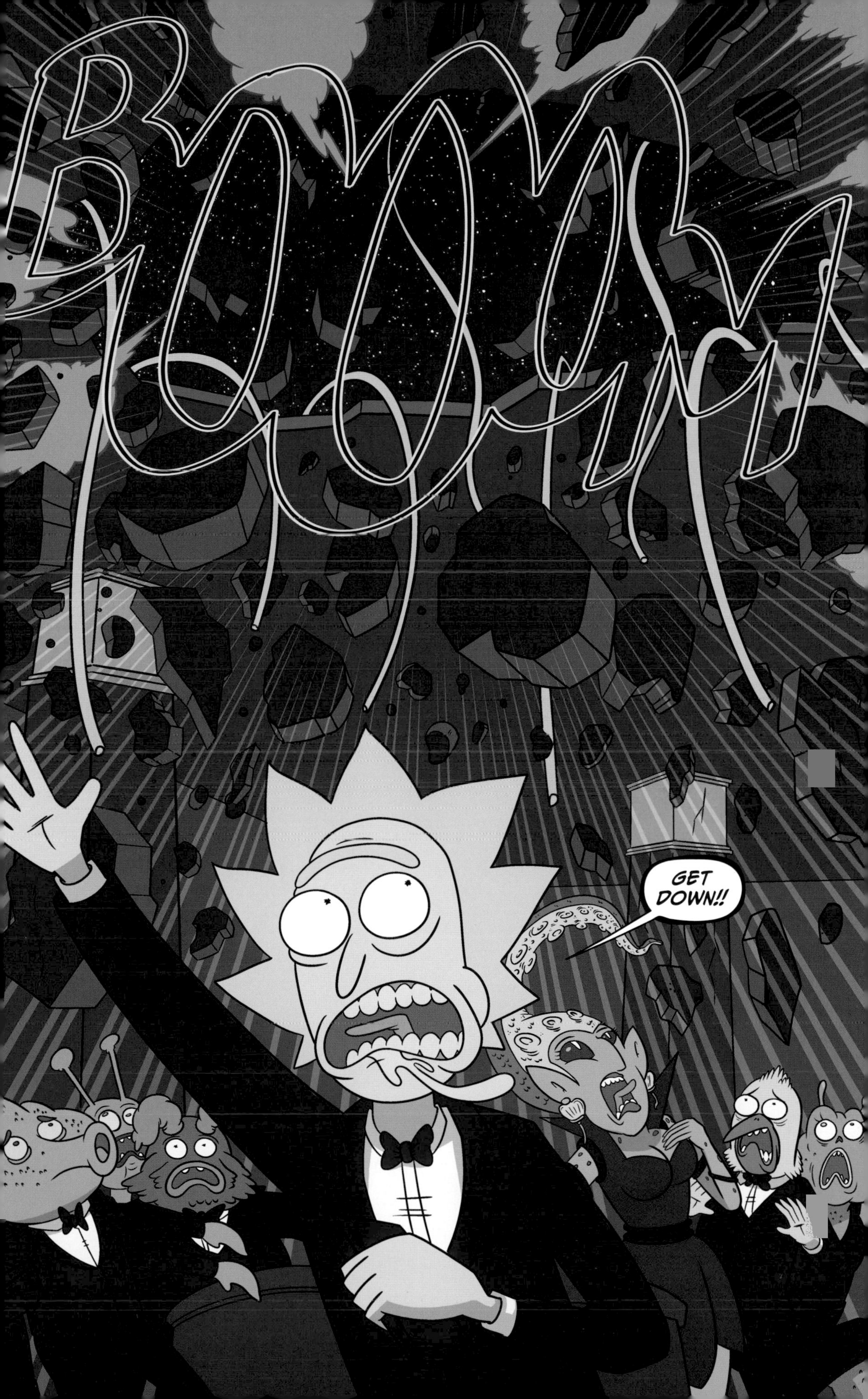
GET DOWN!!

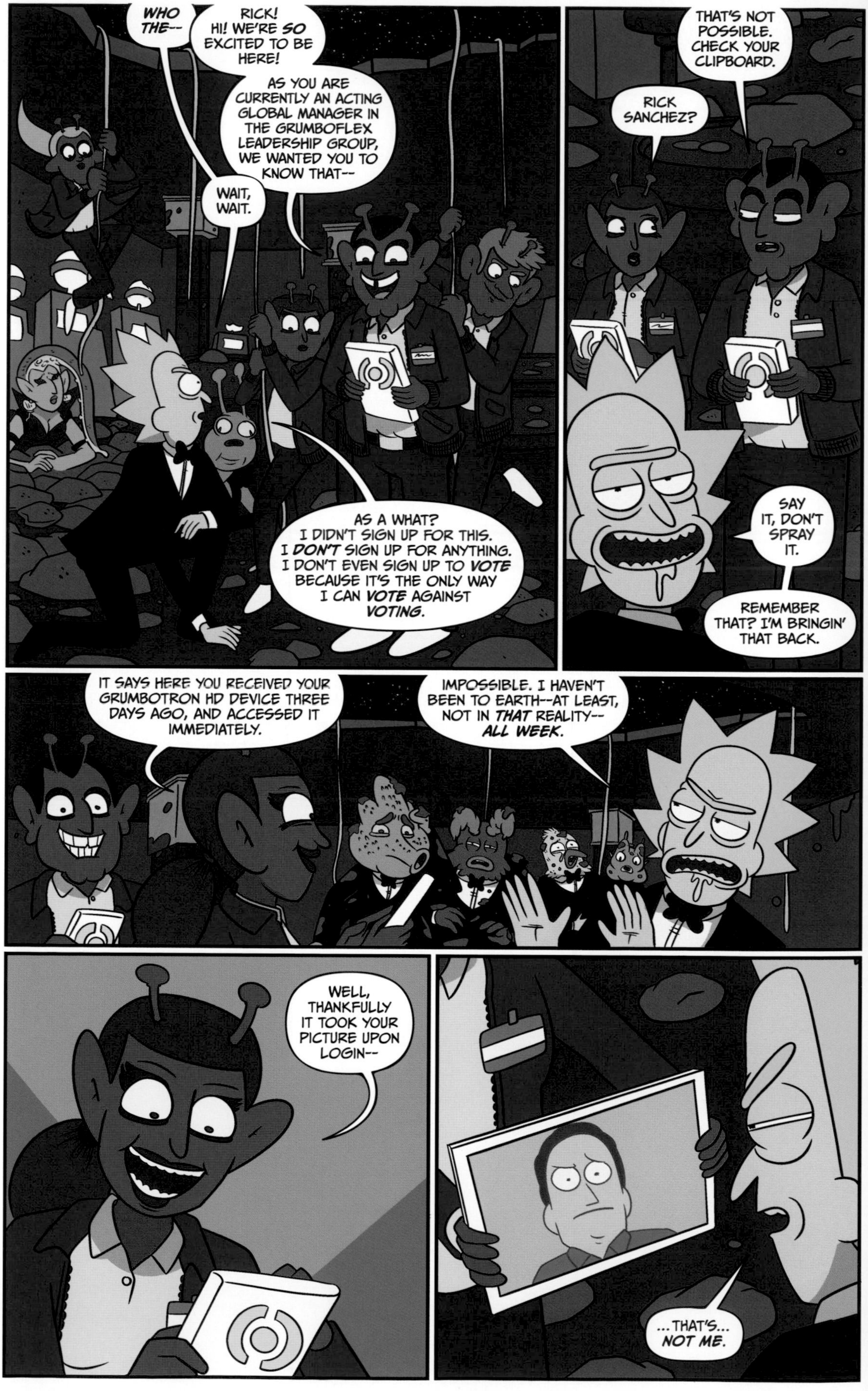
WHO THE--
RICK! HI! WE'RE SO EXCITED TO BE HERE!
AS YOU ARE CURRENTLY AN ACTING GLOBAL MANAGER IN THE GRUMBOFLEX LEADERSHIP GROUP, WE WANTED YOU TO KNOW THAT--
WAIT, WAIT.
AS A WHAT? I DIDN'T SIGN UP FOR THIS. I DON'T SIGN UP FOR ANYTHING. I DON'T EVEN SIGN UP TO VOTE BECAUSE IT'S THE ONLY WAY I CAN VOTE AGAINST VOTING.
THAT'S NOT POSSIBLE. CHECK YOUR CLIPBOARD.
RICK SANCHEZ?
SAY IT, DON'T SPRAY IT.
REMEMBER THAT? I'M BRINGIN' THAT BACK.
IT SAYS HERE YOU RECEIVED YOUR GRUMBOTRON HD DEVICE THREE DAYS AGO, AND ACCESSED IT IMMEDIATELY.
IMPOSSIBLE. I HAVEN'T BEEN TO EARTH--AT LEAST, NOT IN THAT REALITY-- ALL WEEK.
WELL, THANKFULLY IT TOOK YOUR PICTURE UPON LOGIN--
...THAT'S... NOT ME.

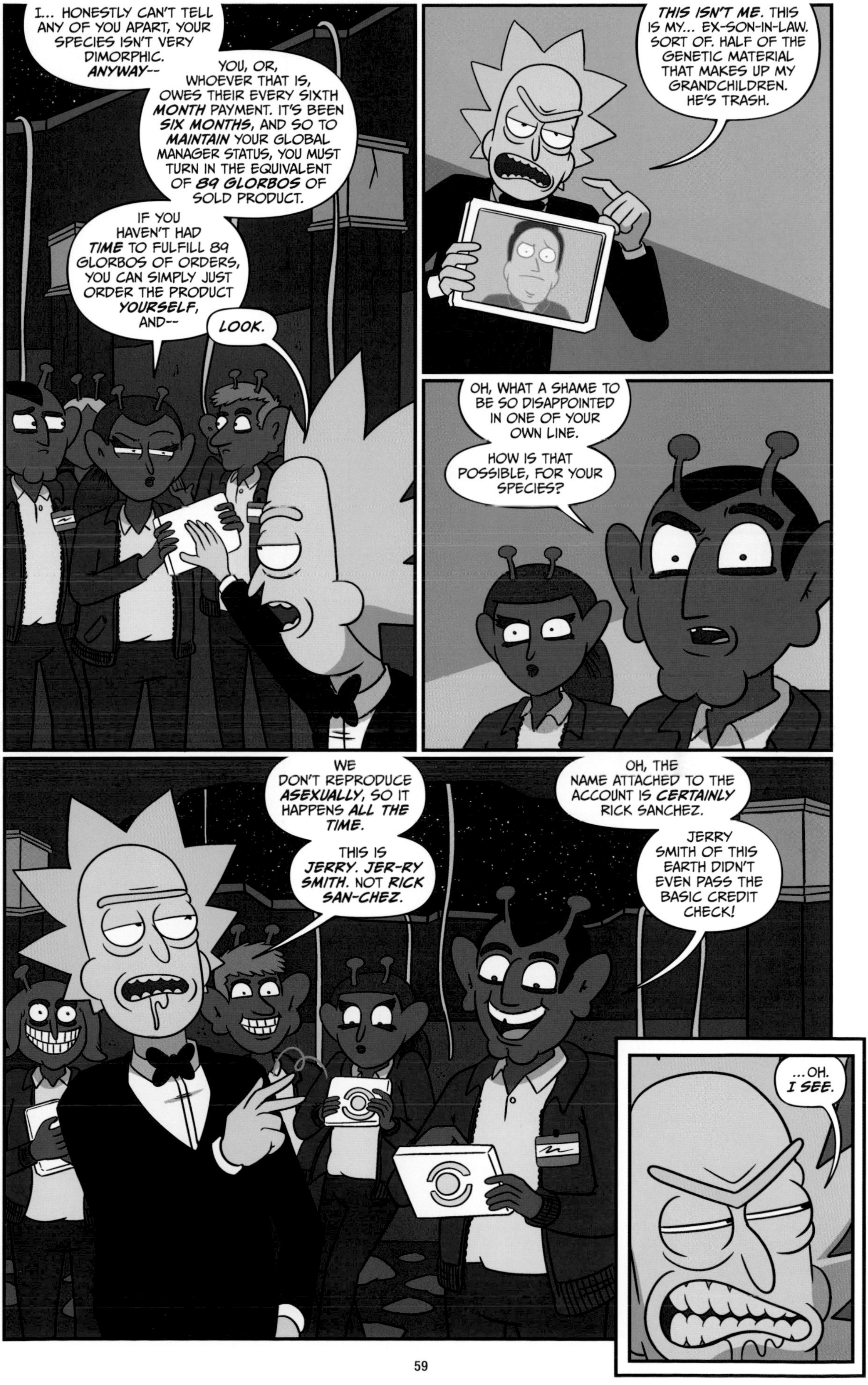
I... HONESTLY CAN'T TELL ANY OF YOU APART, YOUR SPECIES ISN'T VERY DIMORPHIC. ANYWAY--
YOU, OR, WHOEVER THAT IS, OWES THEIR EVERY SIXTH MONTH PAYMENT. IT'S BEEN SIX MONTHS, AND SO TO MAINTAIN YOUR GLOBAL MANAGER STATUS, YOU MUST TURN IN THE EQUIVALENT OF 89 GLORBOS OF SOLD PRODUCT.
IF YOU HAVEN'T HAD TIME TO FULFILL 89 GLORBOS OF ORDERS, YOU CAN SIMPLY JUST ORDER THE PRODUCT YOURSELF, AND--
LOOK.
THIS ISN'T ME. THIS IS MY... EX-SON-IN-LAW. SORT OF. HALF OF THE GENETIC MATERIAL THAT MAKES UP MY GRANDCHILDREN. HE'S TRASH.
OH, WHAT A SHAME TO BE SO DISAPPOINTED IN ONE OF YOUR OWN LINE.
HOW IS THAT POSSIBLE, FOR YOUR SPECIES?
WE DON'T REPRODUCE ASEXUALLY, SO IT HAPPENS ALL THE TIME.
THIS IS JERRY. JER-RY SMITH. NOT RICK SAN-CHEZ.
OH, THE NAME ATTACHED TO THE ACCOUNT IS CERTAINLY RICK SANCHEZ.
JERRY SMITH OF THIS EARTH DIDN'T EVEN PASS THE BASIC CREDIT CHECK!
...OH. I SEE.

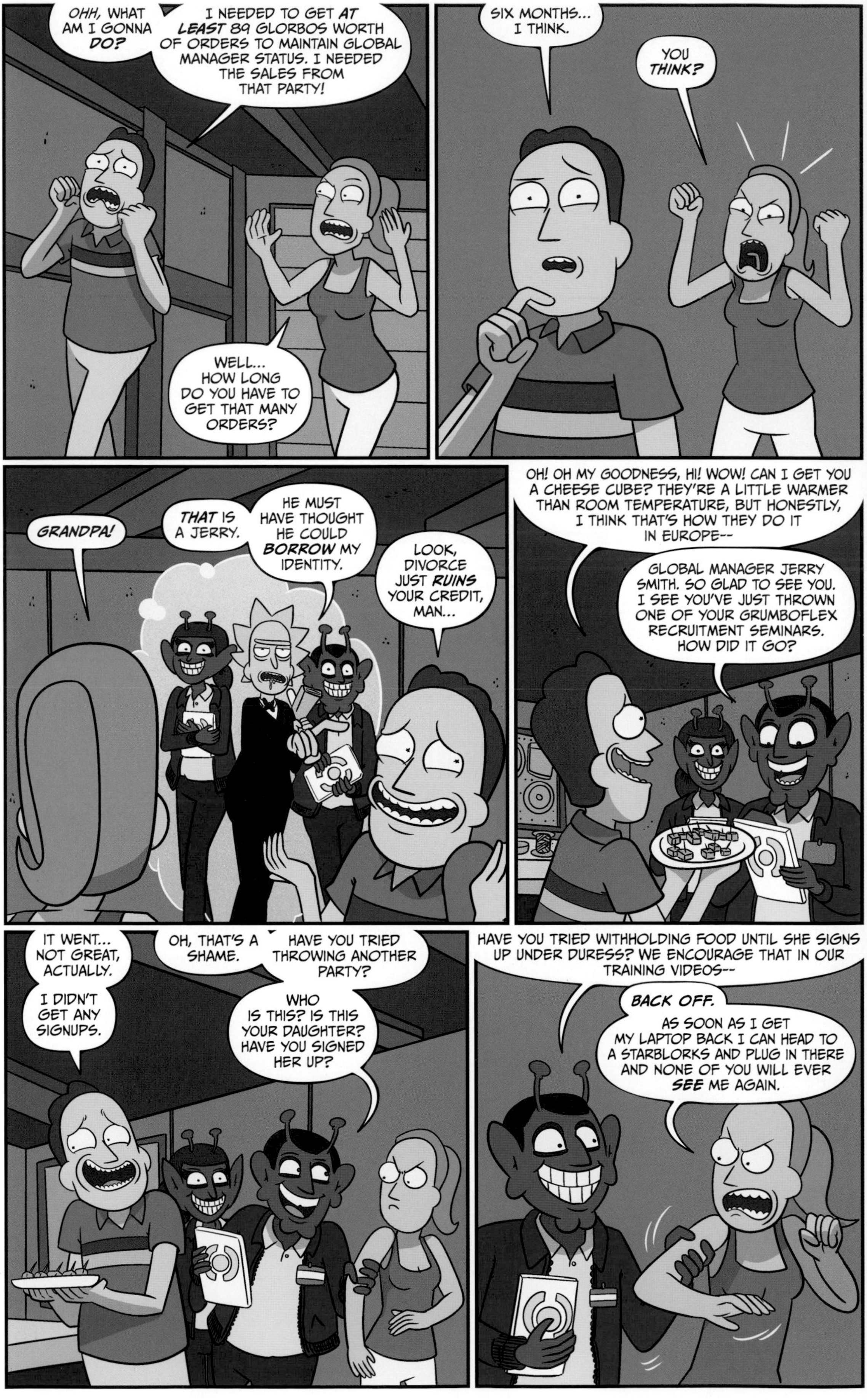
OHH, WHAT AM I GONNA DO?
I NEEDED TO GET AT LEAST 89 GLORBOS WORTH OF ORDERS TO MAINTAIN GLOBAL MANAGER STATUS. I NEEDED THE SALES FROM THAT PARTY!
WELL... HOW LONG DO YOU HAVE TO GET THAT MANY ORDERS?
SIX MONTHS... I THINK.
YOU THINK?
GRANDPA!
THAT IS A JERRY.
HE MUST HAVE THOUGHT HE COULD BORROW MY IDENTITY.
LOOK, DIVORCE JUST RUINS YOUR CREDIT, MAN...
OH! OH MY GOODNESS, HI! WOW! CAN I GET YOU A CHEESE CUBE? THEY'RE A LITTLE WARMER THAN ROOM TEMPERATURE, BUT HONESTLY, I THINK THAT'S HOW THEY DO IT IN EUROPE--
GLOBAL MANAGER JERRY SMITH. SO GLAD TO SEE YOU. I SEE YOU'VE JUST THROWN ONE OF YOUR GRUMBOFLEX RECRUITMENT SEMINARS. HOW DID IT GO?
IT WENT... NOT GREAT, ACTUALLY.
I DIDN'T GET ANY SIGNUPS.
OH, THAT'S A SHAME.
HAVE YOU TRIED THROWING ANOTHER PARTY?
WHO IS THIS? IS THIS YOUR DAUGHTER? HAVE YOU SIGNED HER UP?
HAVE YOU TRIED WITHHOLDING FOOD UNTIL SHE SIGNS UP UNDER DURESS? WE ENCOURAGE THAT IN OUR TRAINING VIDEOS--
BACK OFF.
AS SOON AS I GET MY LAPTOP BACK I CAN HEAD TO A STARBLORKS AND PLUG IN THERE AND NONE OF YOU WILL EVER SEE ME AGAIN.

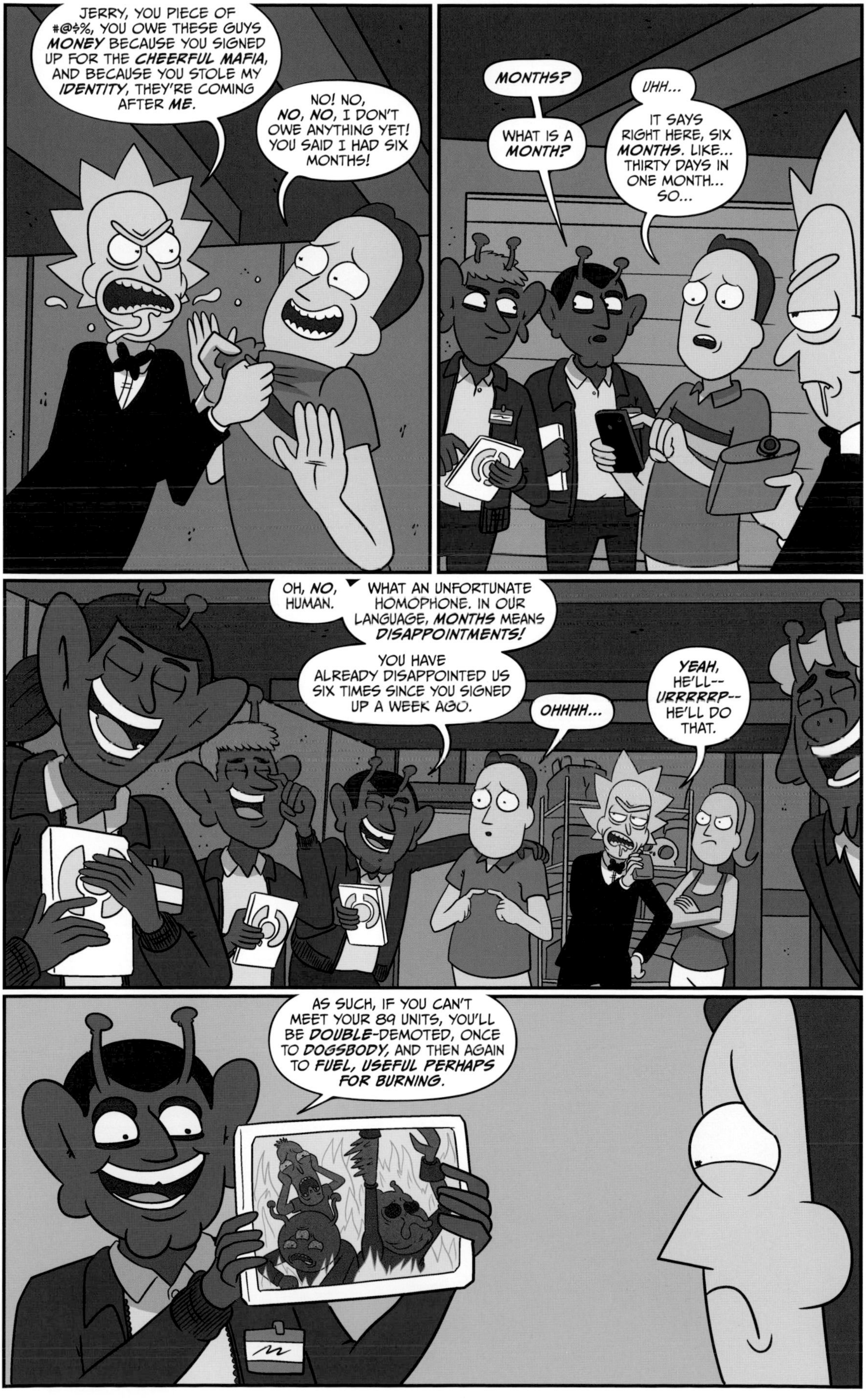
JERRY, YOU PIECE OF #@$%, YOU OWE THESE GUYS MONEY BECAUSE YOU SIGNED UP FOR THE CHEERFUL MAFIA, AND BECAUSE YOU STOLE MY IDENTITY, THEY'RE COMING AFTER ME.
NO! NO, NO, NO, I DON'T OWE ANYTHING YET! YOU SAID I HAD SIX MONTHS!
MONTHS?
WHAT IS A MONTH?
UHH...
IT SAYS RIGHT HERE, SIX MONTHS. LIKE... THIRTY DAYS IN ONE MONTH... SO...
OH, NO, HUMAN.
WHAT AN UNFORTUNATE HOMOPHONE. IN OUR LANGUAGE, MONTHS MEANS DISAPPOINTMENTS!
YOU HAVE ALREADY DISAPPOINTED US SIX TIMES SINCE YOU SIGNED UP A WEEK AGO.
OHHHH...
YEAH, HE'LL-- URRRRRP-- HE'LL DO THAT.
AS SUCH, IF YOU CAN'T MEET YOUR 89 UNITS, YOU'LL BE DOUBLE-DEMOTED, ONCE TO DOGSBODY, AND THEN AGAIN TO FUEL, USEFUL PERHAPS FOR BURNING.

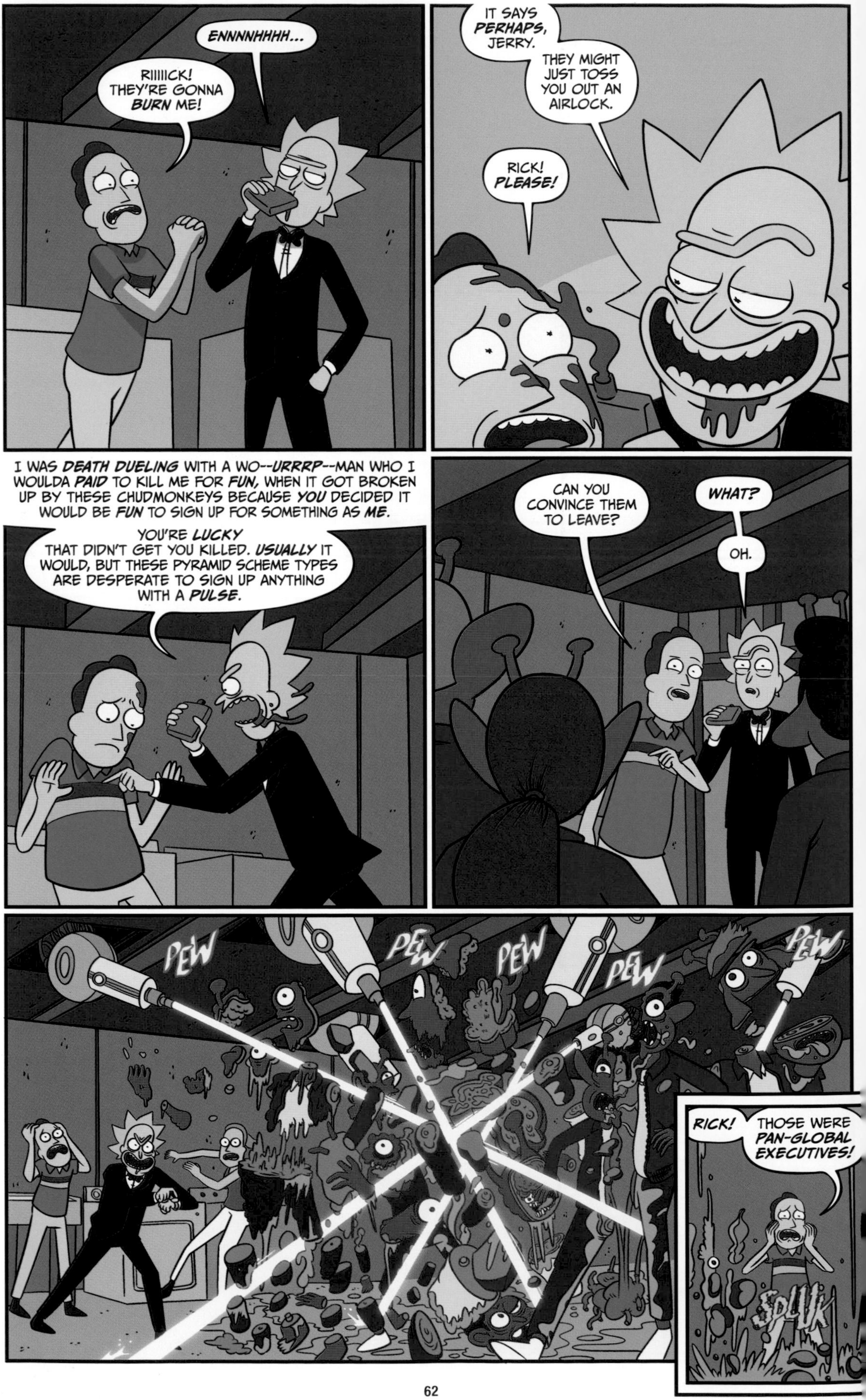
RIIIIICK! THEY'RE GONNA *BURN* ME!
ENNNNHHHH...
IT SAYS *PERHAPS,* JERRY.
THEY MIGHT JUST TOSS YOU OUT AN AIRLOCK.
RICK! *PLEASE!*
I WAS *DEATH DUELING* WITH A WO--*URRRP*--MAN WHO I WOULDA *PAID* TO KILL ME FOR *FUN,* WHEN IT GOT BROKEN UP BY THESE CHUDMONKEYS BECAUSE *YOU* DECIDED IT WOULD BE *FUN* TO SIGN UP FOR SOMETHING AS *ME.*
YOU'RE *LUCKY* THAT DIDN'T GET YOU KILLED. *USUALLY* IT WOULD, BUT THESE PYRAMID SCHEME TYPES ARE DESPERATE TO SIGN UP ANYTHING WITH A *PULSE.*
CAN YOU CONVINCE THEM TO LEAVE?
WHAT?
OH.
PEW
PEW
PEW
PEW
PEW
RICK!
THOSE WERE *PAN-GLOBAL EXECUTIVES!*

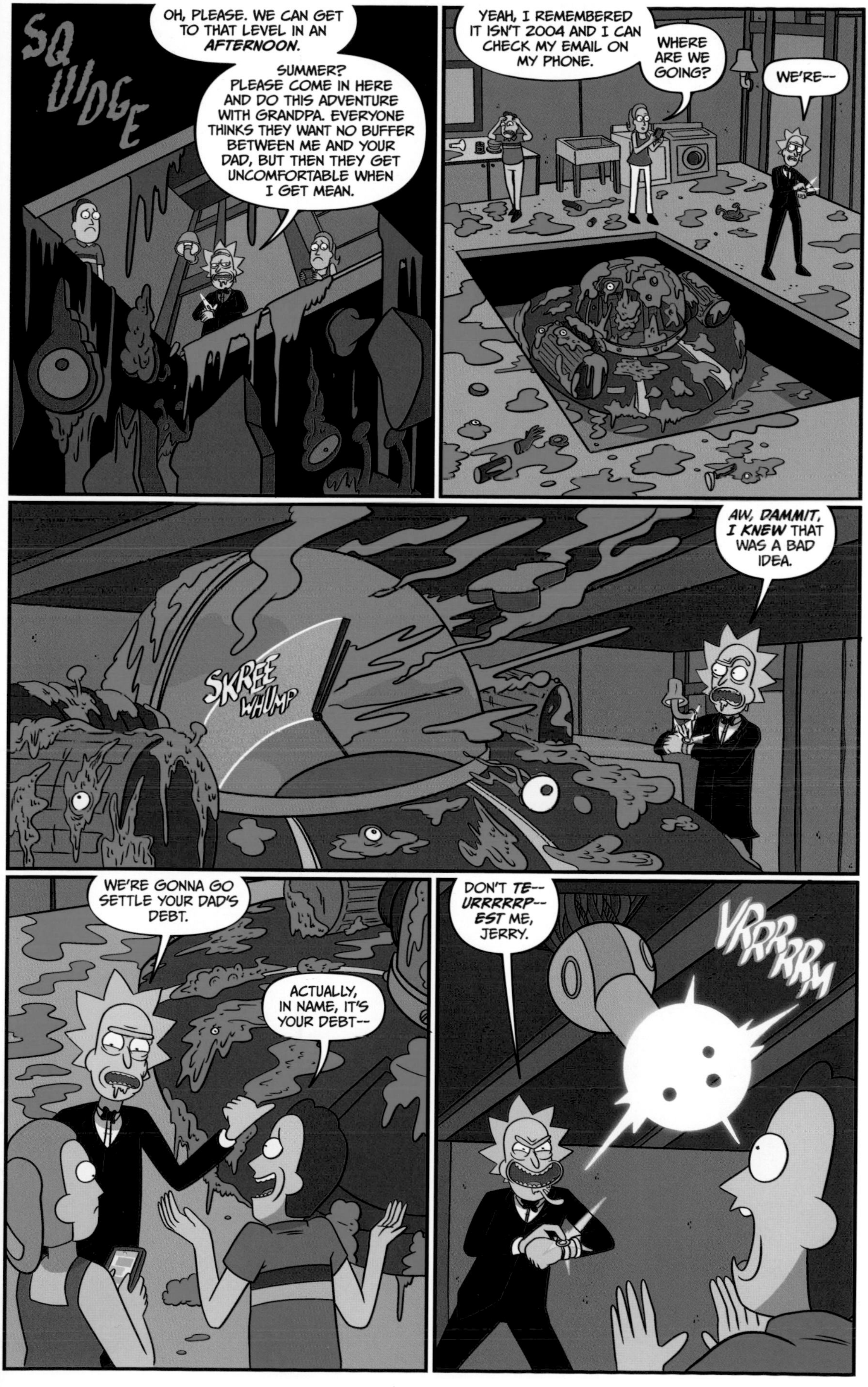
SQUIDGE
OH, PLEASE. WE CAN GET TO THAT LEVEL IN AN *AFTERNOON*.
SUMMER? PLEASE COME IN HERE AND DO THIS ADVENTURE WITH GRANDPA. EVERYONE THINKS THEY WANT NO BUFFER BETWEEN ME AND YOUR DAD, BUT THEN THEY GET UNCOMFORTABLE WHEN I GET MEAN.
YEAH, I REMEMBERED IT ISN'T 2004 AND I CAN CHECK MY EMAIL ON MY PHONE.
WHERE ARE WE GOING?
WE'RE--
AW, *DAMMIT*, *I KNEW* THAT WAS A BAD IDEA.
SKREEE WHUMP
WE'RE GONNA GO SETTLE YOUR DAD'S DEBT.
ACTUALLY, IN NAME, IT'S YOUR DEBT--
DON'T *TE-- URRRRRP-- EST* ME, JERRY.
VRRRRRRM

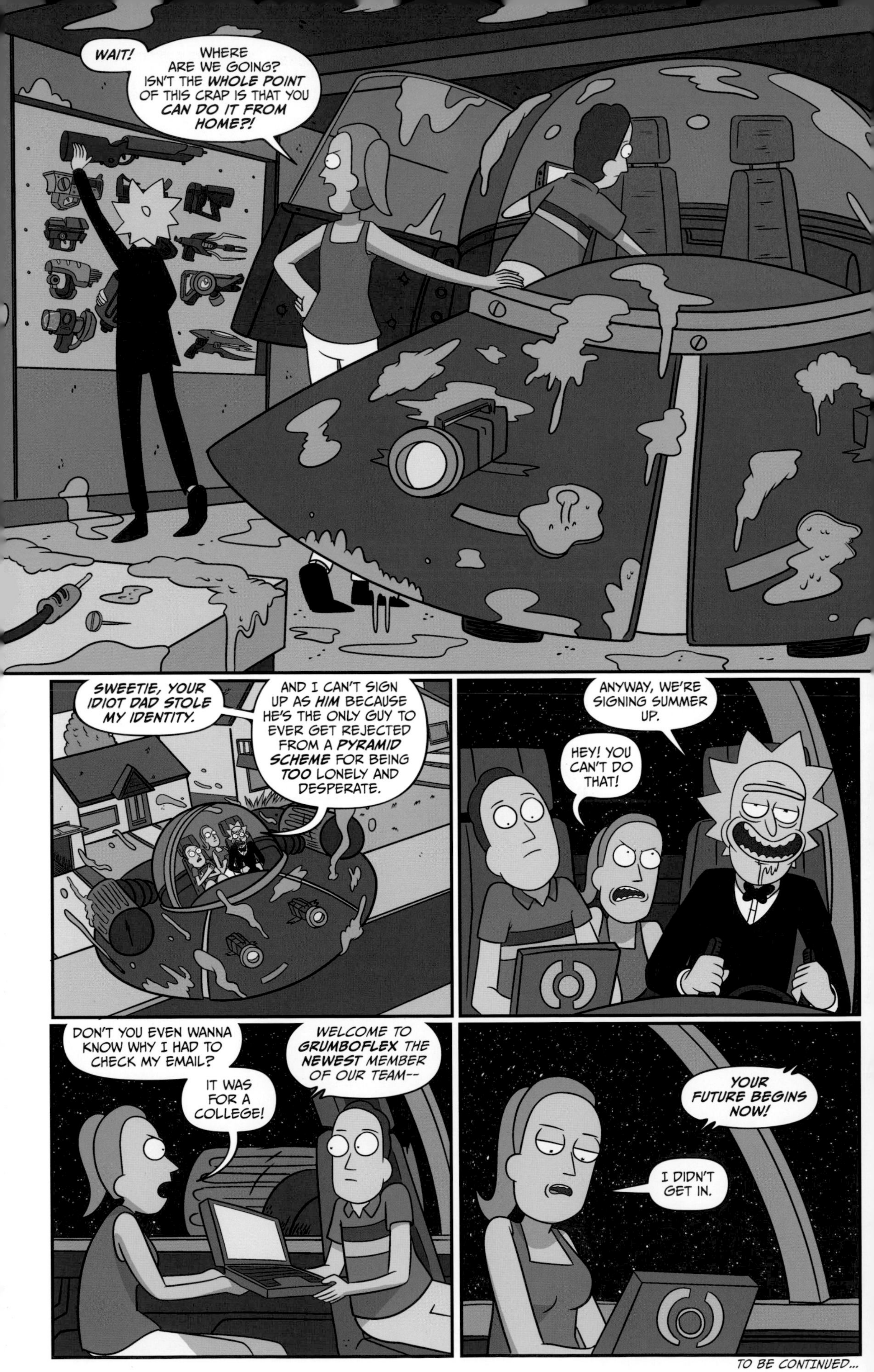
WAIT!
WHERE ARE WE GOING? ISN'T THE WHOLE POINT OF THIS CRAP IS THAT YOU CAN DO IT FROM HOME?!
SWEETIE, YOUR IDIOT DAD STOLE MY IDENTITY.
AND I CAN'T SIGN UP AS HIM BECAUSE HE'S THE ONLY GUY TO EVER GET REJECTED FROM A PYRAMID SCHEME FOR BEING TOO LONELY AND DESPERATE.
ANYWAY, WE'RE SIGNING SUMMER UP.
HEY! YOU CAN'T DO THAT!
DON'T YOU EVEN WANNA KNOW WHY I HAD TO CHECK MY EMAIL?
IT WAS FOR A COLLEGE!
WELCOME TO GRUMBOFLEX THE NEWEST MEMBER OF OUR TEAM--
YOUR FUTURE BEGINS NOW!
I DIDN'T GET IN.

TO BE CONTINUED...

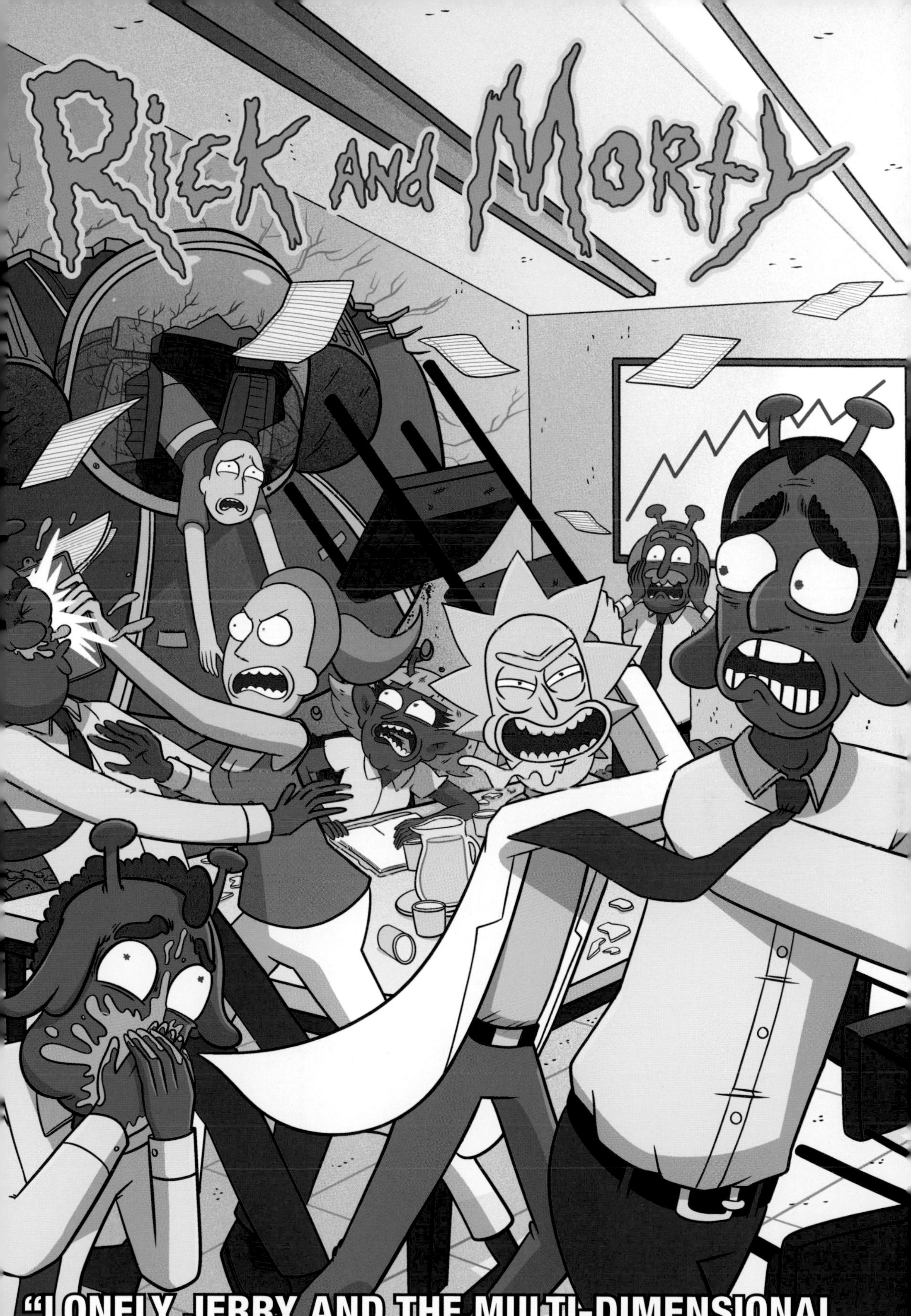
Rick and Morty

"LONELY JERRY AND THE MULTI-DIMENSIONAL SALES OPPORTUNITY" PART 2

WRITTEN BY **TINI HOWARD** ILLUSTRATED BY **MARC ELLERBY** COLORED BY **SARAH STERN** LETTERED BY **CRANK!**

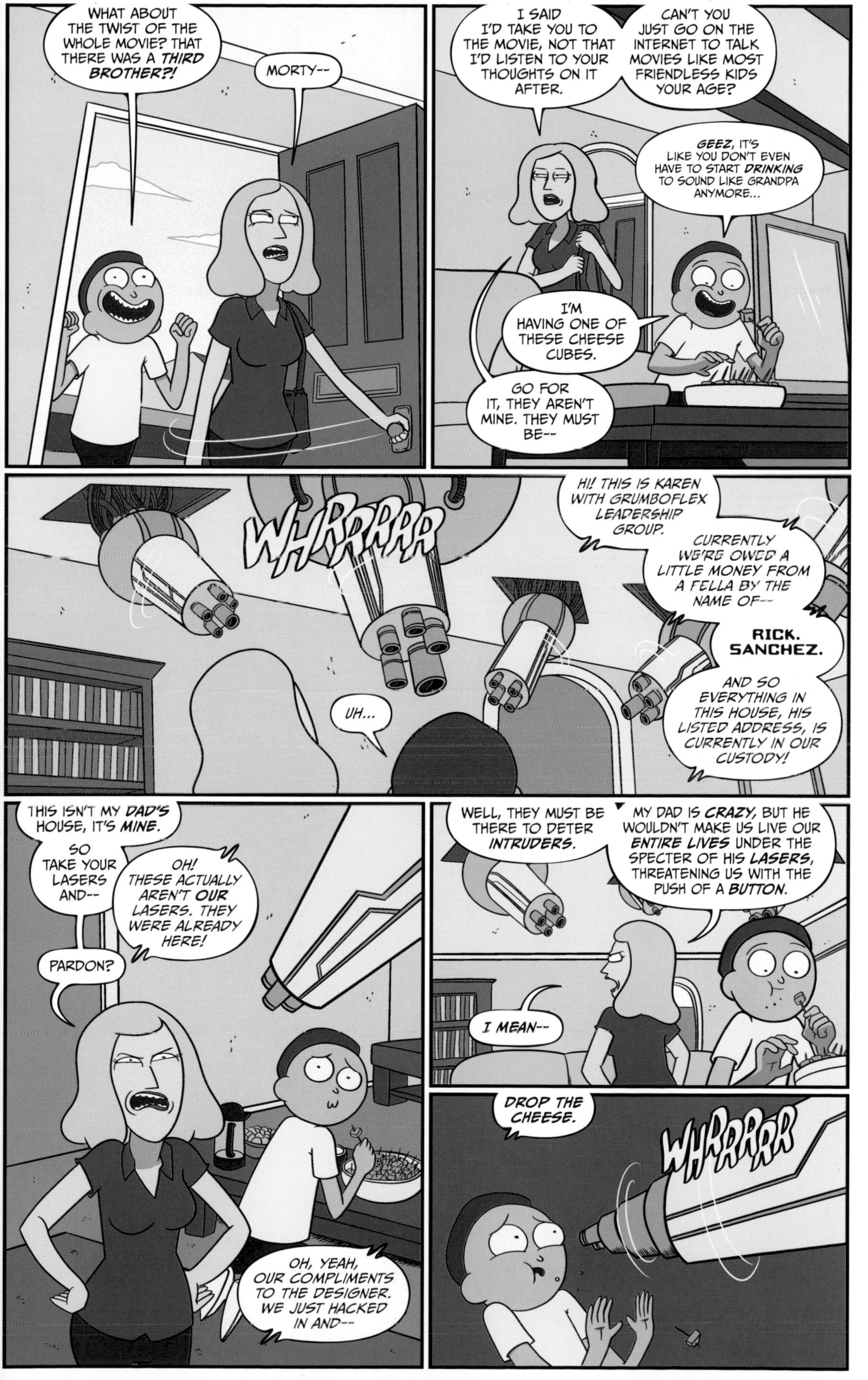
WHAT ABOUT THE TWIST OF THE WHOLE MOVIE? THAT THERE WAS A THIRD BROTHER?!
MORTY--
I SAID I'D TAKE YOU TO THE MOVIE, NOT THAT I'D LISTEN TO YOUR THOUGHTS ON IT AFTER.
CAN'T YOU JUST GO ON THE INTERNET TO TALK MOVIES LIKE MOST FRIENDLESS KIDS YOUR AGE?
GEEZ, IT'S LIKE YOU DON'T EVEN HAVE TO START DRINKING TO SOUND LIKE GRANDPA ANYMORE...
I'M HAVING ONE OF THESE CHEESE CUBES.
GO FOR IT, THEY AREN'T MINE. THEY MUST BE--
WHRRRRR
HI! THIS IS KAREN WITH GRUMBOFLEX LEADERSHIP GROUP.
CURRENTLY WE'RE OWED A LITTLE MONEY FROM A FELLA BY THE NAME OF--
RICK. SANCHEZ.
AND SO EVERYTHING IN THIS HOUSE, HIS LISTED ADDRESS, IS CURRENTLY IN OUR CUSTODY!
UH...
THIS ISN'T MY DAD'S HOUSE, IT'S MINE.
SO TAKE YOUR LASERS AND--
OH! THESE ACTUALLY AREN'T OUR LASERS. THEY WERE ALREADY HERE!
PARDON?
OH, YEAH, OUR COMPLIMENTS TO THE DESIGNER. WE JUST HACKED IN AND--
WELL, THEY MUST BE THERE TO DETER INTRUDERS.
MY DAD IS CRAZY, BUT HE WOULDN'T MAKE US LIVE OUR ENTIRE LIVES UNDER THE SPECTER OF HIS LASERS, THREATENING US WITH THE PUSH OF A BUTTON.
I MEAN--
DROP THE CHEESE.
WHRRRRR

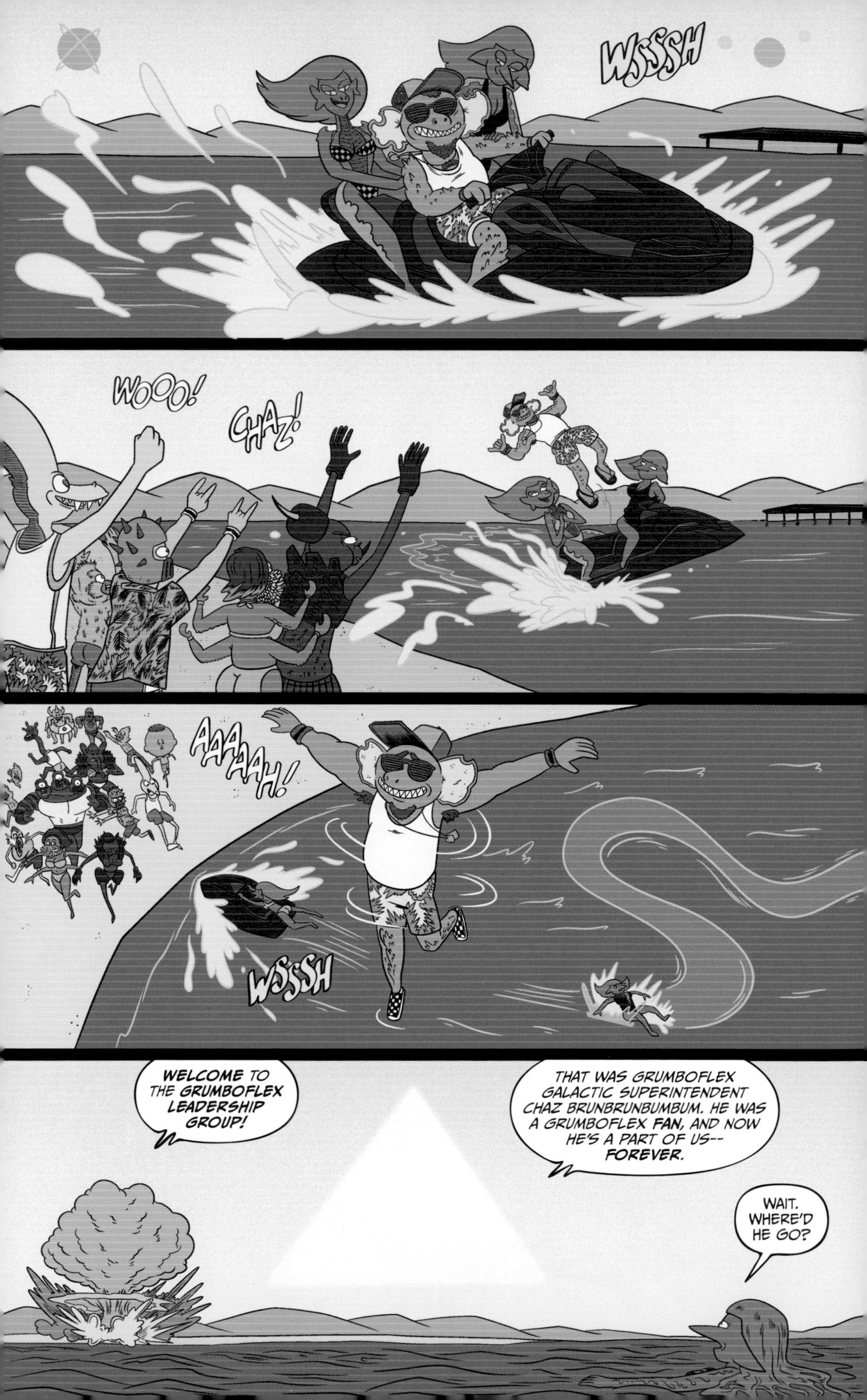
WSSSH
WOOO!
CHAZ!
AAAAAAH!
WSSSH
WELCOME TO THE GRUMBOFLEX LEADERSHIP GROUP!
THAT WAS GRUMBOFLEX GALACTIC SUPERINTENDENT CHAZ BRUNBRUNBUMBUM. HE WAS A GRUMBOFLEX FAN, AND NOW HE'S A PART OF US-- FOREVER.
WAIT. WHERE'D HE GO?

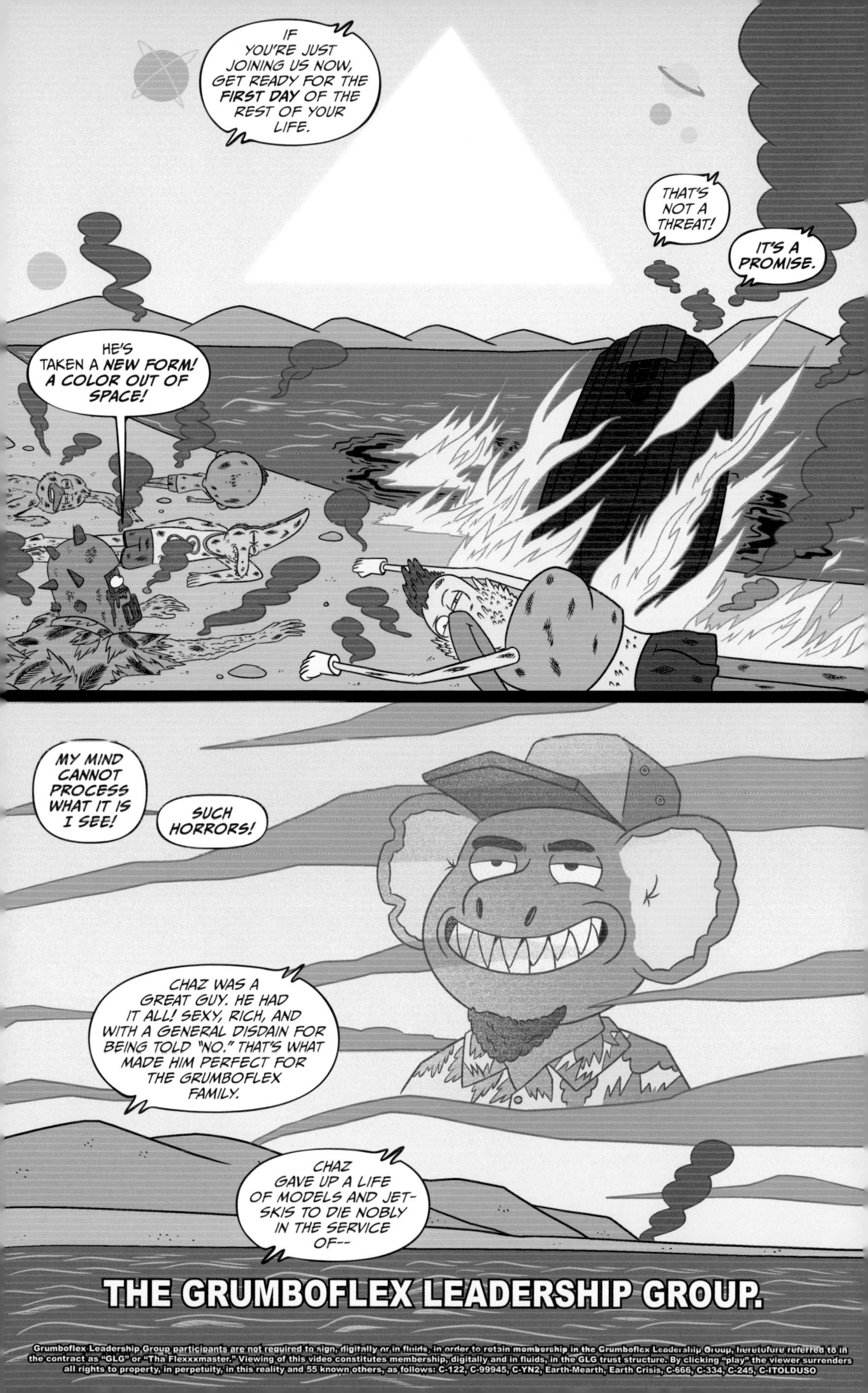
IF YOU'RE JUST JOINING US NOW, GET READY FOR THE FIRST DAY OF THE REST OF YOUR LIFE.
THAT'S NOT A THREAT!
IT'S A PROMISE.
HE'S TAKEN A NEW FORM! A COLOR OUT OF SPACE!
MY MIND CANNOT PROCESS WHAT IT IS I SEE!
SUCH HORRORS!
CHAZ WAS A GREAT GUY. HE HAD IT ALL! SEXY, RICH, AND WITH A GENERAL DISDAIN FOR BEING TOLD "NO." THAT'S WHAT MADE HIM PERFECT FOR THE GRUMBOFLEX FAMILY.
CHAZ GAVE UP A LIFE OF MODELS AND JET-SKIS TO DIE NOBLY IN THE SERVICE OF--
THE GRUMBOFLEX LEADERSHIP GROUP.
Grumboflex Leadership Group participants are not required to sign, digitally or in fluids, in order to retain membership in the Grumboflex Leadership Group, heretofore referred to in the contract as "GLG" or "Tha Flexxxmaster." Viewing of this video constitutes membership, digitally and in fluids, in the GLG trust structure. By clicking "play" the viewer surrenders all rights to property, in perpetuity, in this reality and 55 known others, as follows: C-122, C-99945, C-YN2, Earth-Mearth, Earth Crisis, C-666, C-334, C-245, C-ITOLDUSO

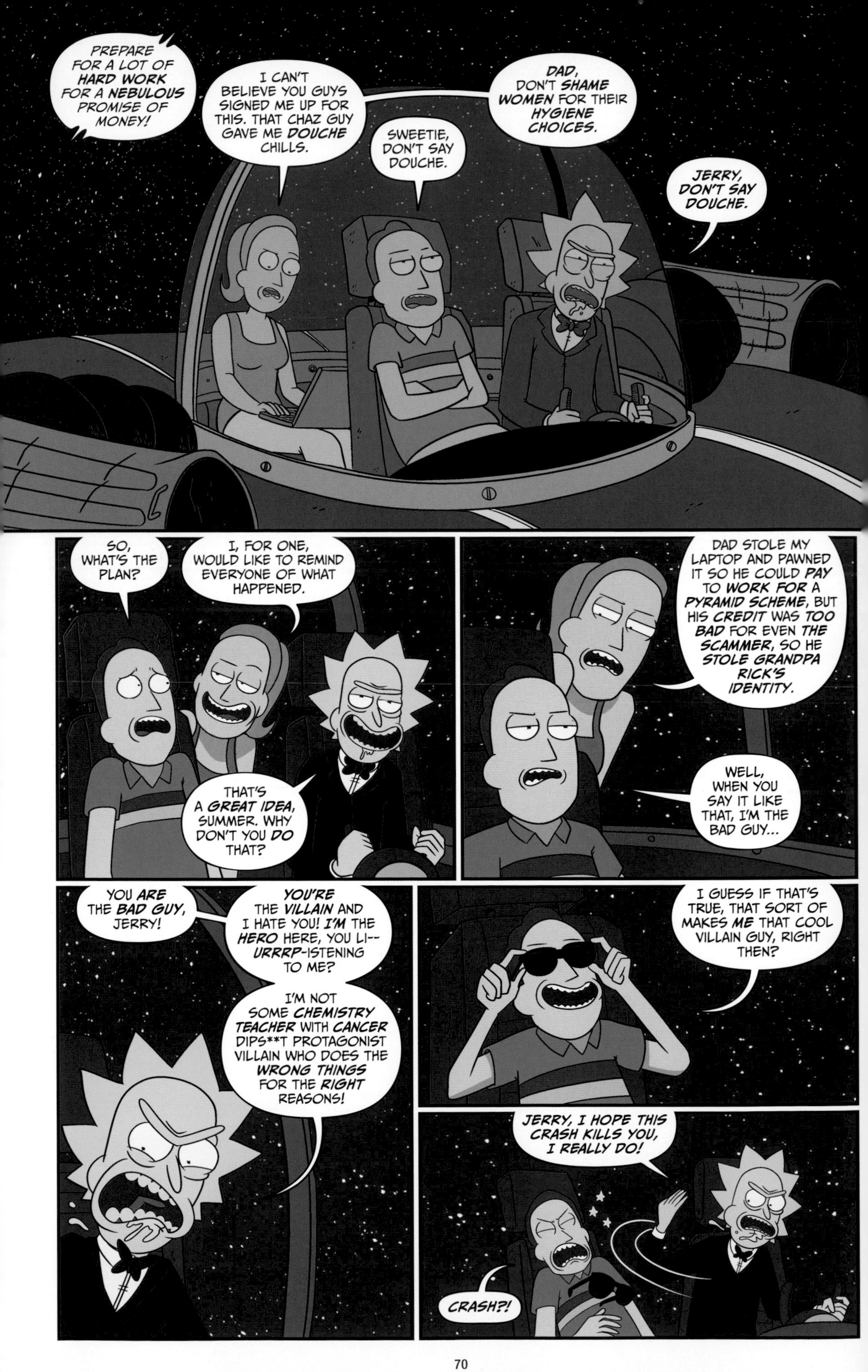
PREPARE FOR A LOT OF HARD WORK FOR A NEBULOUS PROMISE OF MONEY!
I CAN'T BELIEVE YOU GUYS SIGNED ME UP FOR THIS. THAT CHAZ GUY GAVE ME DOUCHE CHILLS.
SWEETIE, DON'T SAY DOUCHE.
DAD, DON'T SHAME WOMEN FOR THEIR HYGIENE CHOICES.
JERRY, DON'T SAY DOUCHE.
SO, WHAT'S THE PLAN?
I, FOR ONE, WOULD LIKE TO REMIND EVERYONE OF WHAT HAPPENED.
THAT'S A GREAT IDEA, SUMMER. WHY DON'T YOU DO THAT?
DAD STOLE MY LAPTOP AND PAWNED IT SO HE COULD PAY TO WORK FOR A PYRAMID SCHEME, BUT HIS CREDIT WAS TOO BAD FOR EVEN THE SCAMMER, SO HE STOLE GRANDPA RICK'S IDENTITY.
WELL, WHEN YOU SAY IT LIKE THAT, I'M THE BAD GUY...
YOU ARE THE BAD GUY, JERRY!
YOU'RE THE VILLAIN AND I HATE YOU! I'M THE HERO HERE, YOU LI-- URRRP-ISTENING TO ME?
I'M NOT SOME CHEMISTRY TEACHER WITH CANCER DIPS**T PROTAGONIST VILLAIN WHO DOES THE WRONG THINGS FOR THE RIGHT REASONS!
I GUESS IF THAT'S TRUE, THAT SORT OF MAKES ME THAT COOL VILLAIN GUY, RIGHT THEN?
JERRY, I HOPE THIS CRASH KILLS YOU, I REALLY DO!
CRASH?!

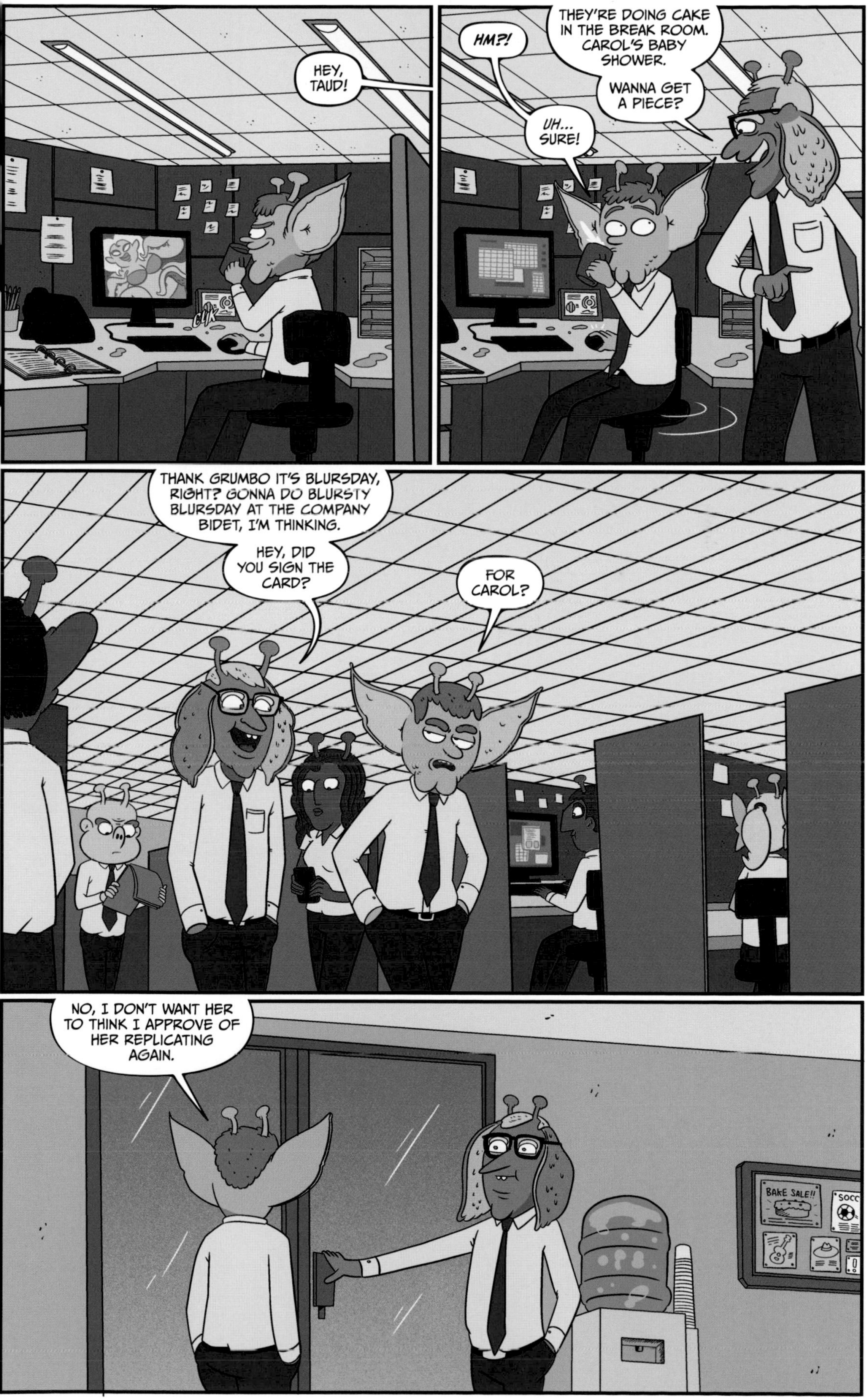
HEY, TAUD!
CLIK
HM?!
THEY'RE DOING CAKE IN THE BREAK ROOM. CAROL'S BABY SHOWER.
WANNA GET A PIECE?
UH... SURE!
THANK GRUMBO IT'S BLURSDAY, RIGHT? GONNA DO BLURSTY BLURSDAY AT THE COMPANY BIDET, I'M THINKING.
HEY, DID YOU SIGN THE CARD?
FOR CAROL?
NO, I DON'T WANT HER TO THINK I APPROVE OF HER REPLICATING AGAIN.
BAKE SALE!!

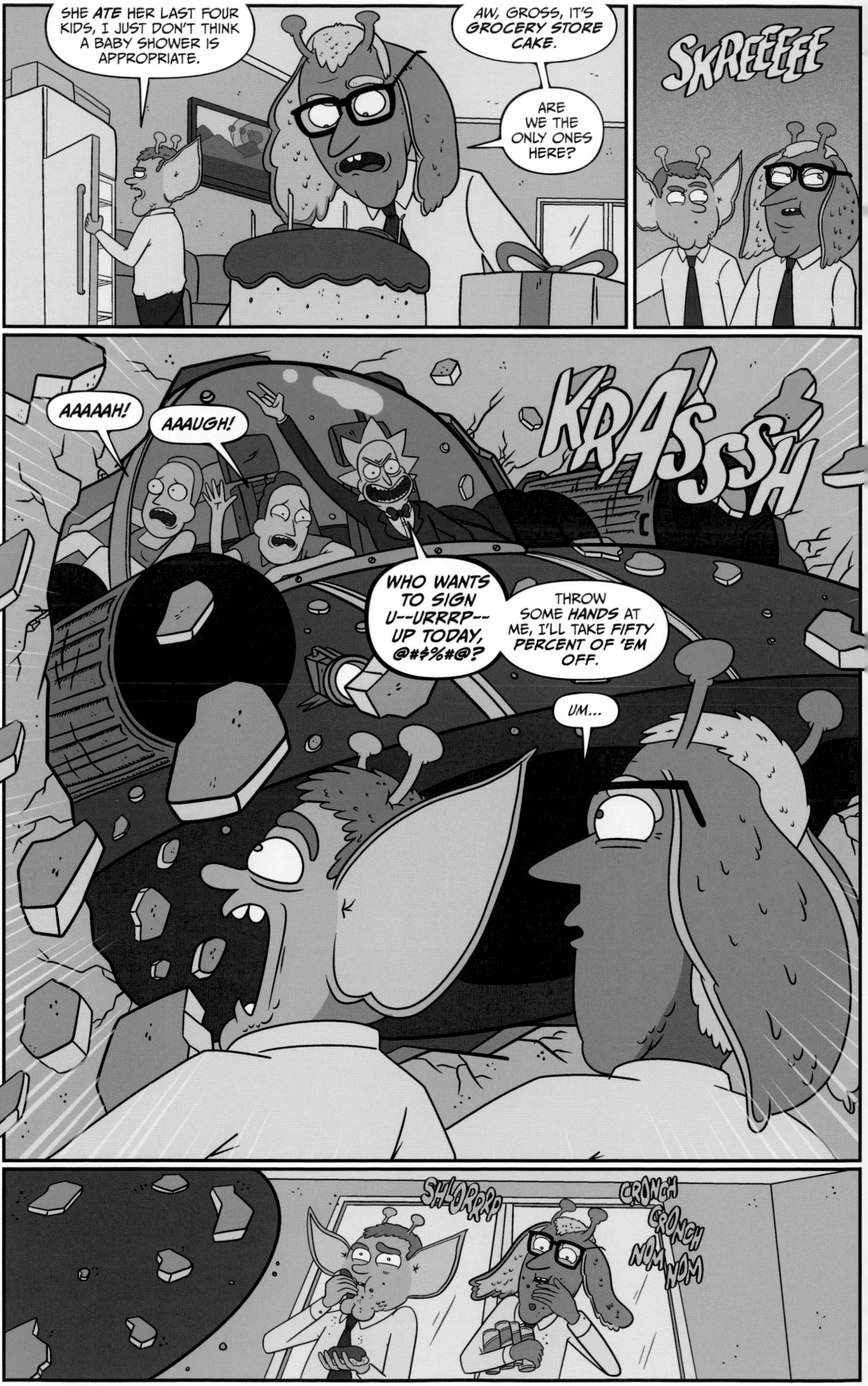
SHE ATE HER LAST FOUR KIDS, I JUST DON'T THINK A BABY SHOWER IS APPROPRIATE.
AW, GROSS, IT'S GROCERY STORE CAKE.
ARE WE THE ONLY ONES HERE?
SKREEEEE
KRASSSH
AAAAAH!
AAAUGH!
WHO WANTS TO SIGN U--URRRP--UP TODAY, @#$%#@?
THROW SOME HANDS AT ME, I'LL TAKE FIFTY PERCENT OF 'EM OFF.
UM...
SHLORRRP
CRONCH
CRONCH
NOM
NOM

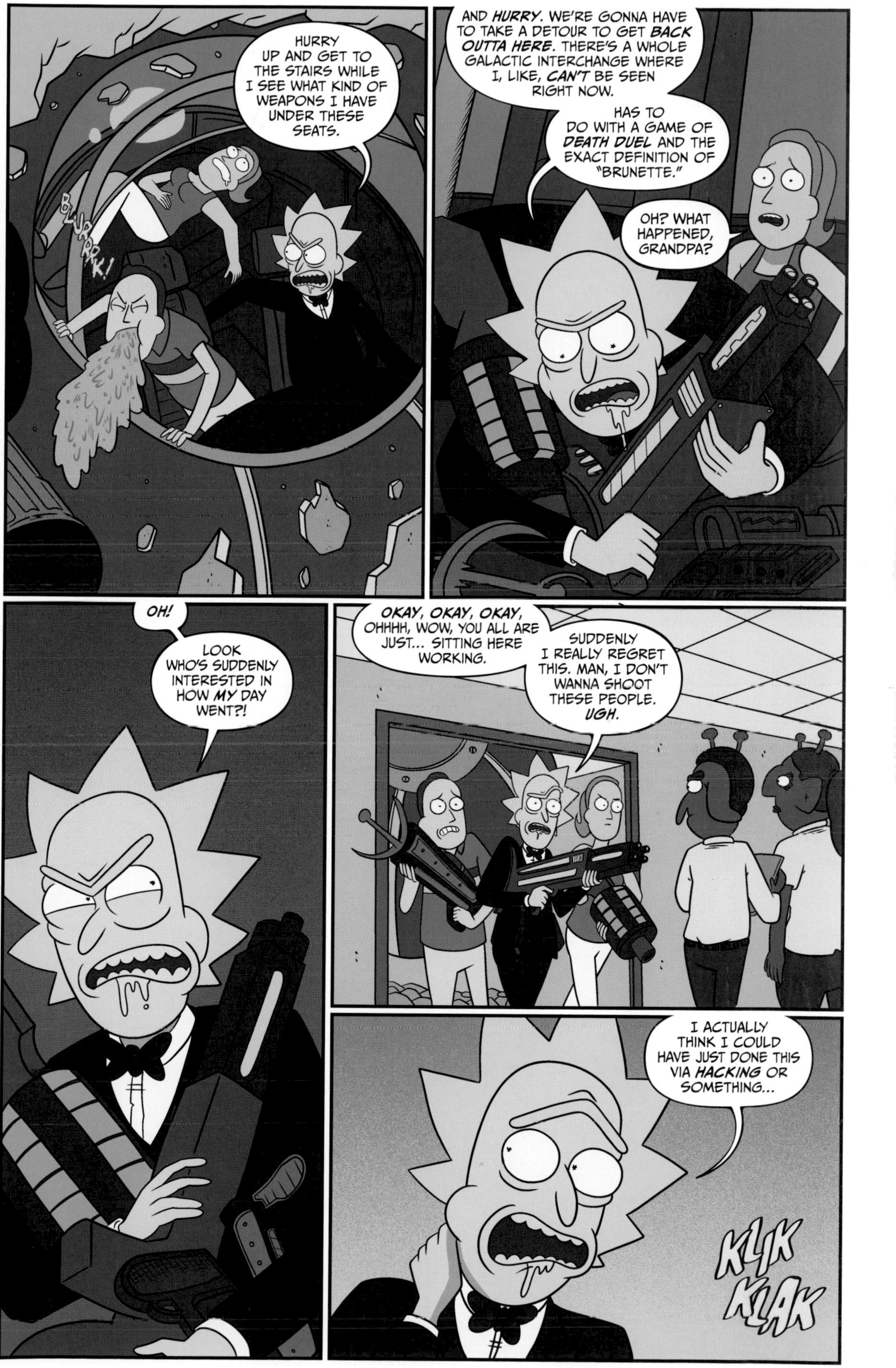

HURRY UP AND GET TO THE STAIRS WHILE I SEE WHAT KIND OF WEAPONS I HAVE UNDER THESE SEATS.
BLURRRK!
AND HURRY. WE'RE GONNA HAVE TO TAKE A DETOUR TO GET BACK OUTTA HERE. THERE'S A WHOLE GALACTIC INTERCHANGE WHERE I, LIKE, CAN'T BE SEEN RIGHT NOW.
HAS TO DO WITH A GAME OF DEATH DUEL AND THE EXACT DEFINITION OF "BRUNETTE."
OH? WHAT HAPPENED, GRANDPA?
OH!
LOOK WHO'S SUDDENLY INTERESTED IN HOW MY DAY WENT?!
OKAY, OKAY, OKAY, OHHHH, WOW, YOU ALL ARE JUST... SITTING HERE WORKING.
SUDDENLY I REALLY REGRET THIS. MAN, I DON'T WANNA SHOOT THESE PEOPLE. UGH.
I ACTUALLY THINK I COULD HAVE JUST DONE THIS VIA HACKING OR SOMETHING...
KLIK KLAK

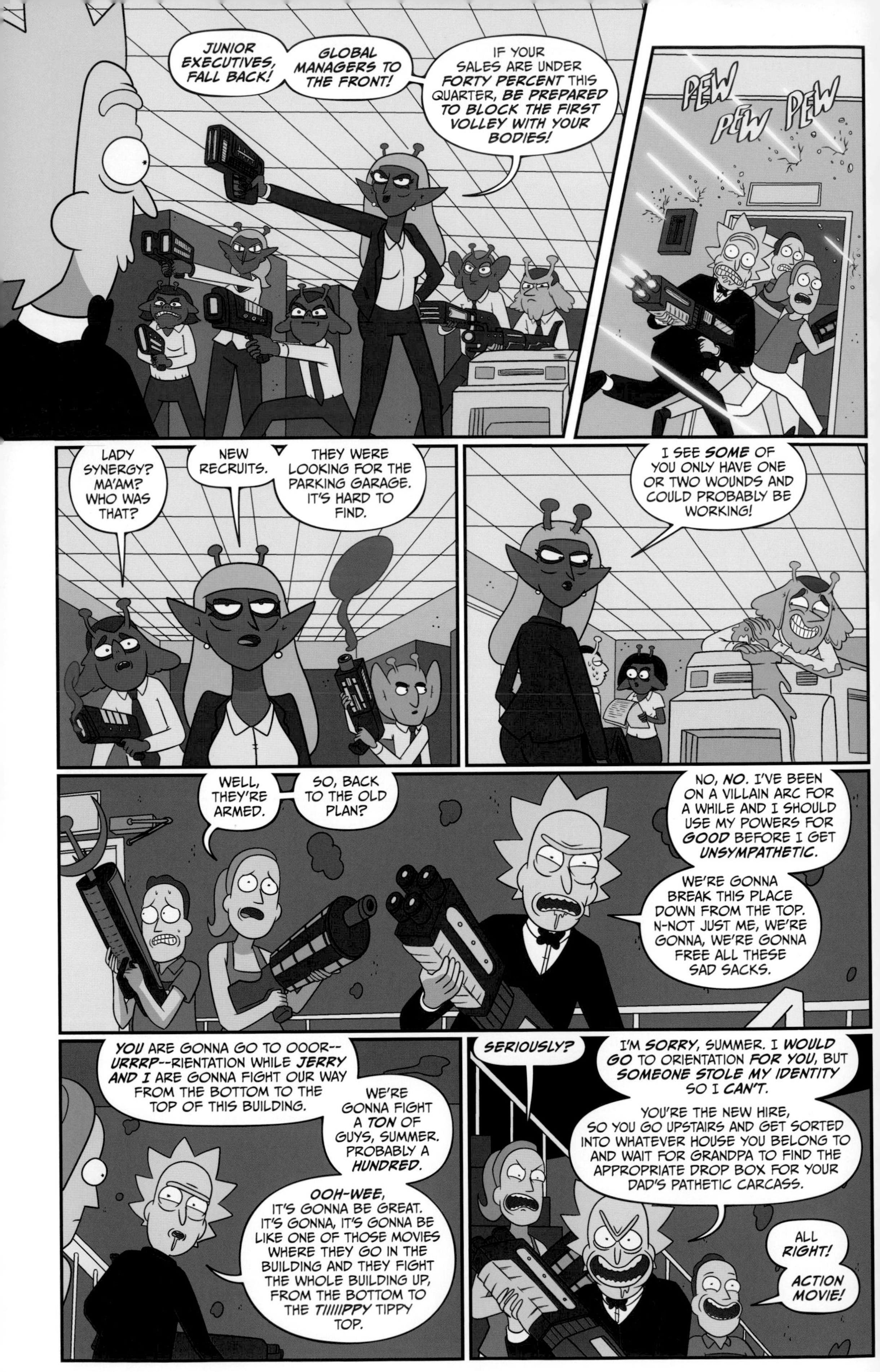
JUNIOR EXECUTIVES, FALL BACK!
GLOBAL MANAGERS TO THE FRONT!
IF YOUR SALES ARE UNDER FORTY PERCENT THIS QUARTER, BE PREPARED TO BLOCK THE FIRST VOLLEY WITH YOUR BODIES!
PEW PEW PEW
LADY SYNERGY? MA'AM? WHO WAS THAT?
NEW RECRUITS.
THEY WERE LOOKING FOR THE PARKING GARAGE. IT'S HARD TO FIND.
I SEE SOME OF YOU ONLY HAVE ONE OR TWO WOUNDS AND COULD PROBABLY BE WORKING!
WELL, THEY'RE ARMED.
SO, BACK TO THE OLD PLAN?
NO, NO. I'VE BEEN ON A VILLAIN ARC FOR A WHILE AND I SHOULD USE MY POWERS FOR GOOD BEFORE I GET UNSYMPATHETIC.
WE'RE GONNA BREAK THIS PLACE DOWN FROM THE TOP. N-NOT JUST ME, WE'RE GONNA, WE'RE GONNA FREE ALL THESE SAD SACKS.
YOU ARE GONNA GO TO OOOR--URRRP--RIENTATION WHILE JERRY AND I ARE GONNA FIGHT OUR WAY FROM THE BOTTOM TO THE TOP OF THIS BUILDING.
WE'RE GONNA FIGHT A TON OF GUYS, SUMMER. PROBABLY A HUNDRED.
OOH-WEE, IT'S GONNA BE GREAT. IT'S GONNA, IT'S GONNA BE LIKE ONE OF THOSE MOVIES WHERE THEY GO IN THE BUILDING AND THEY FIGHT THE WHOLE BUILDING UP, FROM THE BOTTOM TO THE TIIIIIPPY TIPPY TOP.
SERIOUSLY?
I'M SORRY, SUMMER. I WOULD GO TO ORIENTATION FOR YOU, BUT SOMEONE STOLE MY IDENTITY SO I CAN'T.
YOU'RE THE NEW HIRE, SO YOU GO UPSTAIRS AND GET SORTED INTO WHATEVER HOUSE YOU BELONG TO AND WAIT FOR GRANDPA TO FIND THE APPROPRIATE DROP BOX FOR YOUR DAD'S PATHETIC CARCASS.
ALL RIGHT!
ACTION MOVIE!

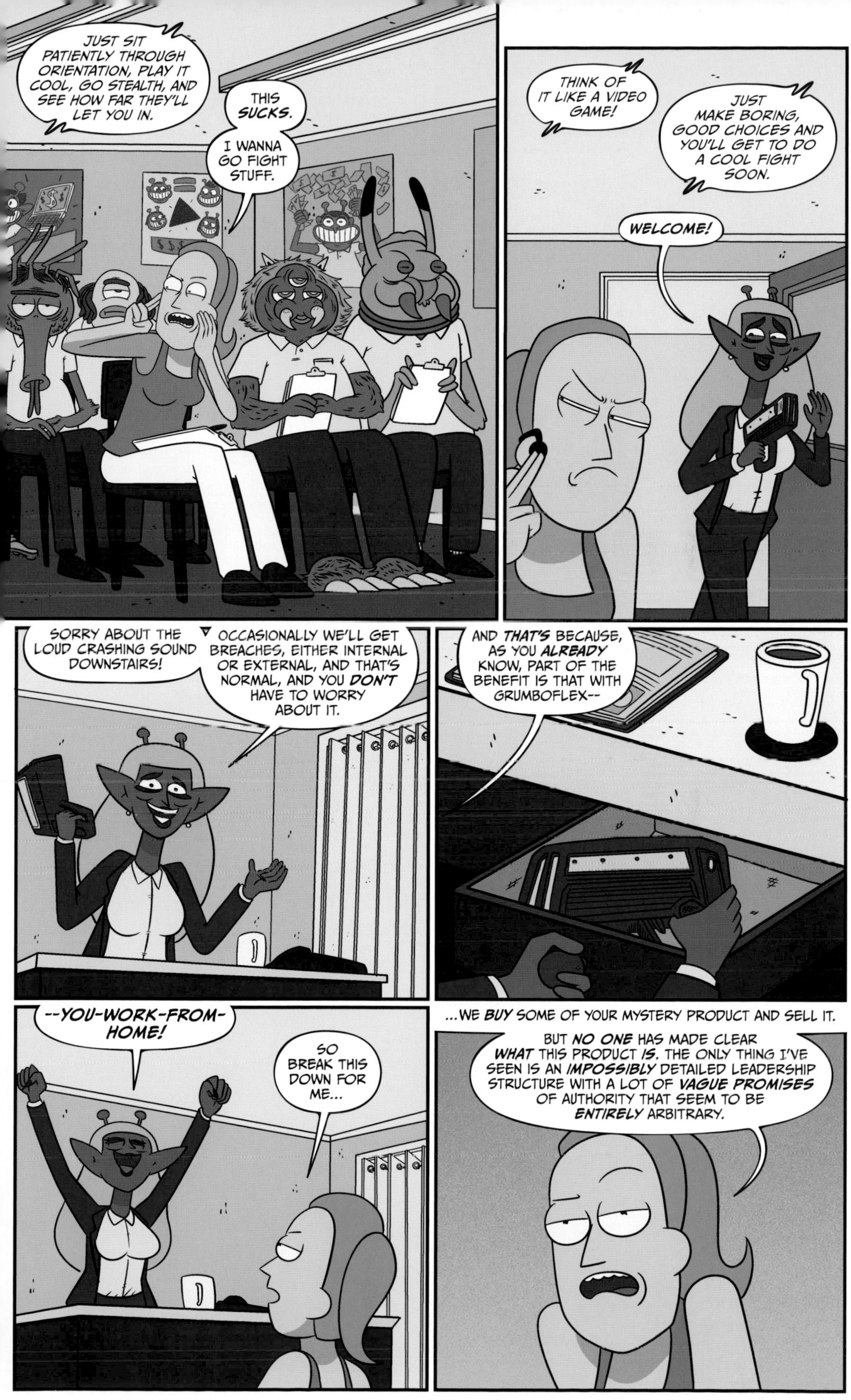
JUST SIT PATIENTLY THROUGH ORIENTATION, PLAY IT COOL, GO STEALTH, AND SEE HOW FAR THEY'LL LET YOU IN.
THIS SUCKS.
I WANNA GO FIGHT STUFF.
THINK OF IT LIKE A VIDEO GAME!
JUST MAKE BORING, GOOD CHOICES AND YOU'LL GET TO DO A COOL FIGHT SOON.
WELCOME!
SORRY ABOUT THE LOUD CRASHING SOUND DOWNSTAIRS!
OCCASIONALLY WE'LL GET BREACHES, EITHER INTERNAL OR EXTERNAL, AND THAT'S NORMAL, AND YOU DON'T HAVE TO WORRY ABOUT IT.
AND THAT'S BECAUSE, AS YOU ALREADY KNOW, PART OF THE BENEFIT IS THAT WITH GRUMBOFLEX--
--YOU-WORK-FROM-HOME!
SO BREAK THIS DOWN FOR ME...
...WE BUY SOME OF YOUR MYSTERY PRODUCT AND SELL IT.
BUT NO ONE HAS MADE CLEAR WHAT THIS PRODUCT IS. THE ONLY THING I'VE SEEN IS AN IMPOSSIBLY DETAILED LEADERSHIP STRUCTURE WITH A LOT OF VAGUE PROMISES OF AUTHORITY THAT SEEM TO BE ENTIRELY ARBITRARY.

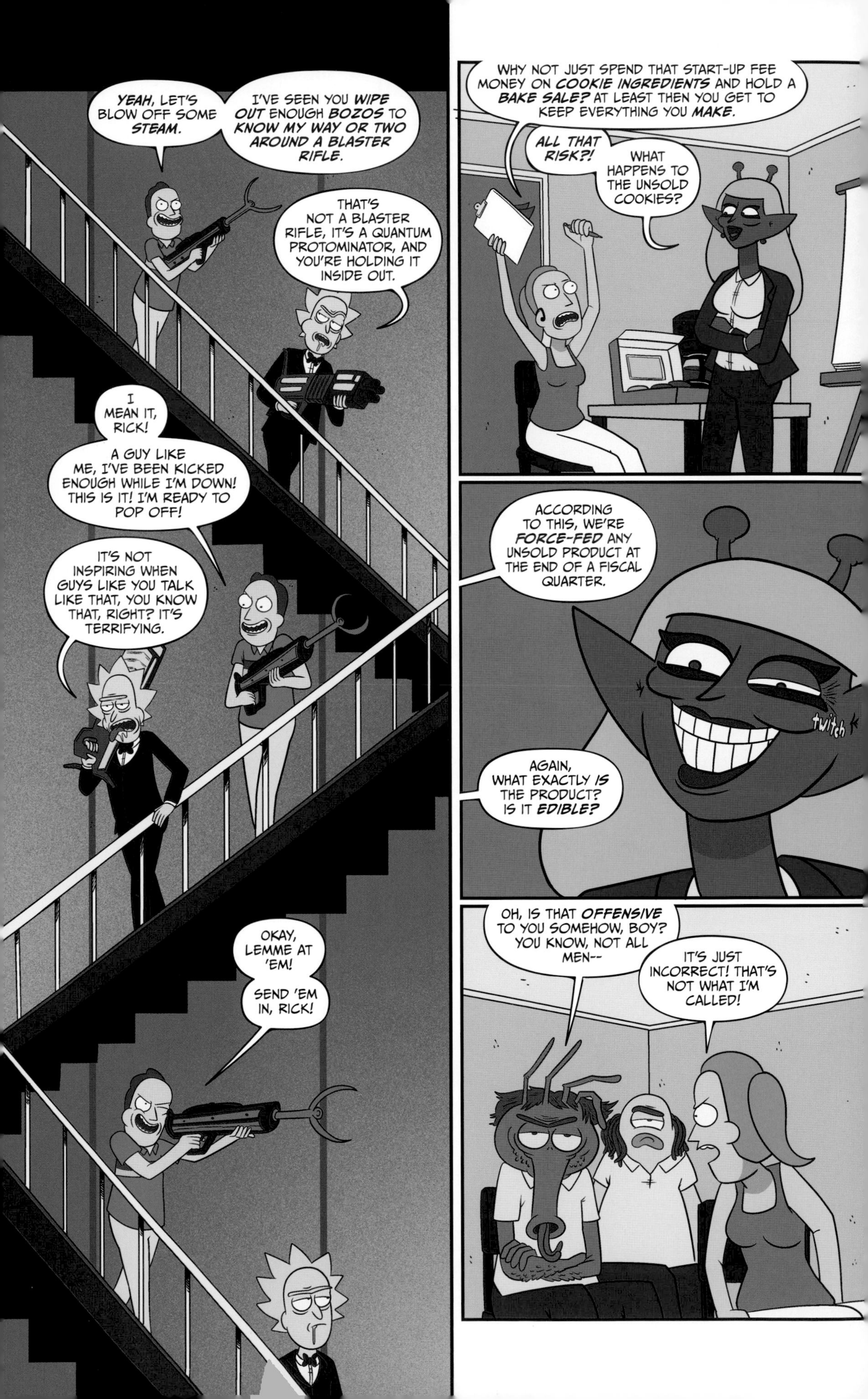
YEAH, LET'S BLOW OFF SOME STEAM.
I'VE SEEN YOU WIPE OUT ENOUGH BOZOS TO KNOW MY WAY OR TWO AROUND A BLASTER RIFLE.
THAT'S NOT A BLASTER RIFLE, IT'S A QUANTUM PROTOMINATOR, AND YOU'RE HOLDING IT INSIDE OUT.
I MEAN IT, RICK!
A GUY LIKE ME, I'VE BEEN KICKED ENOUGH WHILE I'M DOWN! THIS IS IT! I'M READY TO POP OFF!
IT'S NOT INSPIRING WHEN GUYS LIKE YOU TALK LIKE THAT, YOU KNOW THAT, RIGHT? IT'S TERRIFYING.
OKAY, LEMME AT 'EM!
SEND 'EM IN, RICK!
WHY NOT JUST SPEND THAT START-UP FEE MONEY ON COOKIE INGREDIENTS AND HOLD A BAKE SALE? AT LEAST THEN YOU GET TO KEEP EVERYTHING YOU MAKE.
ALL THAT RISK?!
WHAT HAPPENS TO THE UNSOLD COOKIES?
ACCORDING TO THIS, WE'RE FORCE-FED ANY UNSOLD PRODUCT AT THE END OF A FISCAL QUARTER.
twitch
AGAIN, WHAT EXACTLY IS THE PRODUCT? IS IT EDIBLE?
OH, IS THAT OFFENSIVE TO YOU SOMEHOW, BOY? YOU KNOW, NOT ALL MEN--
IT'S JUST INCORRECT! THAT'S NOT WHAT I'M CALLED!

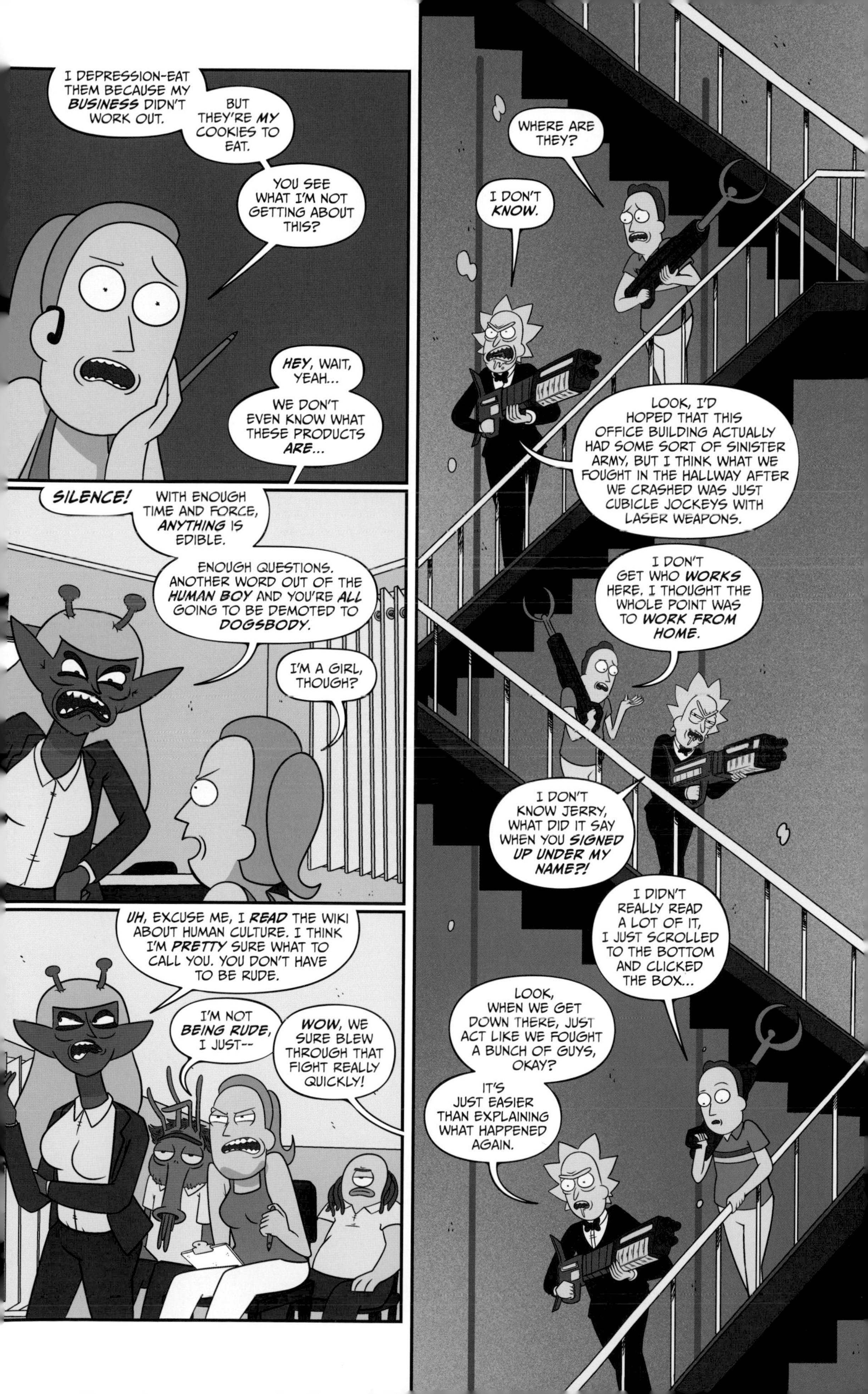

I DEPRESSION-EAT THEM BECAUSE MY BUSINESS DIDN'T WORK OUT.
BUT THEY'RE MY COOKIES TO EAT.
YOU SEE WHAT I'M NOT GETTING ABOUT THIS?
HEY, WAIT, YEAH...
WE DON'T EVEN KNOW WHAT THESE PRODUCTS ARE...
SILENCE!
WITH ENOUGH TIME AND FORCE, ANYTHING IS EDIBLE.
ENOUGH QUESTIONS. ANOTHER WORD OUT OF THE HUMAN BOY AND YOU'RE ALL GOING TO BE DEMOTED TO DOGSBODY.
I'M A GIRL, THOUGH?
UH, EXCUSE ME, I READ THE WIKI ABOUT HUMAN CULTURE. I THINK I'M PRETTY SURE WHAT TO CALL YOU. YOU DON'T HAVE TO BE RUDE.
I'M NOT BEING RUDE, I JUST--
WOW, WE SURE BLEW THROUGH THAT FIGHT REALLY QUICKLY!
WHERE ARE THEY?
I DON'T KNOW.
LOOK, I'D HOPED THAT THIS OFFICE BUILDING ACTUALLY HAD SOME SORT OF SINISTER ARMY, BUT I THINK WHAT WE FOUGHT IN THE HALLWAY AFTER WE CRASHED WAS JUST CUBICLE JOCKEYS WITH LASER WEAPONS.
I DON'T GET WHO WORKS HERE. I THOUGHT THE WHOLE POINT WAS TO WORK FROM HOME.
I DON'T KNOW JERRY, WHAT DID IT SAY WHEN YOU SIGNED UP UNDER MY NAME?!
I DIDN'T REALLY READ A LOT OF IT, I JUST SCROLLED TO THE BOTTOM AND CLICKED THE BOX...
LOOK, WHEN WE GET DOWN THERE, JUST ACT LIKE WE FOUGHT A BUNCH OF GUYS, OKAY?
IT'S JUST EASIER THAN EXPLAINING WHAT HAPPENED AGAIN.

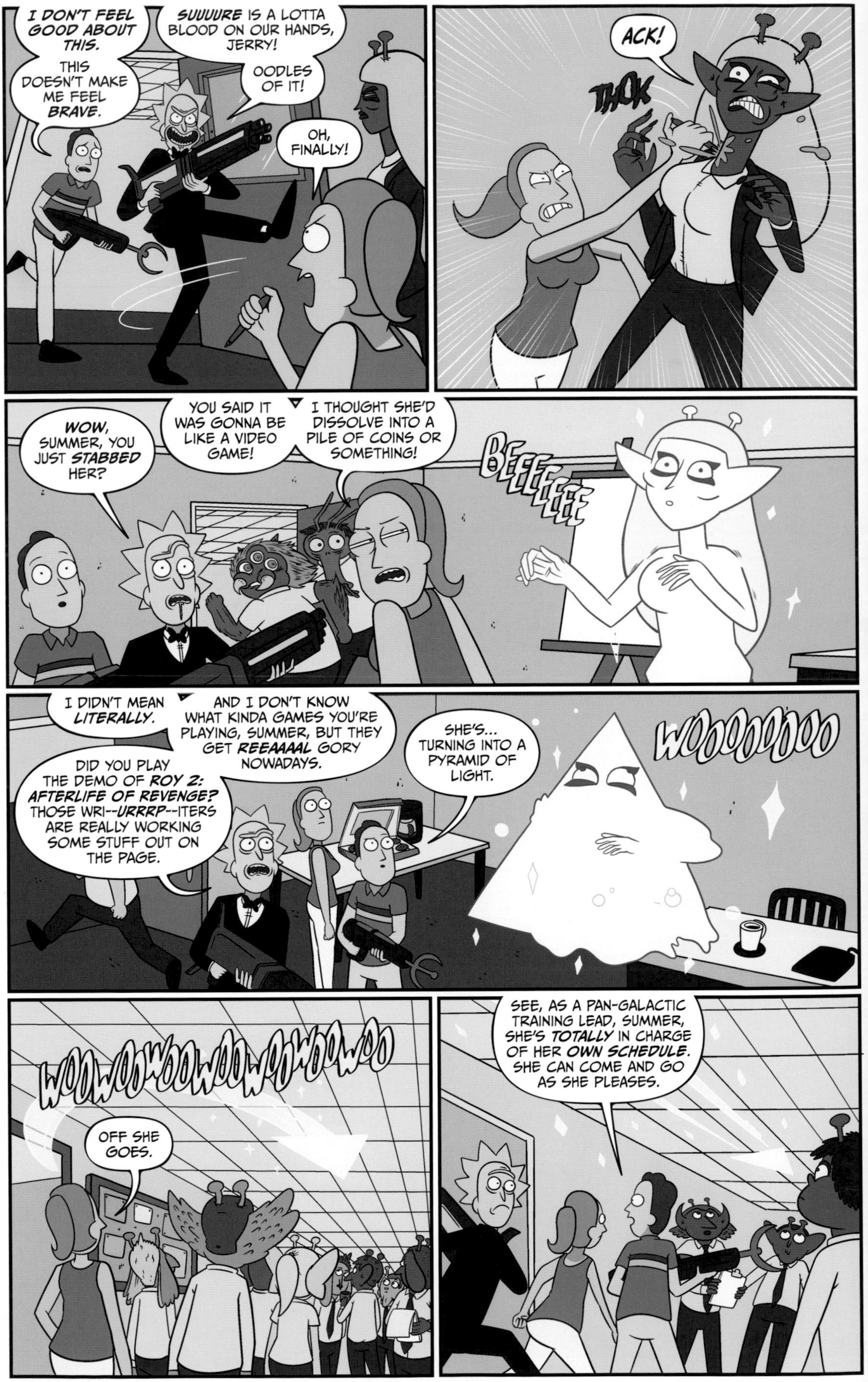
I DON'T FEEL GOOD ABOUT THIS.
THIS DOESN'T MAKE ME FEEL BRAVE.
SUUUURE IS A LOTTA BLOOD ON OUR HANDS, JERRY!
OODLES OF IT!
OH, FINALLY!
ACK!
THOK
WOW, SUMMER, YOU JUST STABBED HER?
YOU SAID IT WAS GONNA BE LIKE A VIDEO GAME!
I THOUGHT SHE'D DISSOLVE INTO A PILE OF COINS OR SOMETHING!
BEEEEEEE
I DIDN'T MEAN LITERALLY.
AND I DON'T KNOW WHAT KINDA GAMES YOU'RE PLAYING, SUMMER, BUT THEY GET REEAAAAL GORY NOWADAYS.
DID YOU PLAY THE DEMO OF ROY 2: AFTERLIFE OF REVENGE? THOSE WRI--URRRP--ITERS ARE REALLY WORKING SOME STUFF OUT ON THE PAGE.
SHE'S... TURNING INTO A PYRAMID OF LIGHT.
WOOOOOOOO
WOOWOOWOOWOOWOOWOOWOO
OFF SHE GOES.
SEE, AS A PAN-GALACTIC TRAINING LEAD, SUMMER, SHE'S TOTALLY IN CHARGE OF HER OWN SCHEDULE. SHE CAN COME AND GO AS SHE PLEASES.

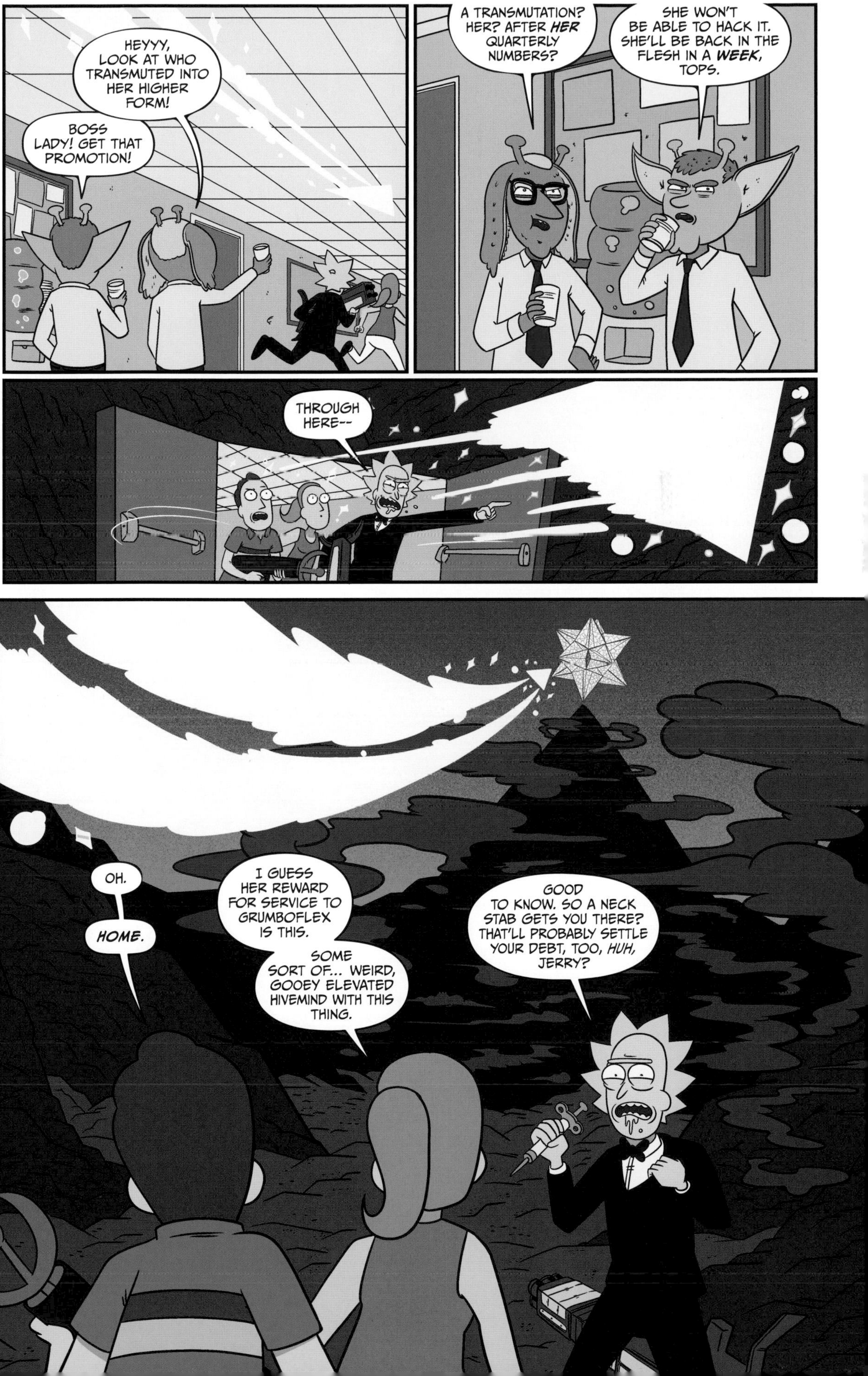
HEYYY, LOOK AT WHO TRANSMUTED INTO HER HIGHER FORM!
BOSS LADY! GET THAT PROMOTION!
A TRANSMUTATION? HER? AFTER *HER* QUARTERLY NUMBERS?
SHE WON'T BE ABLE TO HACK IT. SHE'LL BE BACK IN THE FLESH IN A *WEEK,* TOPS.
THROUGH HERE--
OH.
HOME.
I GUESS HER REWARD FOR SERVICE TO GRUMBOFLEX IS THIS.
SOME SORT OF... WEIRD, GOOEY ELEVATED HIVEMIND WITH THIS THING.
GOOD TO KNOW. SO A NECK STAB GETS YOU THERE? THAT'LL PROBABLY SETTLE YOUR DEBT, TOO, *HUH,* JERRY?

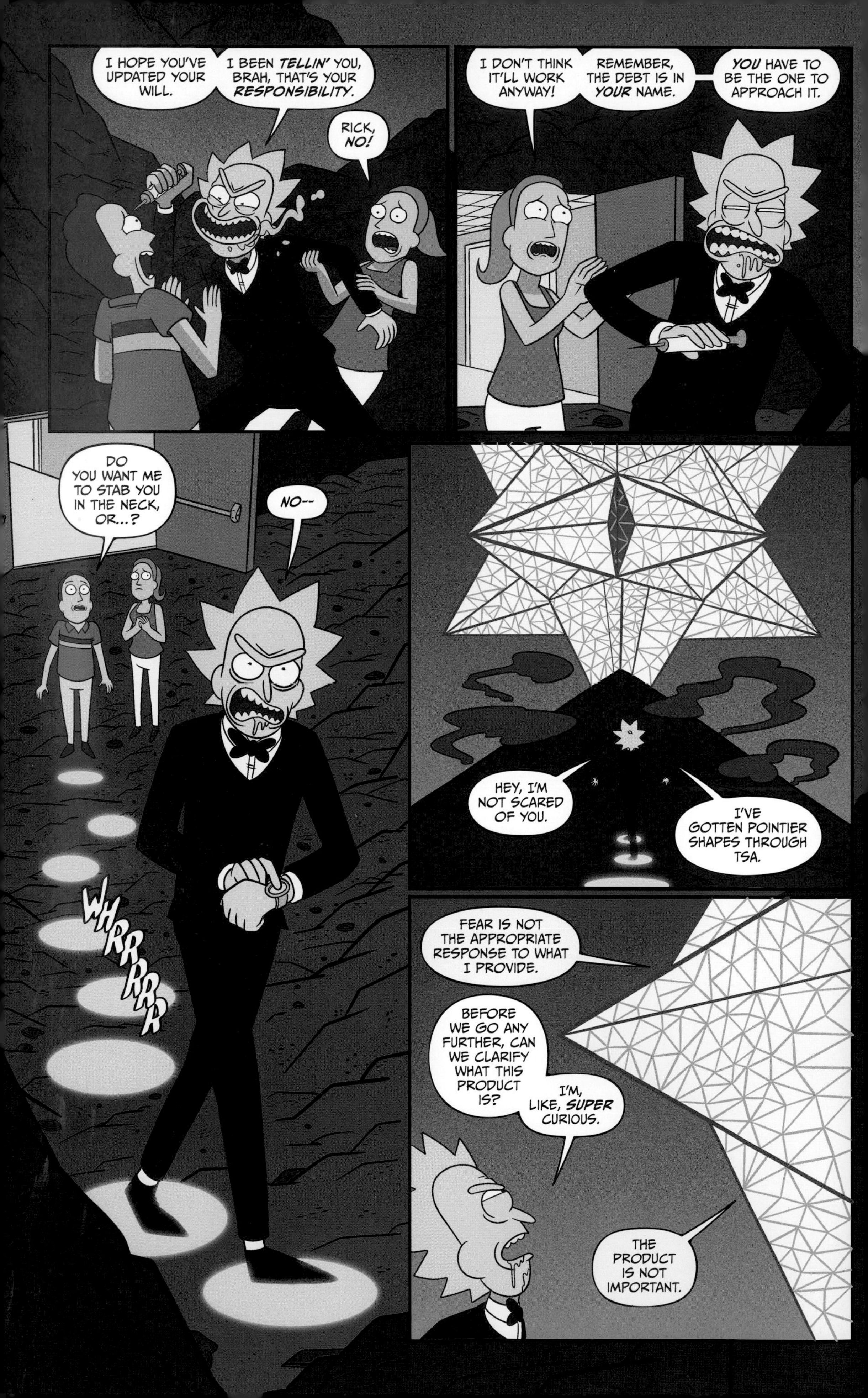
I HOPE YOU'VE UPDATED YOUR WILL.
I BEEN *TELLIN'* YOU, BRAH, THAT'S YOUR *RESPONSIBILITY*.
RICK, *NO!*
I DON'T THINK IT'LL WORK ANYWAY!
REMEMBER, THE DEBT IS IN *YOUR* NAME.
YOU HAVE TO BE THE ONE TO APPROACH IT.
DO YOU WANT ME TO STAB YOU IN THE NECK, OR...?
NO--
WHRRRRRR
HEY, I'M NOT SCARED OF YOU.
I'VE GOTTEN POINTIER SHAPES THROUGH TSA.
FEAR IS NOT THE APPROPRIATE RESPONSE TO WHAT I PROVIDE.
BEFORE WE GO ANY FURTHER, CAN WE CLARIFY WHAT THIS PRODUCT IS?
I'M, LIKE, *SUPER* CURIOUS.
THE PRODUCT IS NOT IMPORTANT.

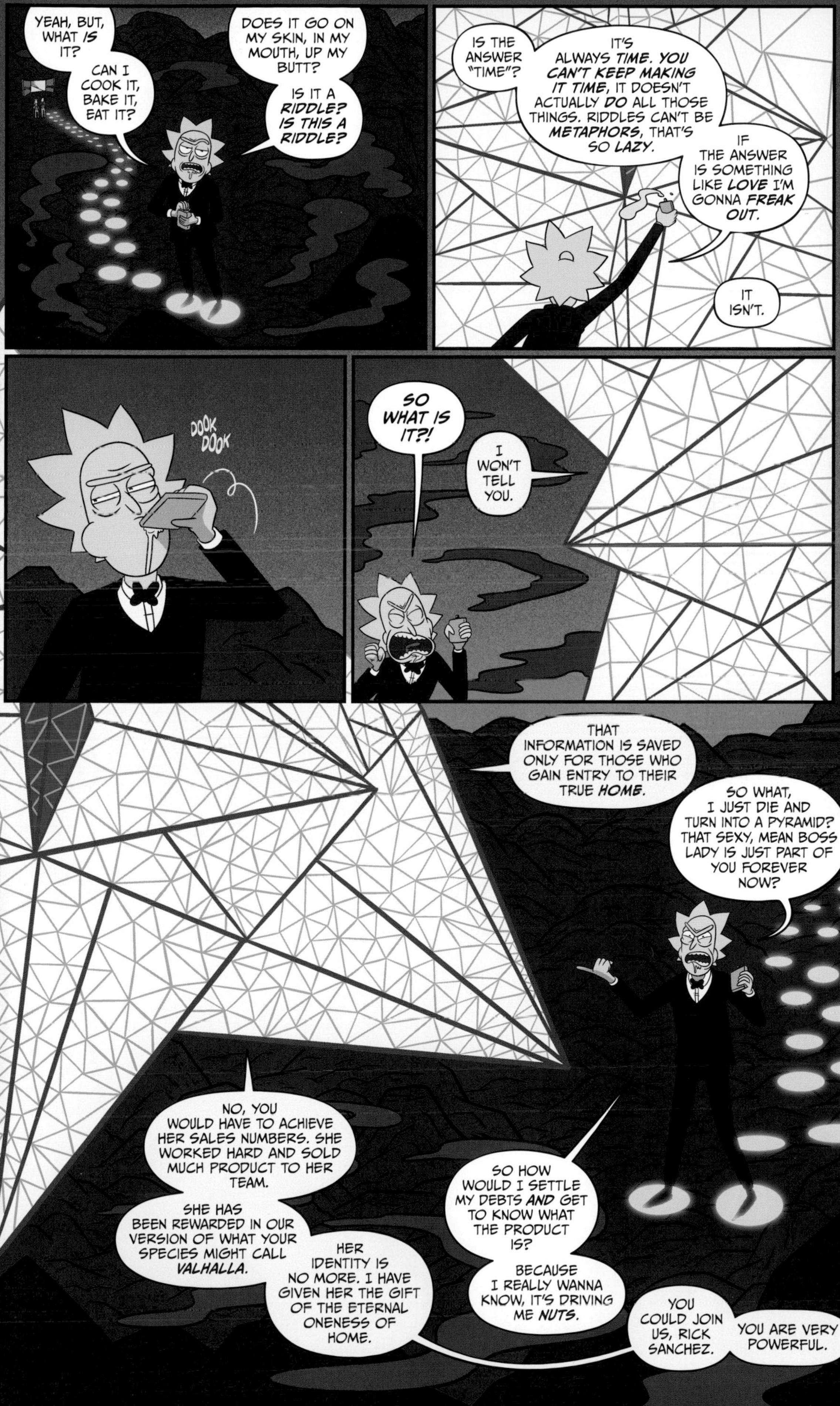

YEAH, BUT, WHAT *IS* IT?
CAN I COOK IT, BAKE IT, EAT IT?
DOES IT GO ON MY SKIN, IN MY MOUTH, UP MY BUTT?
IS IT A *RIDDLE? IS THIS A RIDDLE?*
IS THE ANSWER "TIME"?
IT'S ALWAYS *TIME. YOU CAN'T KEEP MAKING IT TIME,* IT DOESN'T ACTUALLY *DO* ALL THOSE THINGS. RIDDLES CAN'T BE *METAPHORS*, THAT'S SO *LAZY.*
IF THE ANSWER IS SOMETHING LIKE *LOVE* I'M GONNA *FREAK OUT.*
IT ISN'T.
DOOK DOOK
SO WHAT IS IT?!
I WON'T TELL YOU.
THAT INFORMATION IS SAVED ONLY FOR THOSE WHO GAIN ENTRY TO THEIR TRUE *HOME.*
SO WHAT, I JUST DIE AND TURN INTO A PYRAMID? THAT SEXY, MEAN BOSS LADY IS JUST PART OF YOU FOREVER NOW?
NO, YOU WOULD HAVE TO ACHIEVE HER SALES NUMBERS. SHE WORKED HARD AND SOLD MUCH PRODUCT TO HER TEAM.
SHE HAS BEEN REWARDED IN OUR VERSION OF WHAT YOUR SPECIES MIGHT CALL *VALHALLA.*
HER IDENTITY IS NO MORE. I HAVE GIVEN HER THE GIFT OF THE ETERNAL ONENESS OF HOME.
SO HOW WOULD I SETTLE MY DEBTS *AND* GET TO KNOW WHAT THE PRODUCT IS?
BECAUSE I REALLY WANNA KNOW, IT'S DRIVING ME *NUTS.*
YOU COULD JOIN US, RICK SANCHEZ.
YOU ARE VERY POWERFUL.

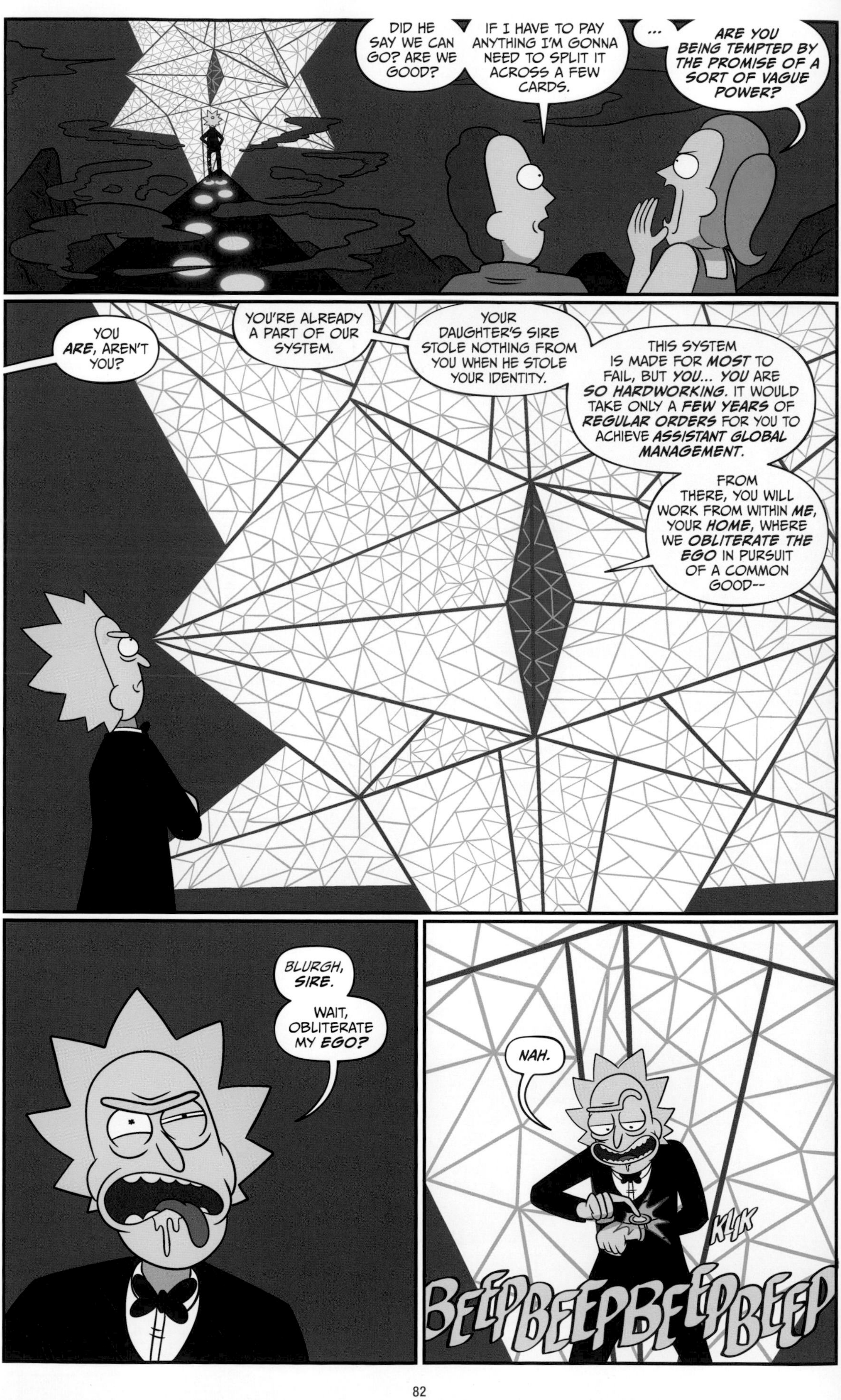
DID HE SAY WE CAN GO? ARE WE GOOD?
IF I HAVE TO PAY ANYTHING I'M GONNA NEED TO SPLIT IT ACROSS A FEW CARDS.
...
ARE YOU BEING TEMPTED BY THE PROMISE OF A SORT OF VAGUE POWER?
YOU ARE, AREN'T YOU?
YOU'RE ALREADY A PART OF OUR SYSTEM.
YOUR DAUGHTER'S SIRE STOLE NOTHING FROM YOU WHEN HE STOLE YOUR IDENTITY.
THIS SYSTEM IS MADE FOR MOST TO FAIL, BUT YOU... YOU ARE SO HARDWORKING. IT WOULD TAKE ONLY A FEW YEARS OF REGULAR ORDERS FOR YOU TO ACHIEVE ASSISTANT GLOBAL MANAGEMENT.
FROM THERE, YOU WILL WORK FROM WITHIN ME, YOUR HOME, WHERE WE OBLITERATE THE EGO IN PURSUIT OF A COMMON GOOD--
BLURGH, SIRE.
WAIT, OBLITERATE MY EGO?
NAH.
KLIK
BEEPBEEPBEEPBEEP

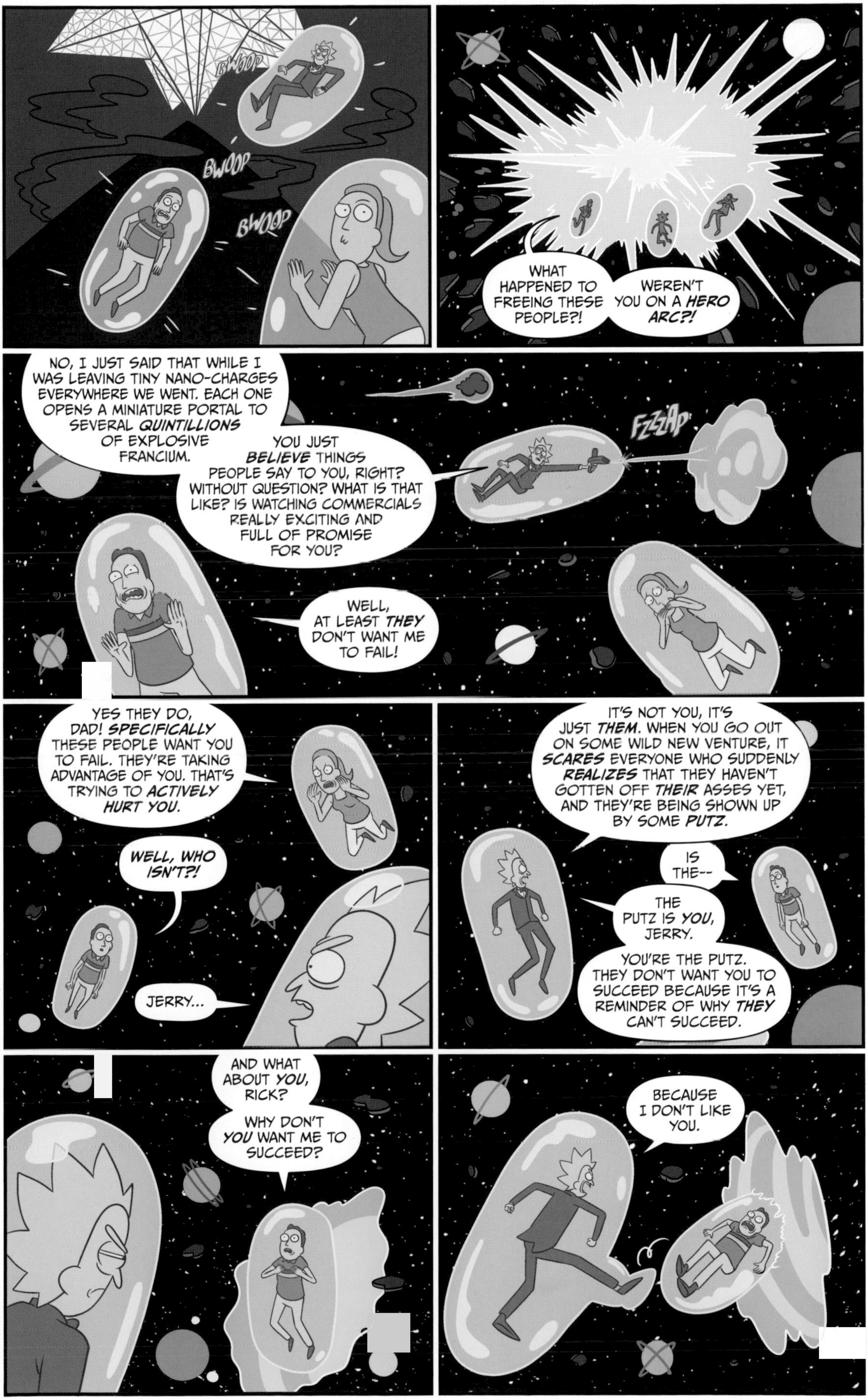
BWOOP
BWOOP
BWOOP
WHAT HAPPENED TO FREEING THESE PEOPLE?!
WEREN'T YOU ON A HERO ARC?!
NO, I JUST SAID THAT WHILE I WAS LEAVING TINY NANO-CHARGES EVERYWHERE WE WENT. EACH ONE OPENS A MINIATURE PORTAL TO SEVERAL QUINTILLIONS OF EXPLOSIVE FRANCIUM.
YOU JUST BELIEVE THINGS PEOPLE SAY TO YOU, RIGHT? WITHOUT QUESTION? WHAT IS THAT LIKE? IS WATCHING COMMERCIALS REALLY EXCITING AND FULL OF PROMISE FOR YOU?
FZZZAP
WELL, AT LEAST THEY DON'T WANT ME TO FAIL!
YES THEY DO, DAD! SPECIFICALLY THESE PEOPLE WANT YOU TO FAIL. THEY'RE TAKING ADVANTAGE OF YOU. THAT'S TRYING TO ACTIVELY HURT YOU.
WELL, WHO ISN'T?!
JERRY...
IT'S NOT YOU, IT'S JUST THEM. WHEN YOU GO OUT ON SOME WILD NEW VENTURE, IT SCARES EVERYONE WHO SUDDENLY REALIZES THAT THEY HAVEN'T GOTTEN OFF THEIR ASSES YET, AND THEY'RE BEING SHOWN UP BY SOME PUTZ.
IS THE--
THE PUTZ IS YOU, JERRY.
YOU'RE THE PUTZ. THEY DON'T WANT YOU TO SUCCEED BECAUSE IT'S A REMINDER OF WHY THEY CAN'T SUCCEED.
AND WHAT ABOUT YOU, RICK?
WHY DON'T YOU WANT ME TO SUCCEED?
BECAUSE I DON'T LIKE YOU.

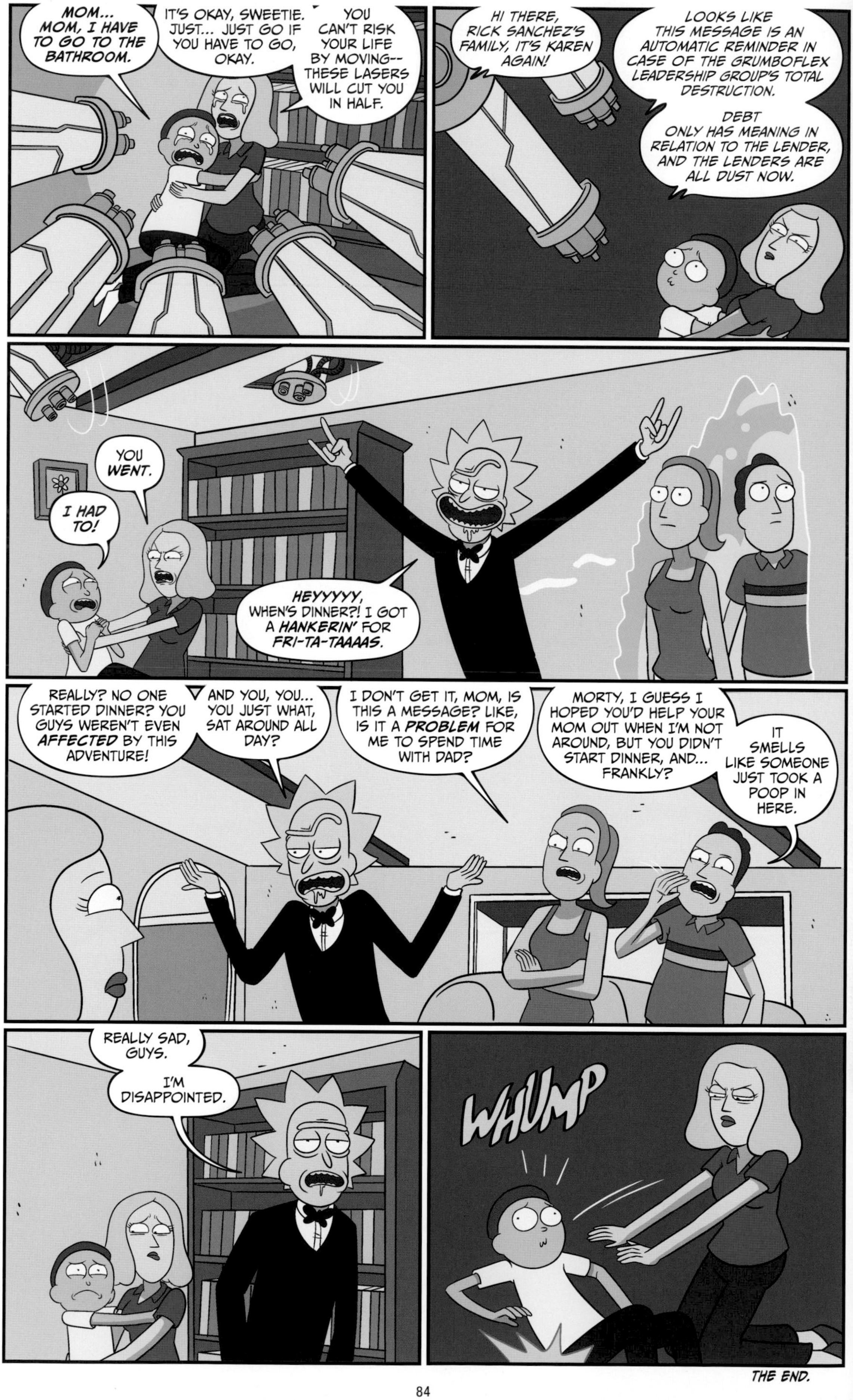
MOM... MOM, I HAVE TO GO TO THE BATHROOM.
IT'S OKAY, SWEETIE. JUST... JUST GO IF YOU HAVE TO GO, OKAY.
YOU CAN'T RISK YOUR LIFE BY MOVING-- THESE LASERS WILL CUT YOU IN HALF.
HI THERE, RICK SANCHEZ'S FAMILY, IT'S KAREN AGAIN!
LOOKS LIKE THIS MESSAGE IS AN AUTOMATIC REMINDER IN CASE OF THE GRUMBOFLEX LEADERSHIP GROUP'S TOTAL DESTRUCTION.
DEBT ONLY HAS MEANING IN RELATION TO THE LENDER, AND THE LENDERS ARE ALL DUST NOW.
YOU WENT.
I HAD TO!
HEYYYYY, WHEN'S DINNER?! I GOT A HANKERIN' FOR FRI-TA-TAAAAS.
REALLY? NO ONE STARTED DINNER? YOU GUYS WEREN'T EVEN AFFECTED BY THIS ADVENTURE!
AND YOU, YOU... YOU JUST WHAT, SAT AROUND ALL DAY?
I DON'T GET IT, MOM, IS THIS A MESSAGE? LIKE, IS IT A PROBLEM FOR ME TO SPEND TIME WITH DAD?
MORTY, I GUESS I HOPED YOU'D HELP YOUR MOM OUT WHEN I'M NOT AROUND, BUT YOU DIDN'T START DINNER, AND... FRANKLY?
IT SMELLS LIKE SOMEONE JUST TOOK A POOP IN HERE.
REALLY SAD, GUYS.
I'M DISAPPOINTED.
WHUMP

THE END.

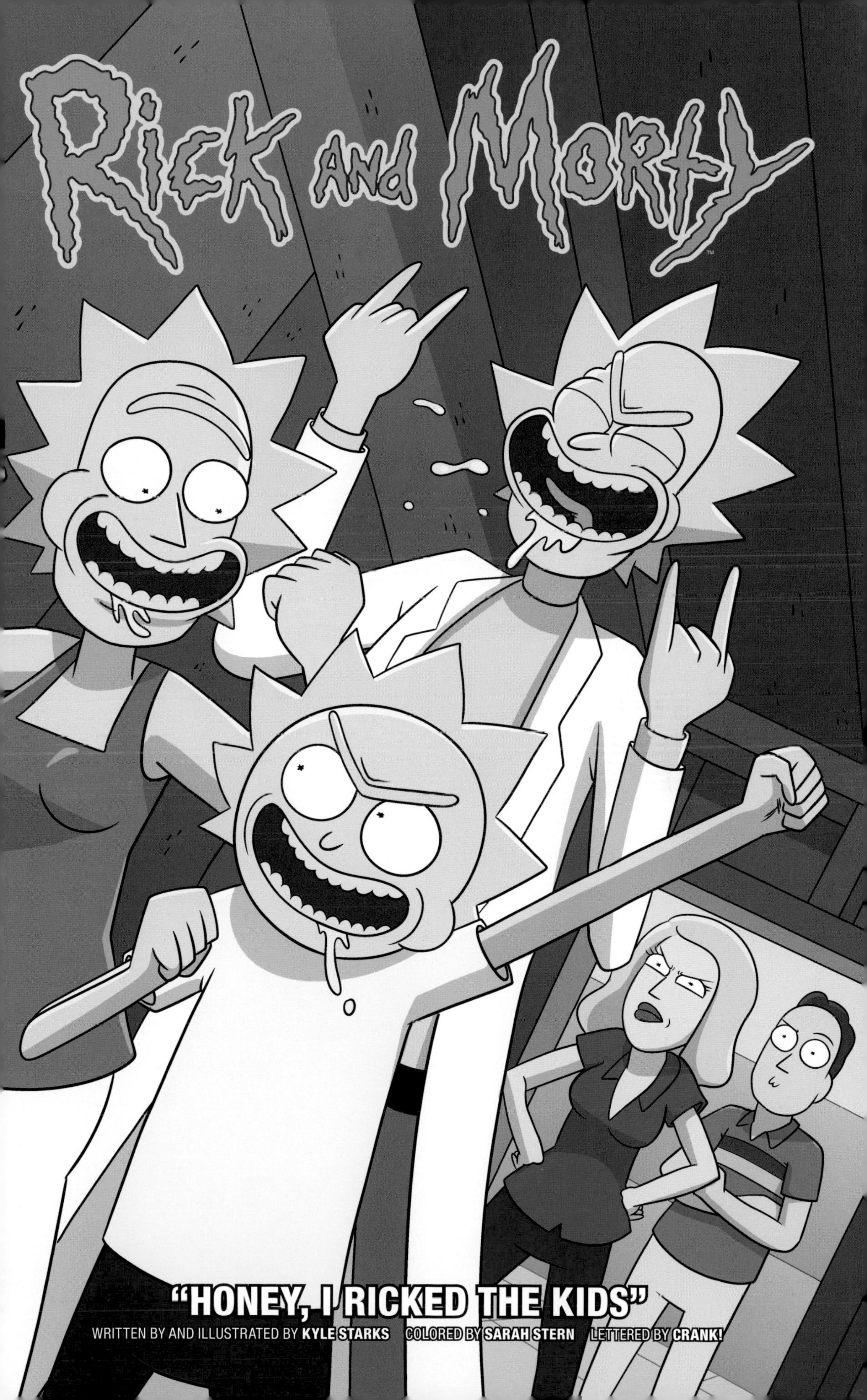

Rick and Morty

"HONEY, I RICKED THE KIDS"

WRITTEN BY AND ILLUSTRATED BY **KYLE STARKS** COLORED BY **SARAH STERN** LETTERED BY **CRANK!**

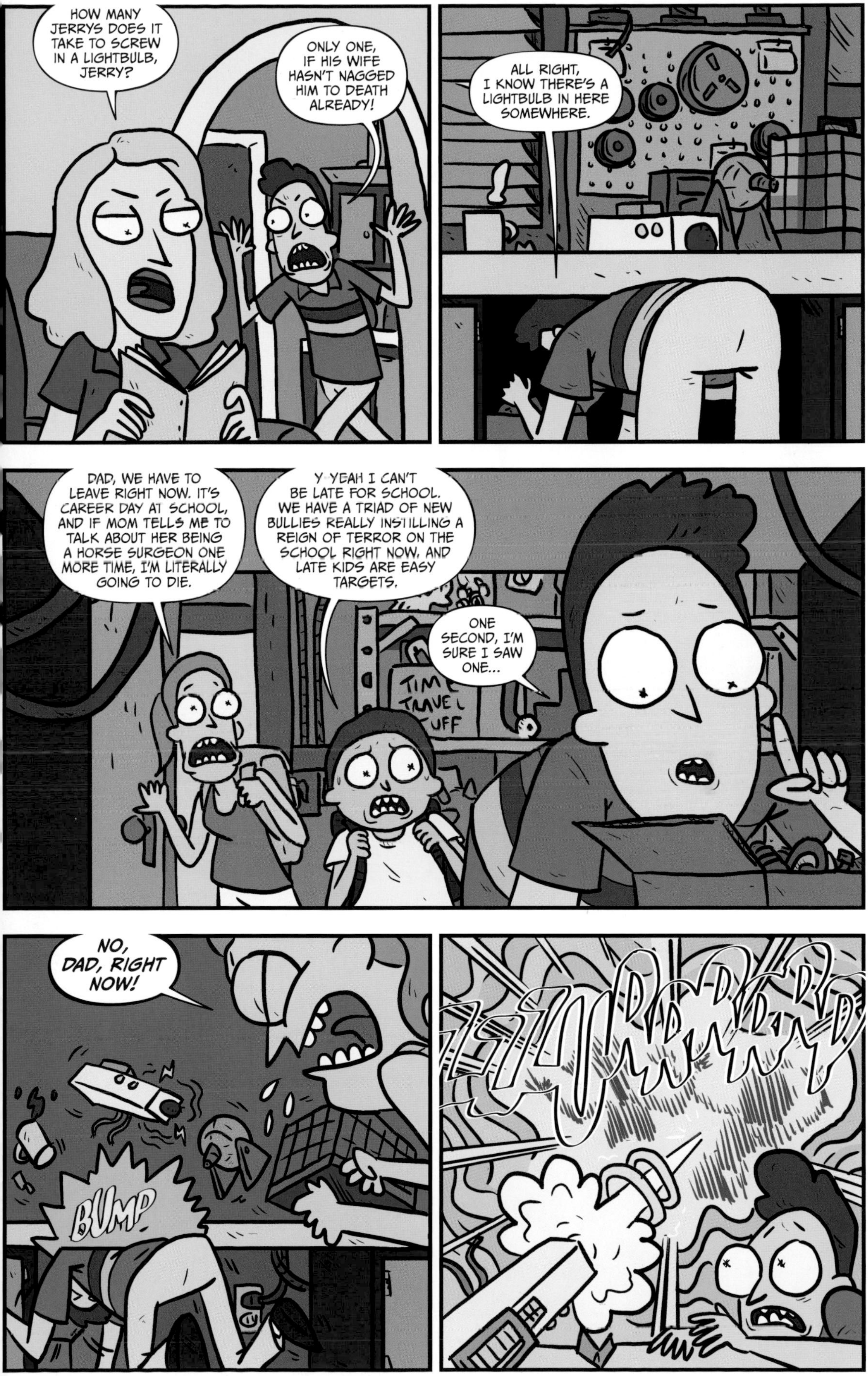
HOW MANY JERRYS DOES IT TAKE TO SCREW IN A LIGHTBULB, JERRY?
ONLY ONE, IF HIS WIFE HASN'T NAGGED HIM TO DEATH ALREADY!
ALL RIGHT, I KNOW THERE'S A LIGHTBULB IN HERE SOMEWHERE.
DAD, WE HAVE TO LEAVE RIGHT NOW. IT'S CAREER DAY AT SCHOOL, AND IF MOM TELLS ME TO TALK ABOUT HER BEING A HORSE SURGEON ONE MORE TIME, I'M LITERALLY GOING TO DIE.
Y-YEAH I CAN'T BE LATE FOR SCHOOL. WE HAVE A TRIAD OF NEW BULLIES REALLY INSTILLING A REIGN OF TERROR ON THE SCHOOL RIGHT NOW, AND LATE KIDS ARE EASY TARGETS.
ONE SECOND, I'M SURE I SAW ONE...
TIME TRAVEL STUFF
NO, DAD, RIGHT NOW!
BUMP

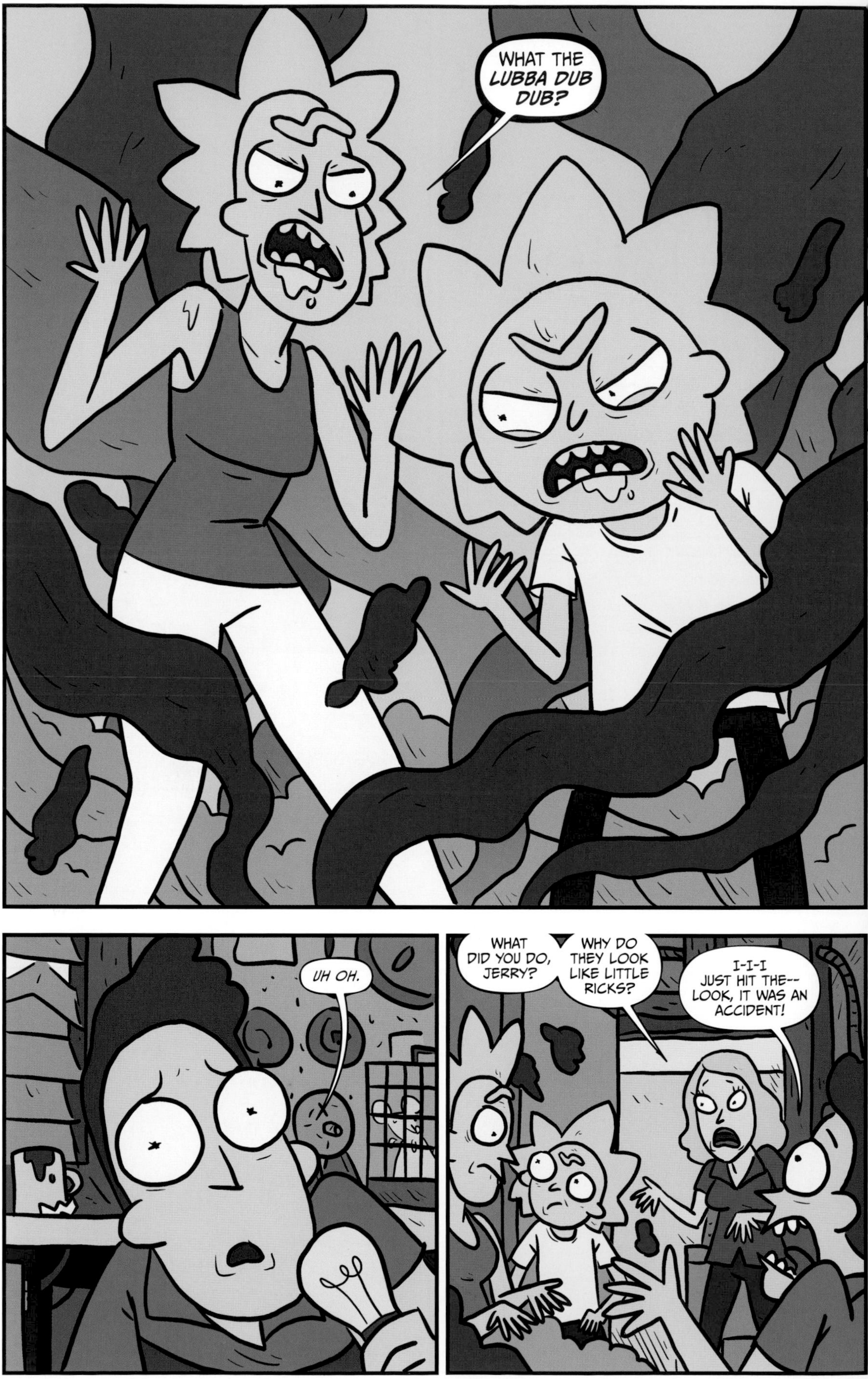
WHAT THE LUBBA DUB DUB?
UH OH.
WHAT DID YOU DO, JERRY?
WHY DO THEY LOOK LIKE LITTLE RICKS?
I-I-I JUST HIT THE-- LOOK, IT WAS AN ACCIDENT!

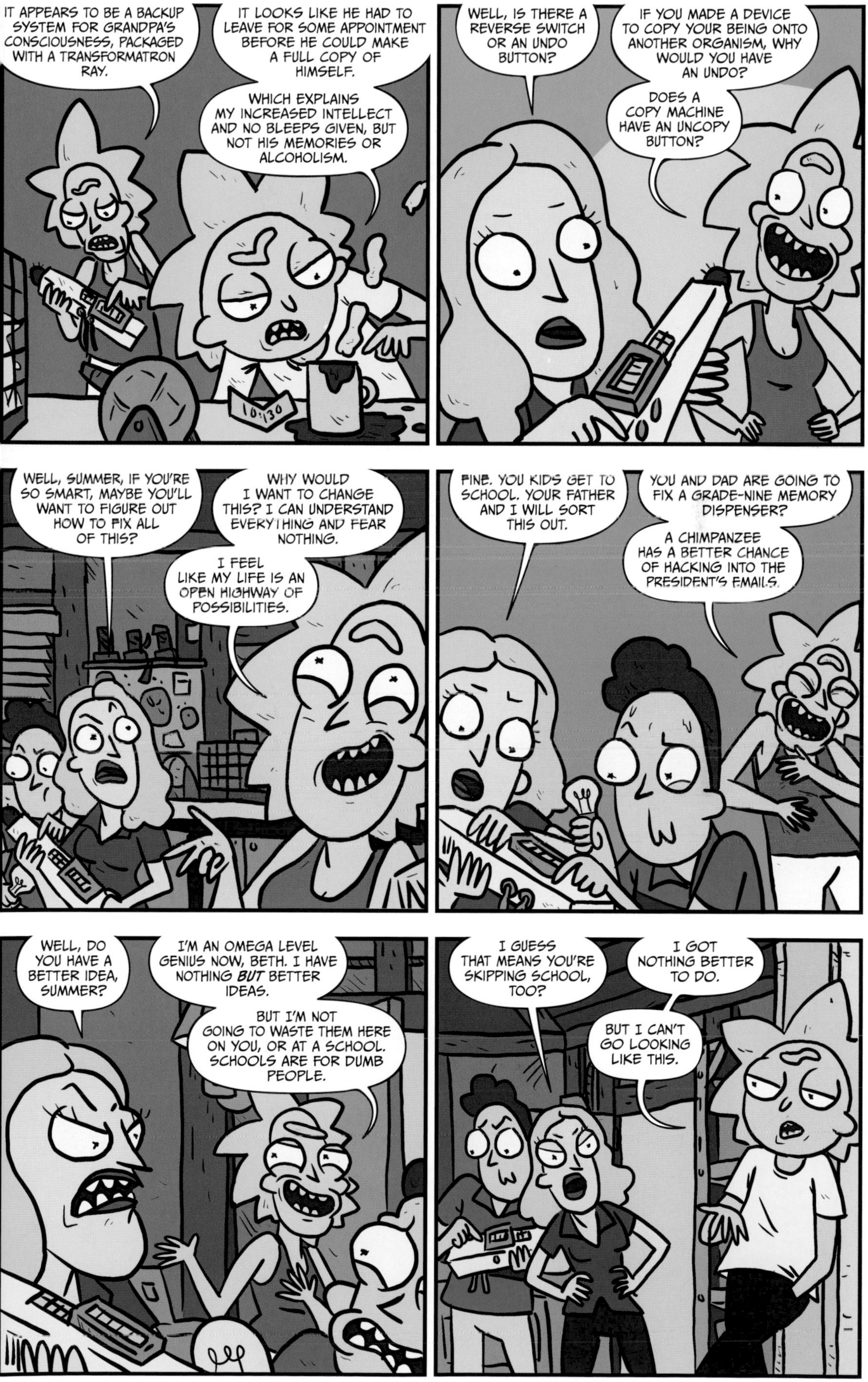
IT APPEARS TO BE A BACKUP SYSTEM FOR GRANDPA'S CONSCIOUSNESS, PACKAGED WITH A TRANSFORMATRON RAY.
IT LOOKS LIKE HE HAD TO LEAVE FOR SOME APPOINTMENT BEFORE HE COULD MAKE A FULL COPY OF HIMSELF.
WHICH EXPLAINS MY INCREASED INTELLECT AND NO BLEEPS GIVEN, BUT NOT HIS MEMORIES OR ALCOHOLISM.
10:30
WELL, IS THERE A REVERSE SWITCH OR AN UNDO BUTTON?
IF YOU MADE A DEVICE TO COPY YOUR BEING ONTO ANOTHER ORGANISM, WHY WOULD YOU HAVE AN UNDO?
DOES A COPY MACHINE HAVE AN UNCOPY BUTTON?
WELL, SUMMER, IF YOU'RE SO SMART, MAYBE YOU'LL WANT TO FIGURE OUT HOW TO FIX ALL OF THIS?
WHY WOULD I WANT TO CHANGE THIS? I CAN UNDERSTAND EVERYTHING AND FEAR NOTHING.
I FEEL LIKE MY LIFE IS AN OPEN HIGHWAY OF POSSIBILITIES.
FINE. YOU KIDS GET TO SCHOOL. YOUR FATHER AND I WILL SORT THIS OUT.
YOU AND DAD ARE GOING TO FIX A GRADE-NINE MEMORY DISPENSER?
A CHIMPANZEE HAS A BETTER CHANCE OF HACKING INTO THE PRESIDENT'S EMAILS.
WELL, DO YOU HAVE A BETTER IDEA, SUMMER?
I'M AN OMEGA LEVEL GENIUS NOW, BETH. I HAVE NOTHING *BUT* BETTER IDEAS.
BUT I'M NOT GOING TO WASTE THEM HERE ON YOU, OR AT A SCHOOL. SCHOOLS ARE FOR DUMB PEOPLE.
I GUESS THAT MEANS YOU'RE SKIPPING SCHOOL, TOO?
I GOT NOTHING BETTER TO DO.
BUT I CAN'T GO LOOKING LIKE THIS.

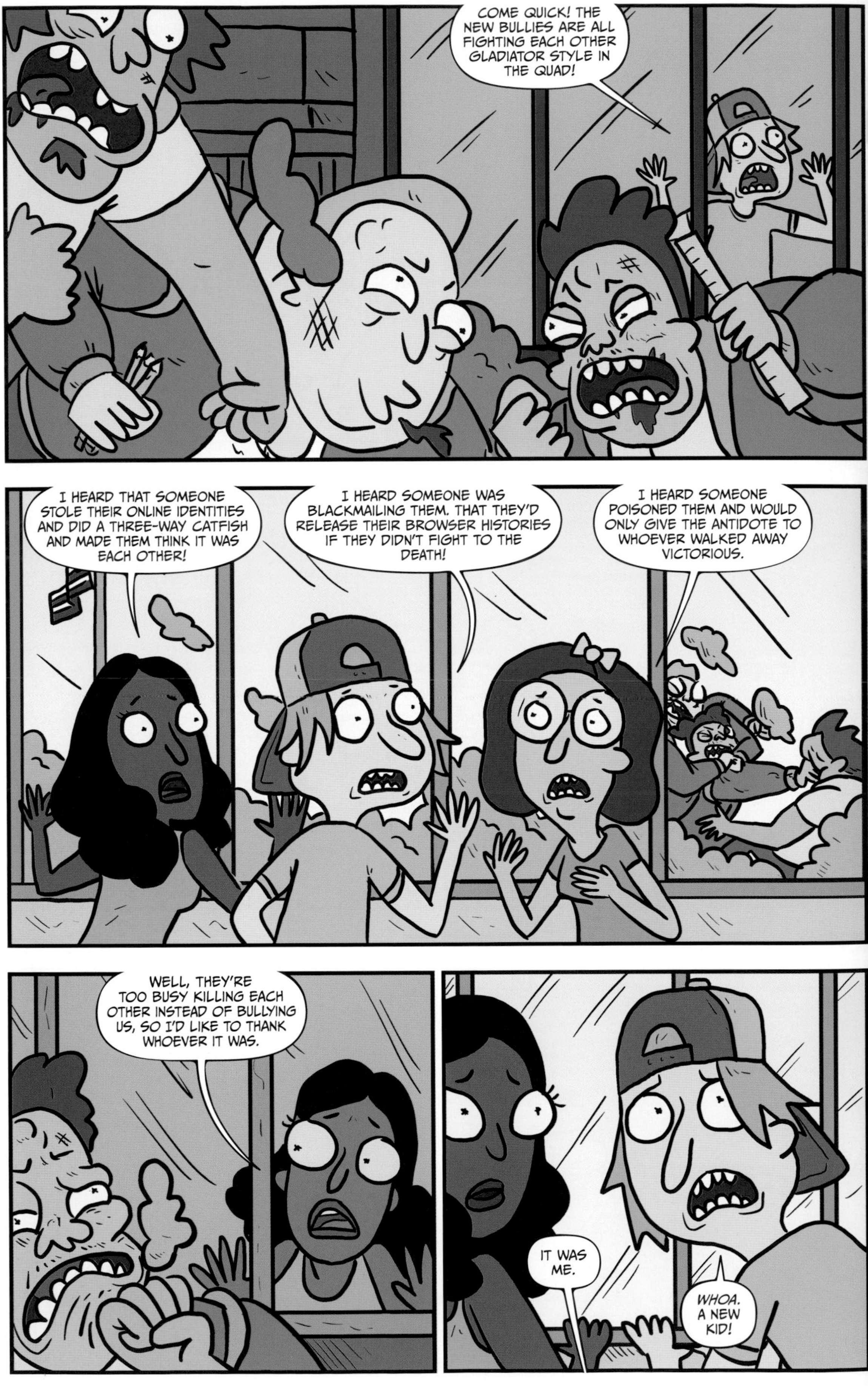
COME QUICK! THE NEW BULLIES ARE ALL FIGHTING EACH OTHER GLADIATOR STYLE IN THE QUAD!
I HEARD THAT SOMEONE STOLE THEIR ONLINE IDENTITIES AND DID A THREE-WAY CATFISH AND MADE THEM THINK IT WAS EACH OTHER!
I HEARD SOMEONE WAS BLACKMAILING THEM. THAT THEY'D RELEASE THEIR BROWSER HISTORIES IF THEY DIDN'T FIGHT TO THE DEATH!
I HEARD SOMEONE POISONED THEM AND WOULD ONLY GIVE THE ANTIDOTE TO WHOEVER WALKED AWAY VICTORIOUS.
WELL, THEY'RE TOO BUSY KILLING EACH OTHER INSTEAD OF BULLYING US, SO I'D LIKE TO THANK WHOEVER IT WAS.
IT WAS ME.
WHOA. A NEW KID!

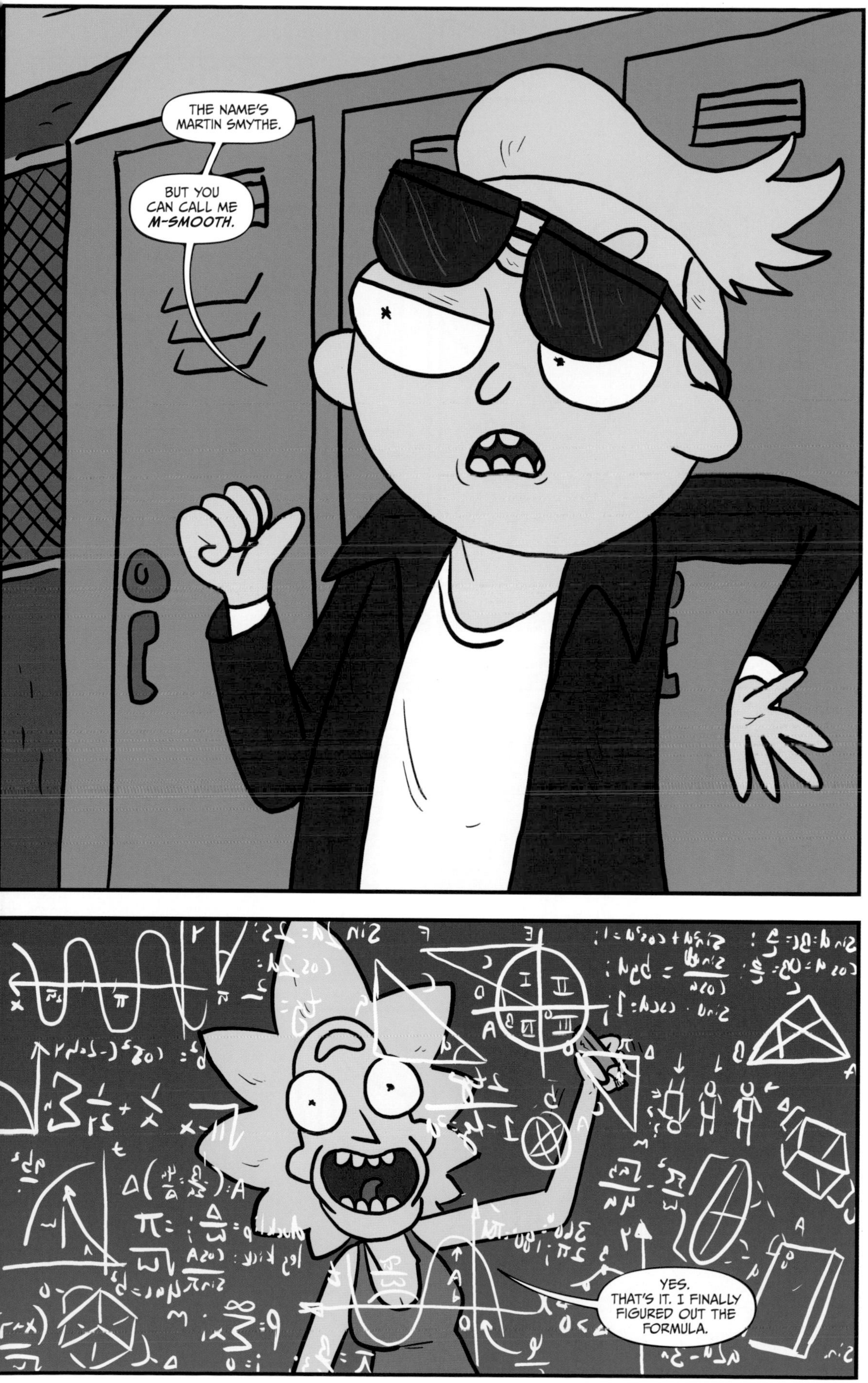
THE NAME'S MARTIN SMYTHE.
BUT YOU CAN CALL ME *M-SMOOTH.*
YES. THAT'S IT. I FINALLY FIGURED OUT THE FORMULA.

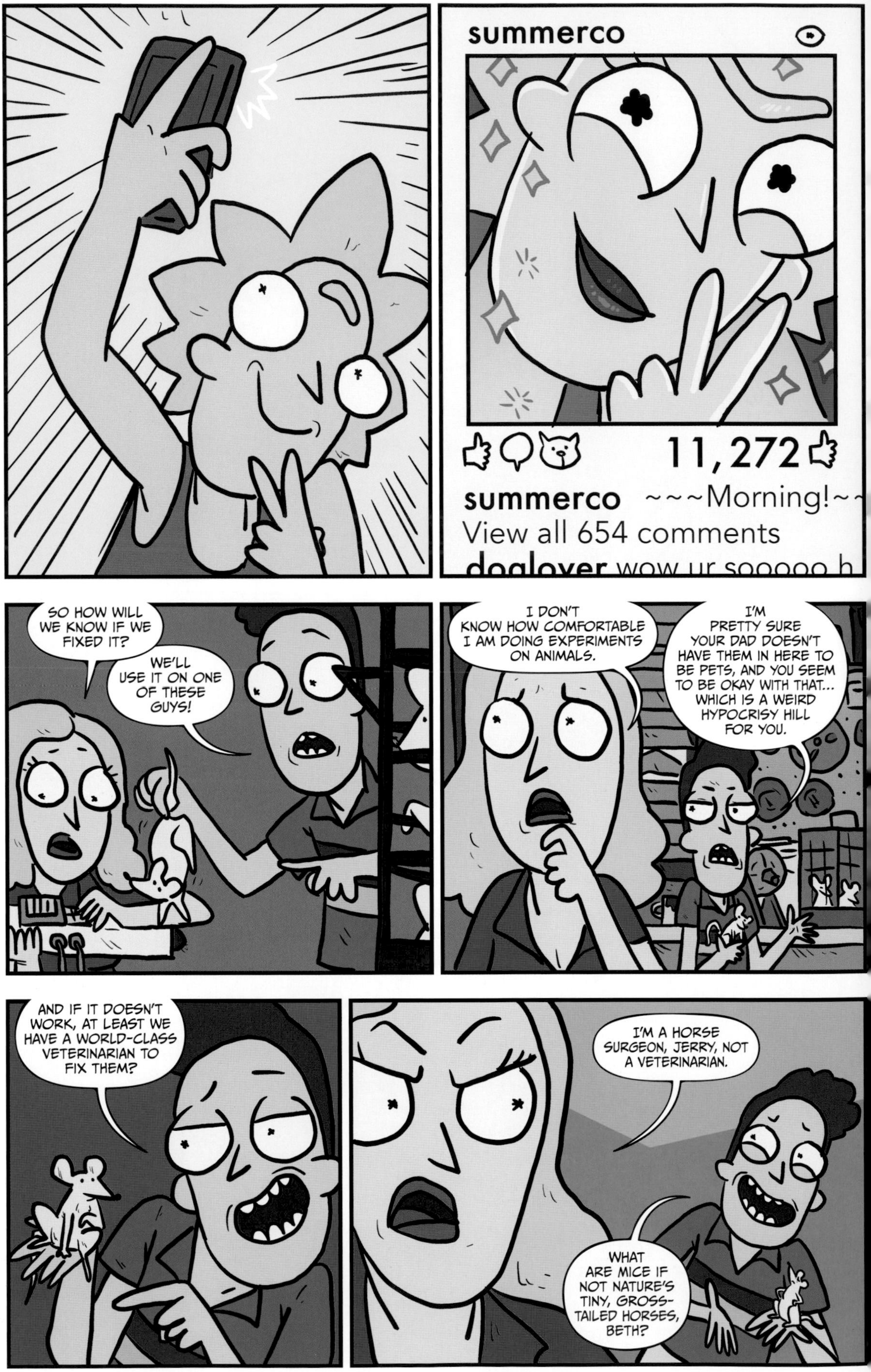

summerco
11,272
summerco ~~~Morning!~~
View all 654 comments
doglover wow ur sooooo h
SO HOW WILL WE KNOW IF WE FIXED IT?
WE'LL USE IT ON ONE OF THESE GUYS!
I DON'T KNOW HOW COMFORTABLE I AM DOING EXPERIMENTS ON ANIMALS.
I'M PRETTY SURE YOUR DAD DOESN'T HAVE THEM IN HERE TO BE PETS, AND YOU SEEM TO BE OKAY WITH THAT... WHICH IS A WEIRD HYPOCRISY HILL FOR YOU.
AND IF IT DOESN'T WORK, AT LEAST WE HAVE A WORLD-CLASS VETERINARIAN TO FIX THEM?
I'M A HORSE SURGEON, JERRY, NOT A VETERINARIAN.
WHAT ARE MICE IF NOT NATURE'S TINY, GROSS-TAILED HORSES, BETH?

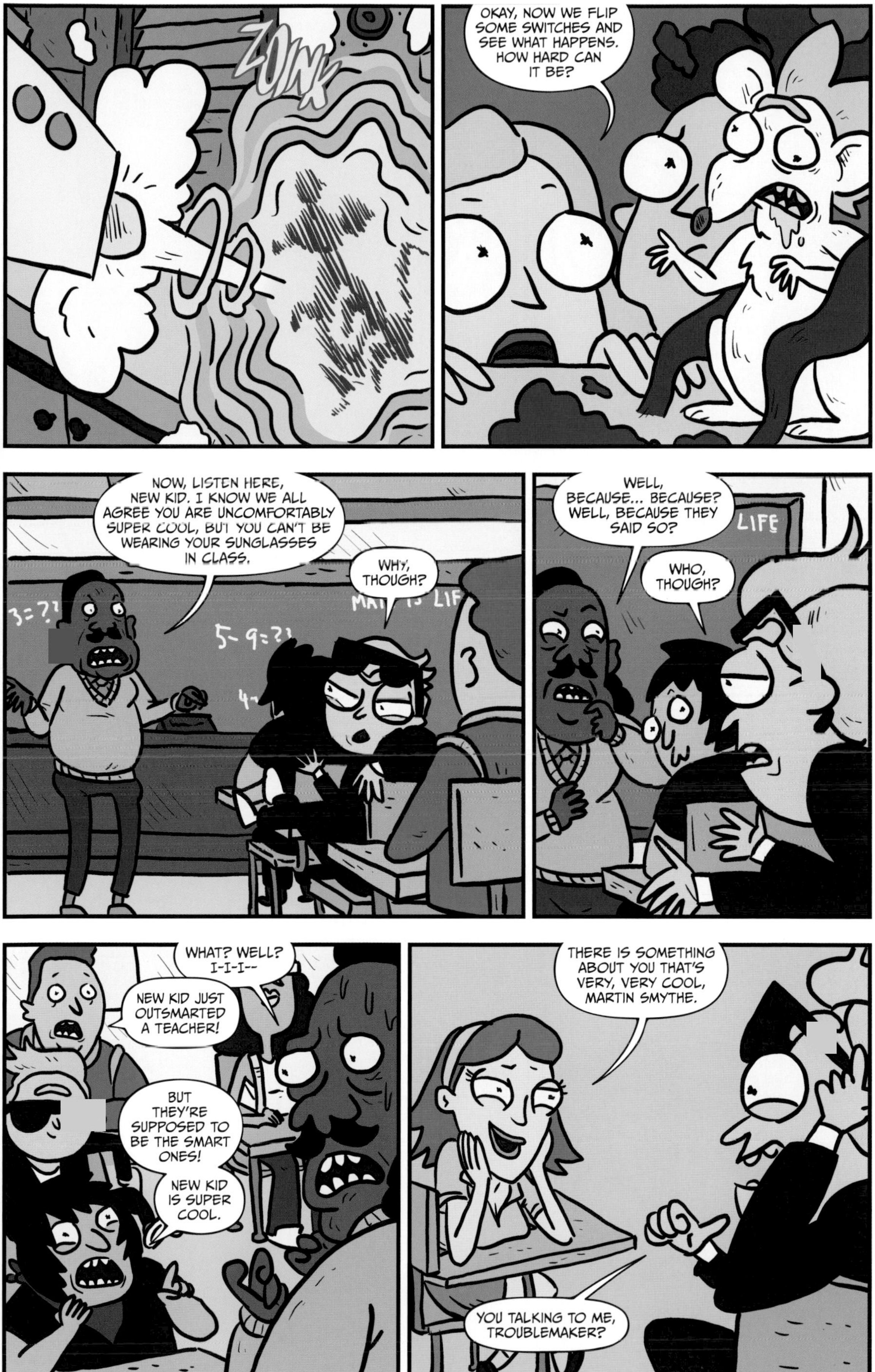
ZONK
OKAY, NOW WE FLIP SOME SWITCHES AND SEE WHAT HAPPENS. HOW HARD CAN IT BE?
NOW, LISTEN HERE, NEW KID. I KNOW WE ALL AGREE YOU ARE UNCOMFORTABLY SUPER COOL, BUT YOU CAN'T BE WEARING YOUR SUNGLASSES IN CLASS.
WHY, THOUGH?
WELL, BECAUSE... BECAUSE? WELL, BECAUSE THEY SAID SO?
LIFE
WHO, THOUGH?
WHAT? WELL? I-I-I--
NEW KID JUST OUTSMARTED A TEACHER!
BUT THEY'RE SUPPOSED TO BE THE SMART ONES!
NEW KID IS SUPER COOL.
THERE IS SOMETHING ABOUT YOU THAT'S VERY, VERY COOL, MARTIN SMYTHE.
YOU TALKING TO ME, TROUBLEMAKER?

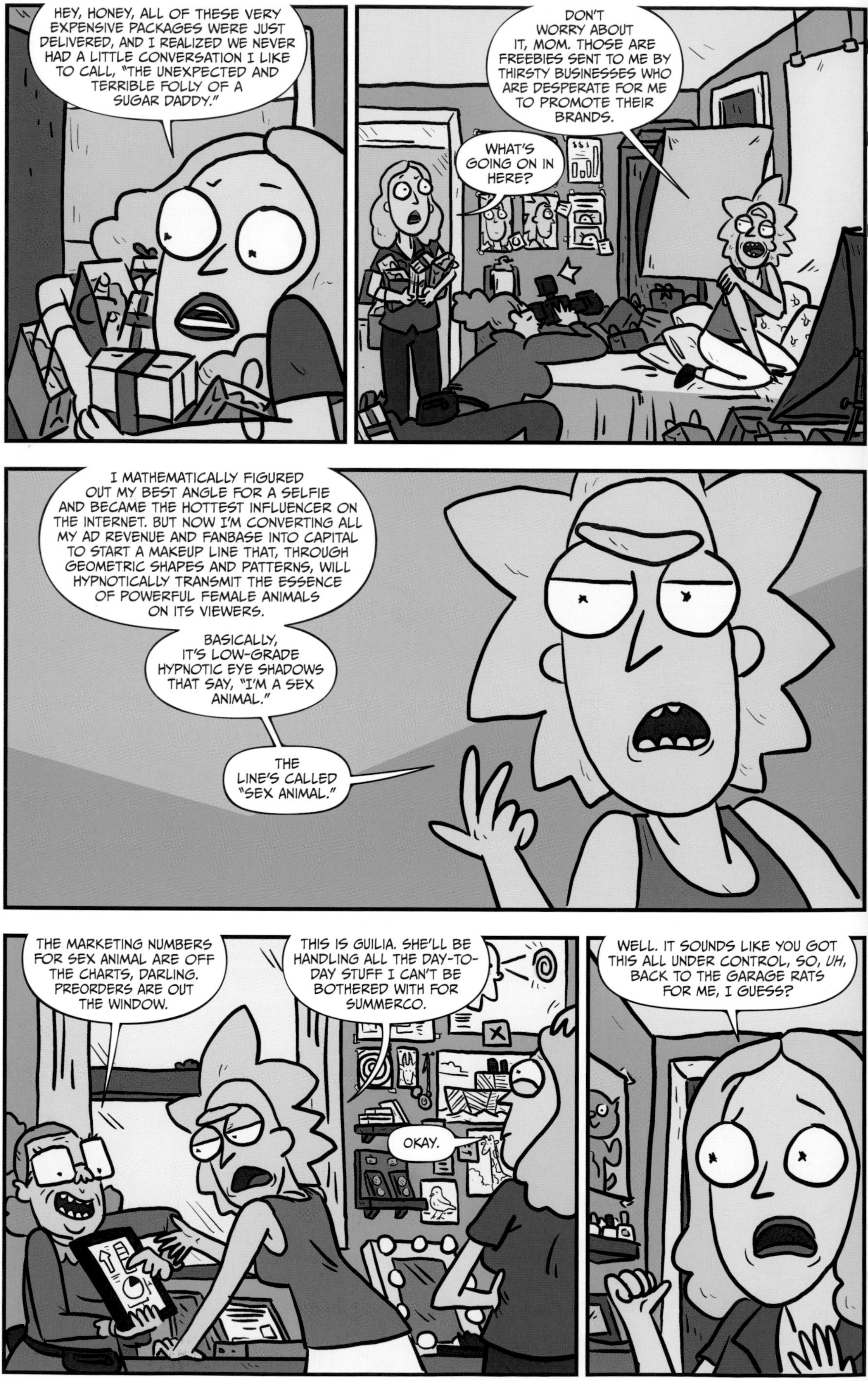
HEY, HONEY, ALL OF THESE VERY EXPENSIVE PACKAGES WERE JUST DELIVERED, AND I REALIZED WE NEVER HAD A LITTLE CONVERSATION I LIKE TO CALL, "THE UNEXPECTED AND TERRIBLE FOLLY OF A SUGAR DADDY."
WHAT'S GOING ON IN HERE?
DON'T WORRY ABOUT IT, MOM. THOSE ARE FREEBIES SENT TO ME BY THIRSTY BUSINESSES WHO ARE DESPERATE FOR ME TO PROMOTE THEIR BRANDS.
I MATHEMATICALLY FIGURED OUT MY BEST ANGLE FOR A SELFIE AND BECAME THE HOTTEST INFLUENCER ON THE INTERNET. BUT NOW I'M CONVERTING ALL MY AD REVENUE AND FANBASE INTO CAPITAL TO START A MAKEUP LINE THAT, THROUGH GEOMETRIC SHAPES AND PATTERNS, WILL HYPNOTICALLY TRANSMIT THE ESSENCE OF POWERFUL FEMALE ANIMALS ON ITS VIEWERS.
BASICALLY, IT'S LOW-GRADE HYPNOTIC EYE SHADOWS THAT SAY, "I'M A SEX ANIMAL."
THE LINE'S CALLED "SEX ANIMAL."
THE MARKETING NUMBERS FOR SEX ANIMAL ARE OFF THE CHARTS, DARLING. PREORDERS ARE OUT THE WINDOW.
THIS IS GUILIA. SHE'LL BE HANDLING ALL THE DAY-TO-DAY STUFF I CAN'T BE BOTHERED WITH FOR SUMMERCO.
OKAY.
WELL. IT SOUNDS LIKE YOU GOT THIS ALL UNDER CONTROL, SO, *UH*, BACK TO THE GARAGE RATS FOR ME, I GUESS?

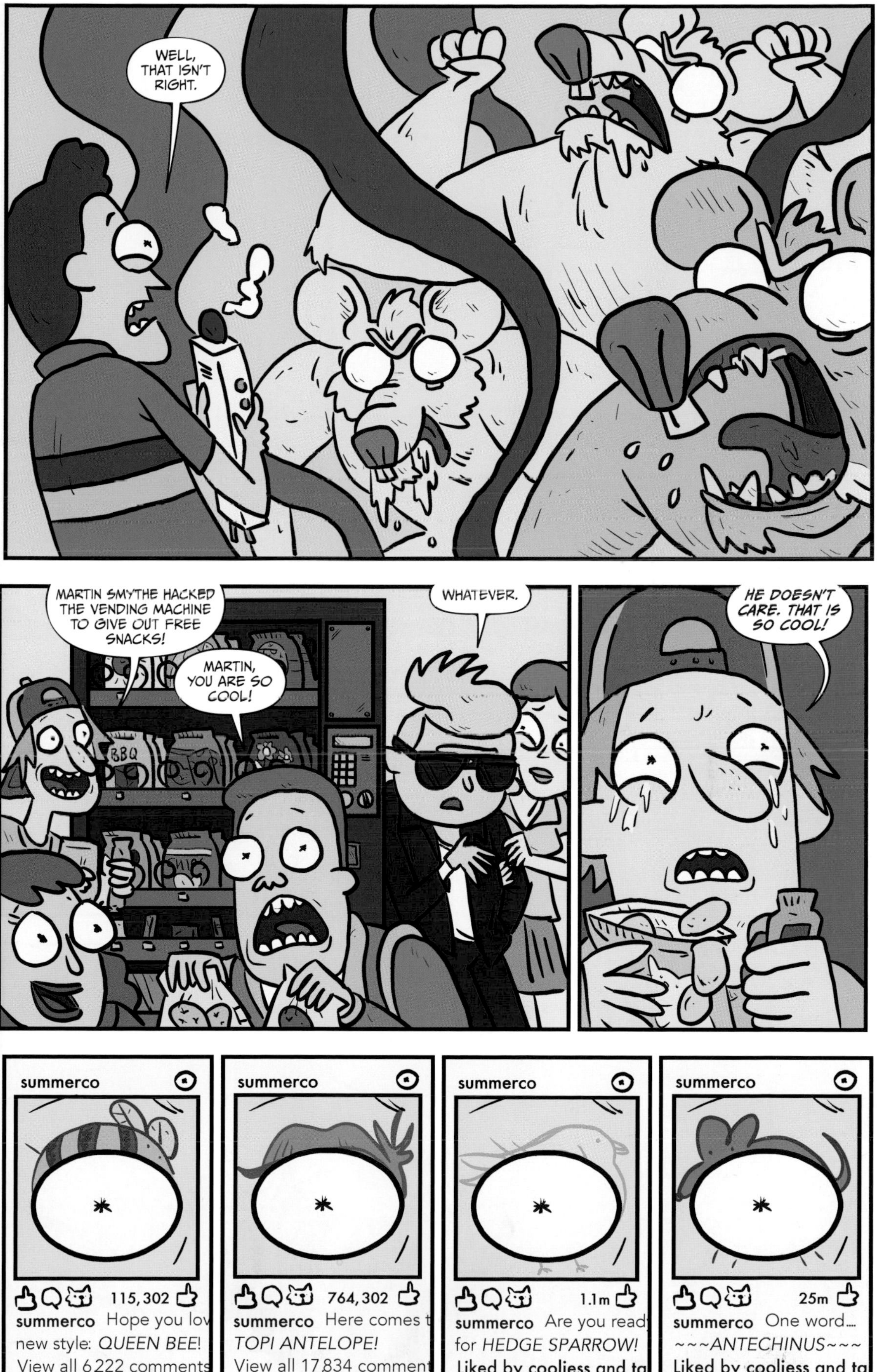
WELL, THAT ISN'T RIGHT.
MARTIN SMYTHE HACKED THE VENDING MACHINE TO GIVE OUT FREE SNACKS!
MARTIN, YOU ARE SO COOL!
WHATEVER.
HE DOESN'T CARE. THAT IS SO COOL!
summerco
115,302
summerco Hope you lov
new style: QUEEN BEE!
View all 6,222 comments
summerco
764,302
summerco Here comes t
TOPI ANTELOPE!
View all 17,834 comment
summerco
1.1m
summerco Are you read
for HEDGE SPARROW!
Liked by cooljess and ta
summerco
25m
summerco One word....
~~~ANTECHINUS~~~
Liked by cooljess and ta
~~~

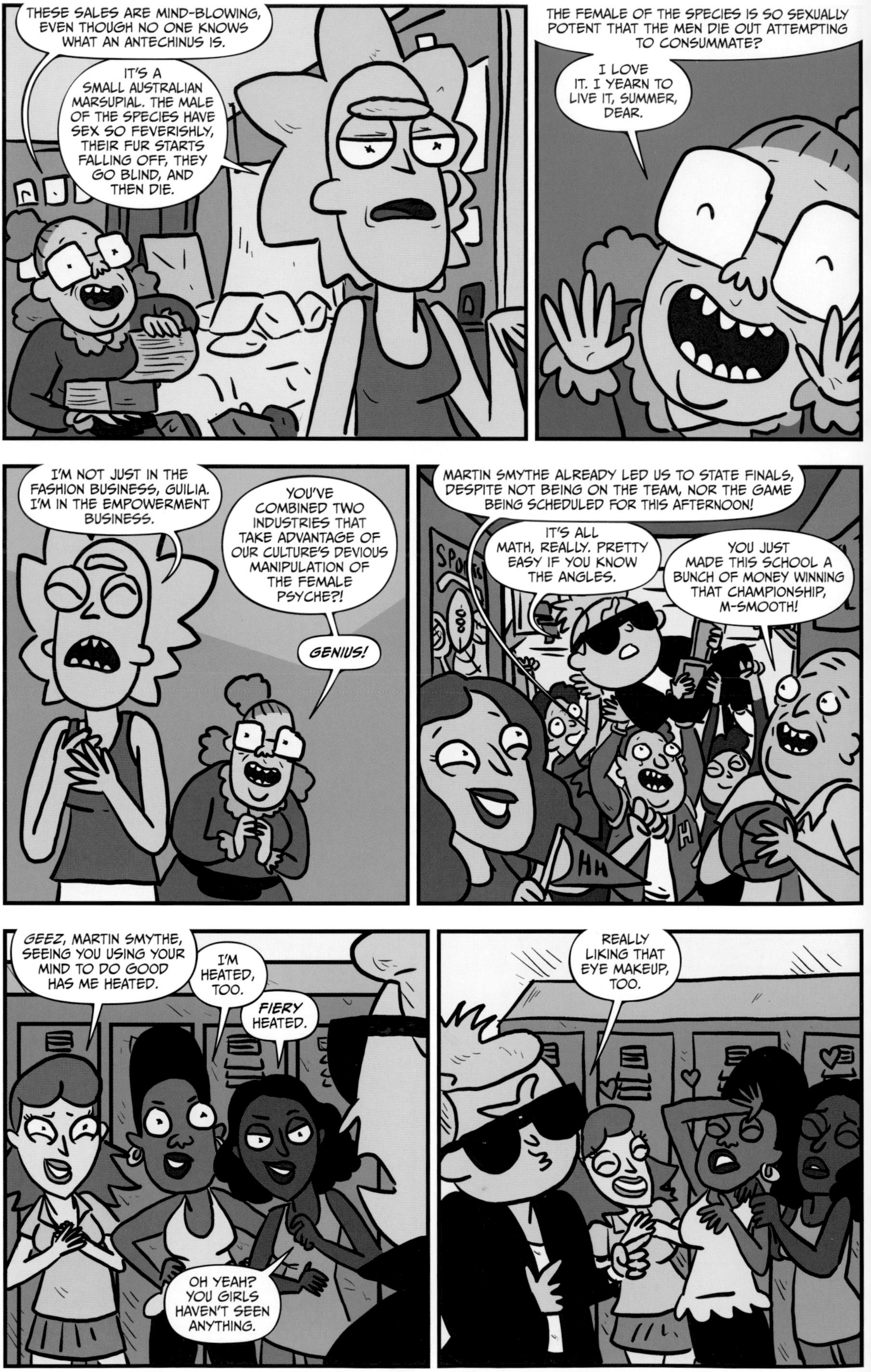
THESE SALES ARE MIND-BLOWING, EVEN THOUGH NO ONE KNOWS WHAT AN ANTECHINUS IS.
IT'S A SMALL AUSTRALIAN MARSUPIAL. THE MALE OF THE SPECIES HAVE SEX SO FEVERISHLY, THEIR FUR STARTS FALLING OFF, THEY GO BLIND, AND THEN DIE.
THE FEMALE OF THE SPECIES IS SO SEXUALLY POTENT THAT THE MEN DIE OUT ATTEMPTING TO CONSUMMATE?
I LOVE IT. I YEARN TO LIVE IT, SUMMER, DEAR.
I'M NOT JUST IN THE FASHION BUSINESS, GUILIA. I'M IN THE EMPOWERMENT BUSINESS.
YOU'VE COMBINED TWO INDUSTRIES THAT TAKE ADVANTAGE OF OUR CULTURE'S DEVIOUS MANIPULATION OF THE FEMALE PSYCHE?!
GENIUS!
MARTIN SMYTHE ALREADY LED US TO STATE FINALS, DESPITE NOT BEING ON THE TEAM, NOR THE GAME BEING SCHEDULED FOR THIS AFTERNOON!
IT'S ALL MATH, REALLY. PRETTY EASY IF YOU KNOW THE ANGLES.
YOU JUST MADE THIS SCHOOL A BUNCH OF MONEY WINNING THAT CHAMPIONSHIP, M-SMOOTH!
GEEZ, MARTIN SMYTHE, SEEING YOU USING YOUR MIND TO DO GOOD HAS ME HEATED.
I'M HEATED, TOO.
FIERY HEATED.
OH YEAH? YOU GIRLS HAVEN'T SEEN ANYTHING.
REALLY LIKING THAT EYE MAKEUP, TOO.

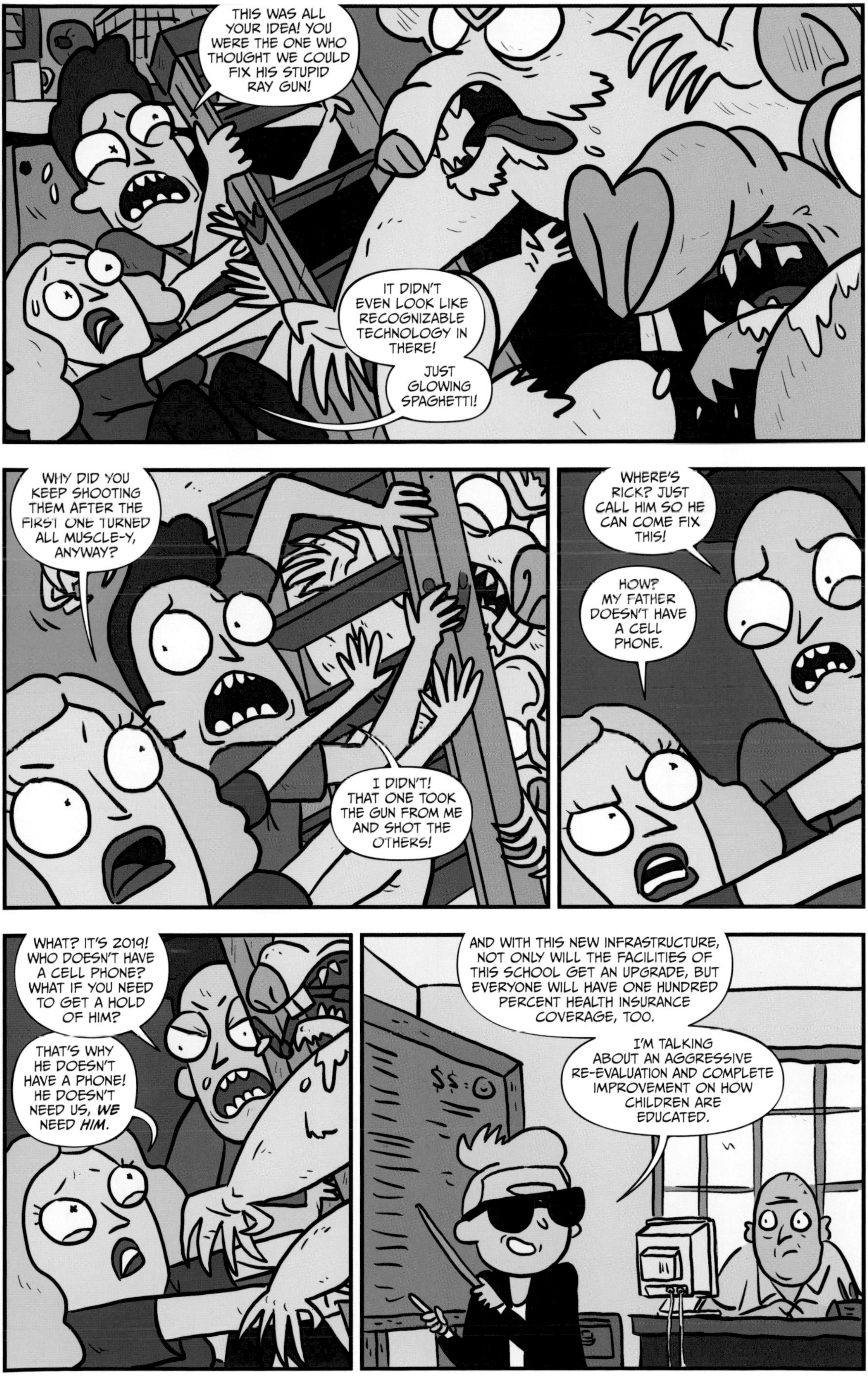
THIS WAS ALL YOUR IDEA! YOU WERE THE ONE WHO THOUGHT WE COULD FIX HIS STUPID RAY GUN!
IT DIDN'T EVEN LOOK LIKE RECOGNIZABLE TECHNOLOGY IN THERE!
JUST GLOWING SPAGHETTI!
WHY DID YOU KEEP SHOOTING THEM AFTER THE FIRST ONE TURNED ALL MUSCLE-Y, ANYWAY?
I DIDN'T! THAT ONE TOOK THE GUN FROM ME AND SHOT THE OTHERS!
WHERE'S RICK? JUST CALL HIM SO HE CAN COME FIX THIS!
HOW? MY FATHER DOESN'T HAVE A CELL PHONE.
WHAT? IT'S 2019! WHO DOESN'T HAVE A CELL PHONE? WHAT IF YOU NEED TO GET A HOLD OF HIM?
THAT'S WHY HE DOESN'T HAVE A PHONE! HE DOESN'T NEED US, *WE* NEED *HIM*.
AND WITH THIS NEW INFRASTRUCTURE, NOT ONLY WILL THE FACILITIES OF THIS SCHOOL GET AN UPGRADE, BUT EVERYONE WILL HAVE ONE HUNDRED PERCENT HEALTH INSURANCE COVERAGE, TOO.
I'M TALKING ABOUT AN AGGRESSIVE RE-EVALUATION AND COMPLETE IMPROVEMENT ON HOW CHILDREN ARE EDUCATED.
$$:©

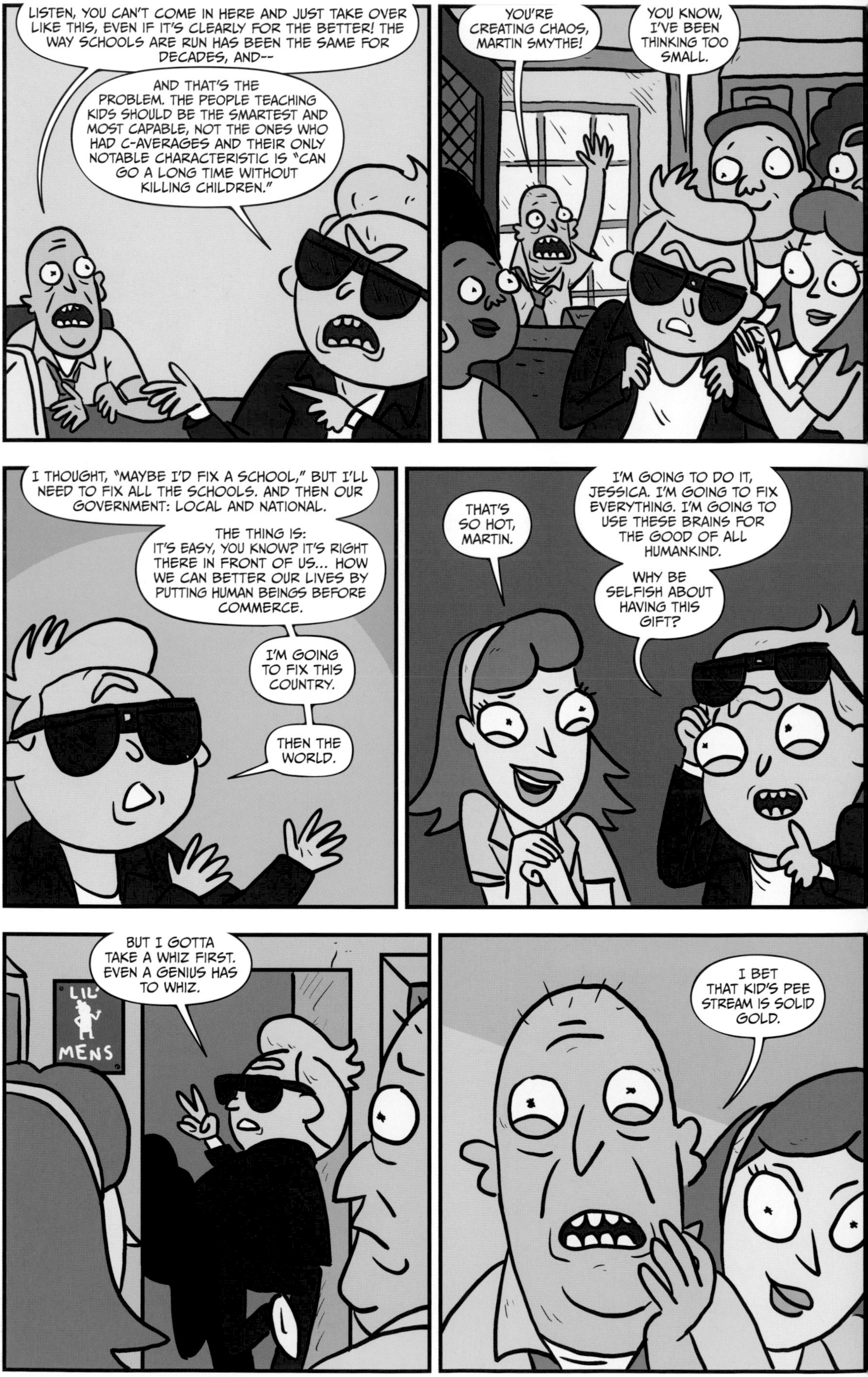
LISTEN, YOU CAN'T COME IN HERE AND JUST TAKE OVER LIKE THIS, EVEN IF IT'S CLEARLY FOR THE BETTER! THE WAY SCHOOLS ARE RUN HAS BEEN THE SAME FOR DECADES, AND--
AND THAT'S THE PROBLEM. THE PEOPLE TEACHING KIDS SHOULD BE THE SMARTEST AND MOST CAPABLE, NOT THE ONES WHO HAD C-AVERAGES AND THEIR ONLY NOTABLE CHARACTERISTIC IS "CAN GO A LONG TIME WITHOUT KILLING CHILDREN."
YOU'RE CREATING CHAOS, MARTIN SMYTHE!
YOU KNOW, I'VE BEEN THINKING TOO SMALL.
I THOUGHT, "MAYBE I'D FIX A SCHOOL," BUT I'LL NEED TO FIX ALL THE SCHOOLS. AND THEN OUR GOVERNMENT: LOCAL AND NATIONAL.
THE THING IS: IT'S EASY, YOU KNOW? IT'S RIGHT THERE IN FRONT OF US... HOW WE CAN BETTER OUR LIVES BY PUTTING HUMAN BEINGS BEFORE COMMERCE.
I'M GOING TO FIX THIS COUNTRY.
THEN THE WORLD.
THAT'S SO HOT, MARTIN.
I'M GOING TO DO IT, JESSICA. I'M GOING TO FIX EVERYTHING. I'M GOING TO USE THESE BRAINS FOR THE GOOD OF ALL HUMANKIND.
WHY BE SELFISH ABOUT HAVING THIS GIFT?
BUT I GOTTA TAKE A WHIZ FIRST. EVEN A GENIUS HAS TO WHIZ.
LIL' MENS
I BET THAT KID'S PEE STREAM IS SOLID GOLD.

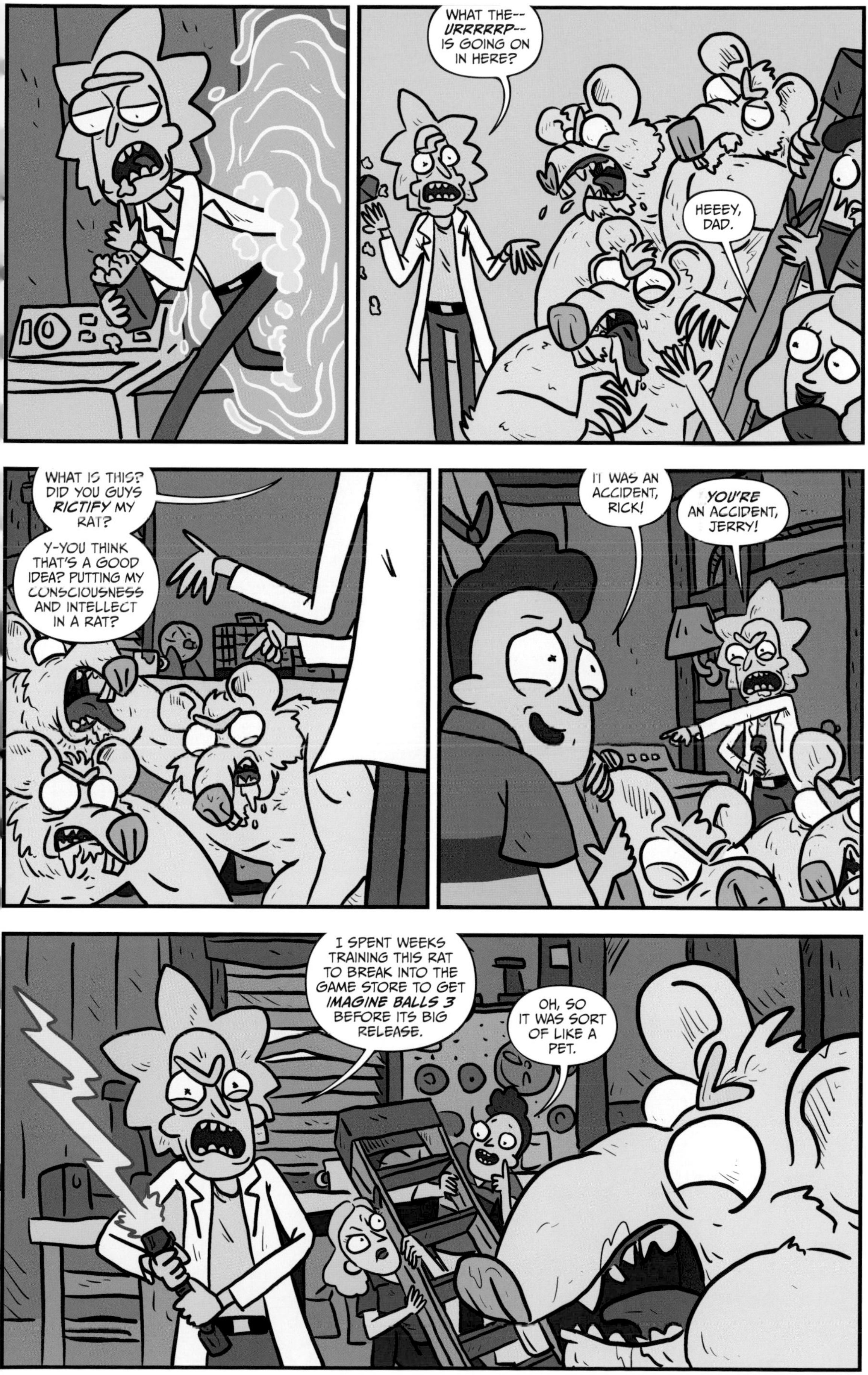
WHAT THE-- *URRRRRP--* IS GOING ON IN HERE?
HEEEY, DAD.
WHAT IS THIS? DID YOU GUYS *RICTIFY* MY RAT?
Y-YOU THINK THAT'S A GOOD IDEA? PUTTING MY CONSCIOUSNESS AND INTELLECT IN A RAT?
IT WAS AN ACCIDENT, RICK!
YOU'RE AN ACCIDENT, JERRY!
I SPENT WEEKS TRAINING THIS RAT TO BREAK INTO THE GAME STORE TO GET *IMAGINE BALLS 3* BEFORE ITS BIG RELEASE.
OH, SO IT WAS SORT OF LIKE A PET.

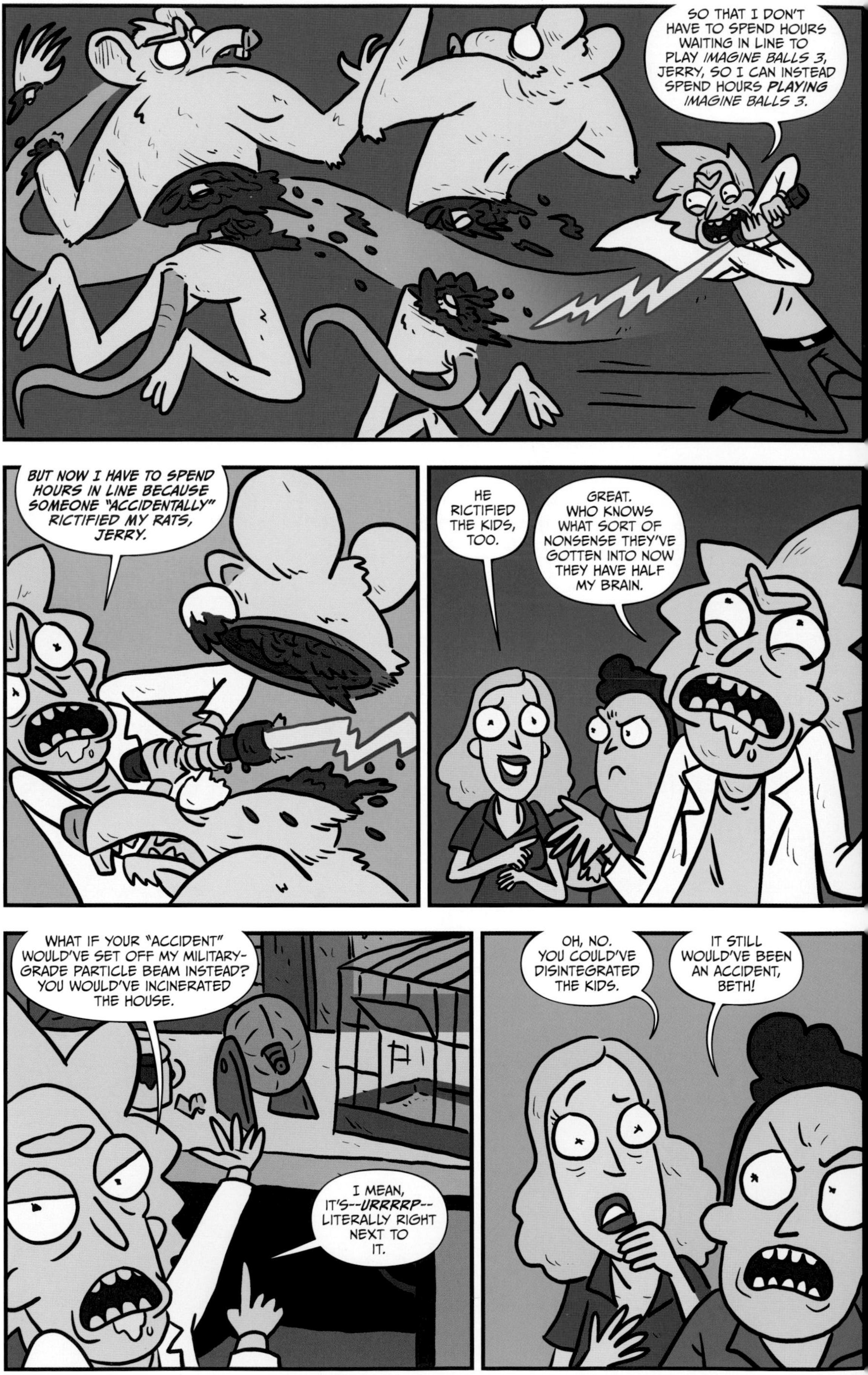
SO THAT I DON'T HAVE TO SPEND HOURS WAITING IN LINE TO PLAY IMAGINE BALLS 3, JERRY, SO I CAN INSTEAD SPEND HOURS PLAYING IMAGINE BALLS 3.
BUT NOW I HAVE TO SPEND HOURS IN LINE BECAUSE SOMEONE "ACCIDENTALLY" RICTIFIED MY RATS, JERRY.
HE RICTIFIED THE KIDS, TOO.
GREAT. WHO KNOWS WHAT SORT OF NONSENSE THEY'VE GOTTEN INTO NOW THEY HAVE HALF MY BRAIN.
WHAT IF YOUR "ACCIDENT" WOULD'VE SET OFF MY MILITARY-GRADE PARTICLE BEAM INSTEAD? YOU WOULD'VE INCINERATED THE HOUSE.
I MEAN, IT'S--URRRRP--LITERALLY RIGHT NEXT TO IT.
OH, NO. YOU COULD'VE DISINTEGRATED THE KIDS.
IT STILL WOULD'VE BEEN AN ACCIDENT, BETH!

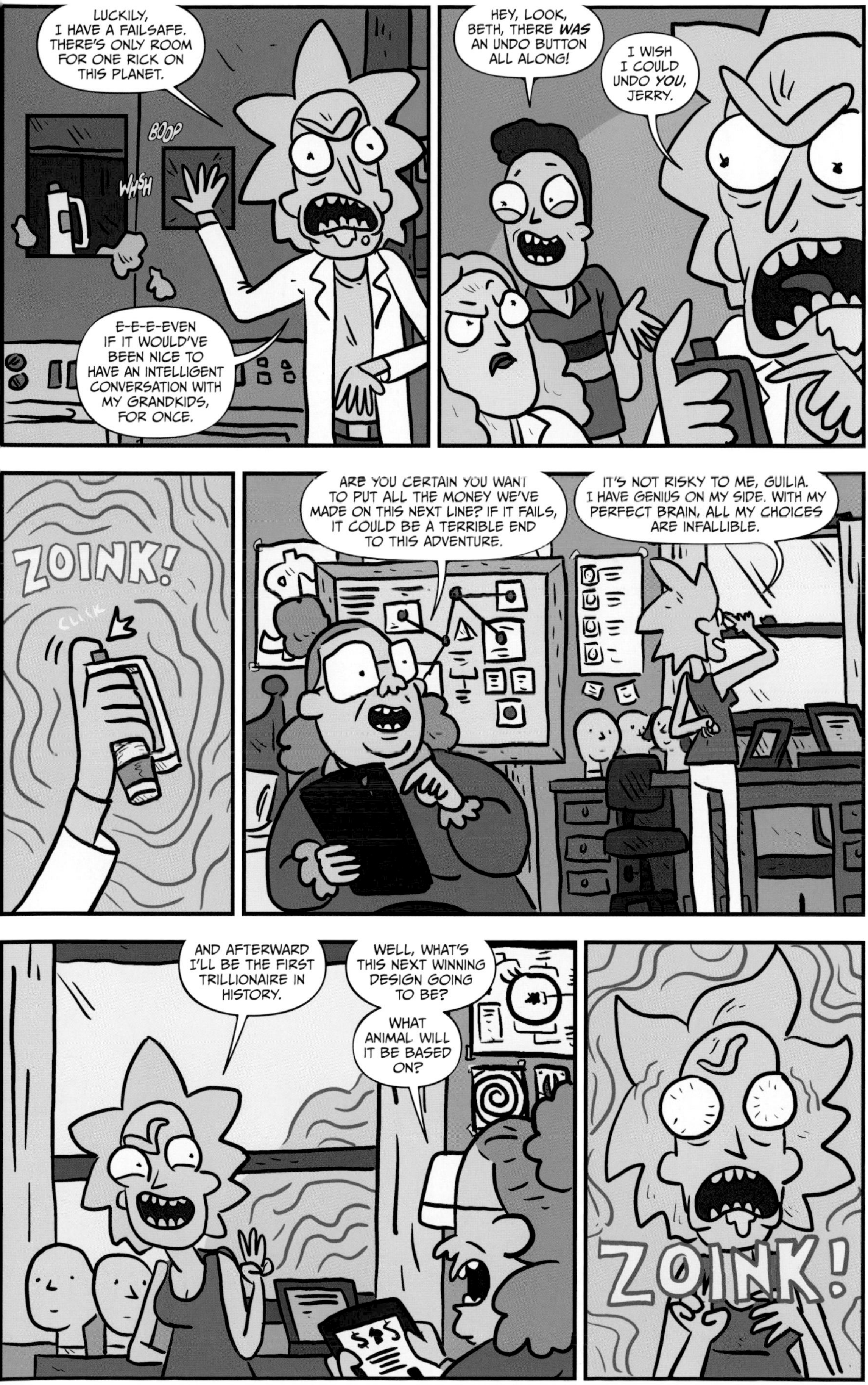
LUCKILY, I HAVE A FAILSAFE. THERE'S ONLY ROOM FOR ONE RICK ON THIS PLANET.
BOOP
WHSH
E-E-E-EVEN IF IT WOULD'VE BEEN NICE TO HAVE AN INTELLIGENT CONVERSATION WITH MY GRANDKIDS, FOR ONCE.
HEY, LOOK, BETH, THERE *WAS* AN UNDO BUTTON ALL ALONG!
I WISH I COULD UNDO *YOU*, JERRY.
ZOINK!
CLICK
ARE YOU CERTAIN YOU WANT TO PUT ALL THE MONEY WE'VE MADE ON THIS NEXT LINE? IF IT FAILS, IT COULD BE A TERRIBLE END TO THIS ADVENTURE.
IT'S NOT RISKY TO ME, GUILIA. I HAVE GENIUS ON MY SIDE. WITH MY PERFECT BRAIN, ALL MY CHOICES ARE INFALLIBLE.
AND AFTERWARD I'LL BE THE FIRST TRILLIONAIRE IN HISTORY.
WELL, WHAT'S THIS NEXT WINNING DESIGN GOING TO BE?
WHAT ANIMAL WILL IT BE BASED ON?
ZOINK!

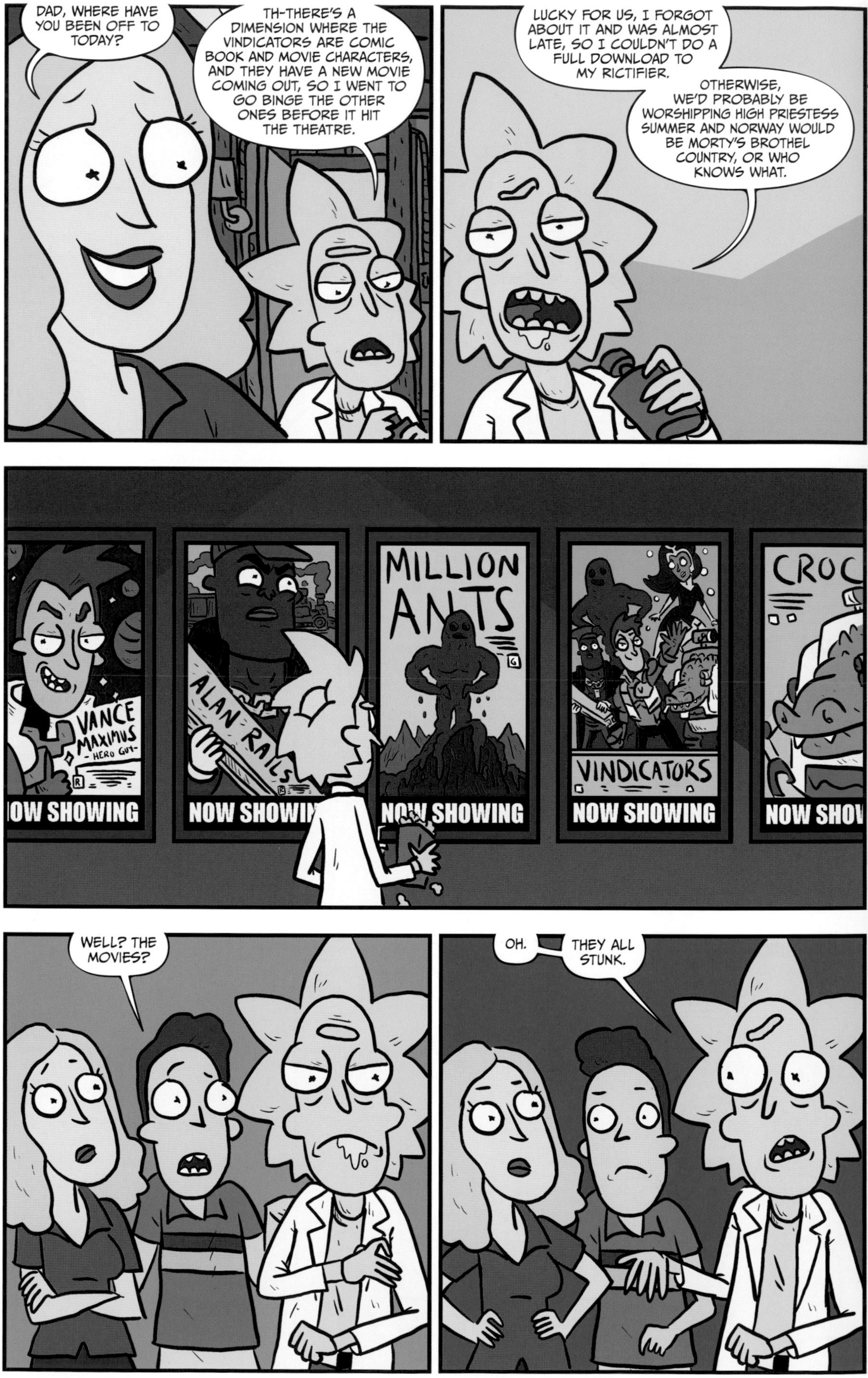
DAD, WHERE HAVE YOU BEEN OFF TO TODAY?
TH-THERE'S A DIMENSION WHERE THE VINDICATORS ARE COMIC BOOK AND MOVIE CHARACTERS, AND THEY HAVE A NEW MOVIE COMING OUT, SO I WENT TO GO BINGE THE OTHER ONES BEFORE IT HIT THE THEATRE.
LUCKY FOR US, I FORGOT ABOUT IT AND WAS ALMOST LATE, SO I COULDN'T DO A FULL DOWNLOAD TO MY RICTIFIER.
OTHERWISE, WE'D PROBABLY BE WORSHIPPING HIGH PRIESTESS SUMMER AND NORWAY WOULD BE MORTY'S BROTHEL COUNTRY, OR WHO KNOWS WHAT.
VANCE MAXIMUS
-HERO GUY-
OW SHOWING
ALAN RAILS
NOW SHOWIN
MILLION ANTS
NOW SHOWING
VINDICATORS
NOW SHOWING
CROC
NOW SHOW
WELL? THE MOVIES?
OH.
THEY ALL STUNK.

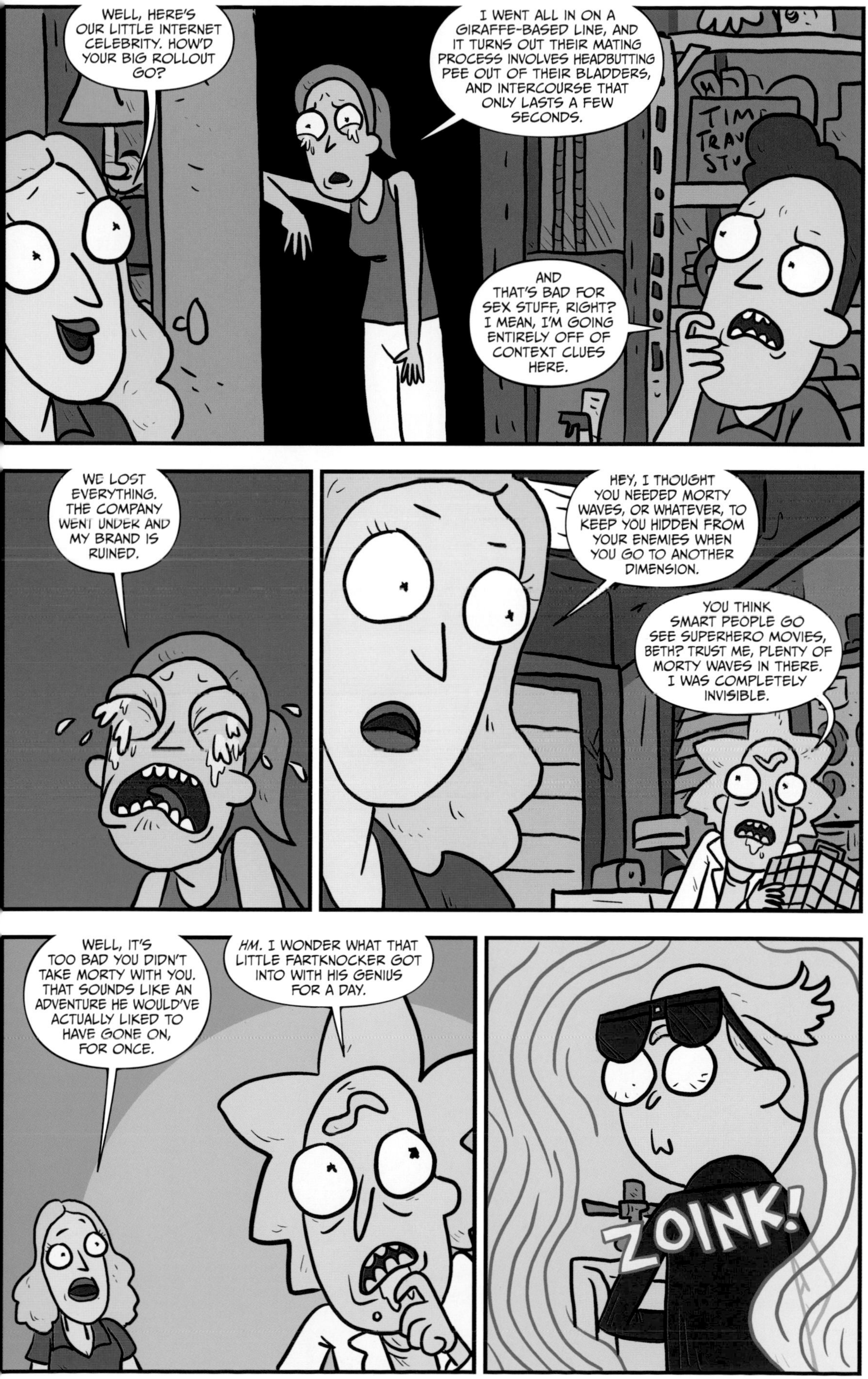
WELL, HERE'S OUR LITTLE INTERNET CELEBRITY. HOW'D YOUR BIG ROLLOUT GO?
I WENT ALL IN ON A GIRAFFE-BASED LINE, AND IT TURNS OUT THEIR MATING PROCESS INVOLVES HEADBUTTING PEE OUT OF THEIR BLADDERS, AND INTERCOURSE THAT ONLY LASTS A FEW SECONDS.
AND THAT'S BAD FOR SEX STUFF, RIGHT? I MEAN, I'M GOING ENTIRELY OFF OF CONTEXT CLUES HERE.
WE LOST EVERYTHING. THE COMPANY WENT UNDER AND MY BRAND IS RUINED.
HEY, I THOUGHT YOU NEEDED MORTY WAVES, OR WHATEVER, TO KEEP YOU HIDDEN FROM YOUR ENEMIES WHEN YOU GO TO ANOTHER DIMENSION.
YOU THINK SMART PEOPLE GO SEE SUPERHERO MOVIES, BETH? TRUST ME, PLENTY OF MORTY WAVES IN THERE. I WAS COMPLETELY INVISIBLE.
WELL, IT'S TOO BAD YOU DIDN'T TAKE MORTY WITH YOU. THAT SOUNDS LIKE AN ADVENTURE HE WOULD'VE ACTUALLY LIKED TO HAVE GONE ON, FOR ONCE.
HM. I WONDER WHAT THAT LITTLE FARTKNOCKER GOT INTO WITH HIS GENIUS FOR A DAY.
ZOINK!

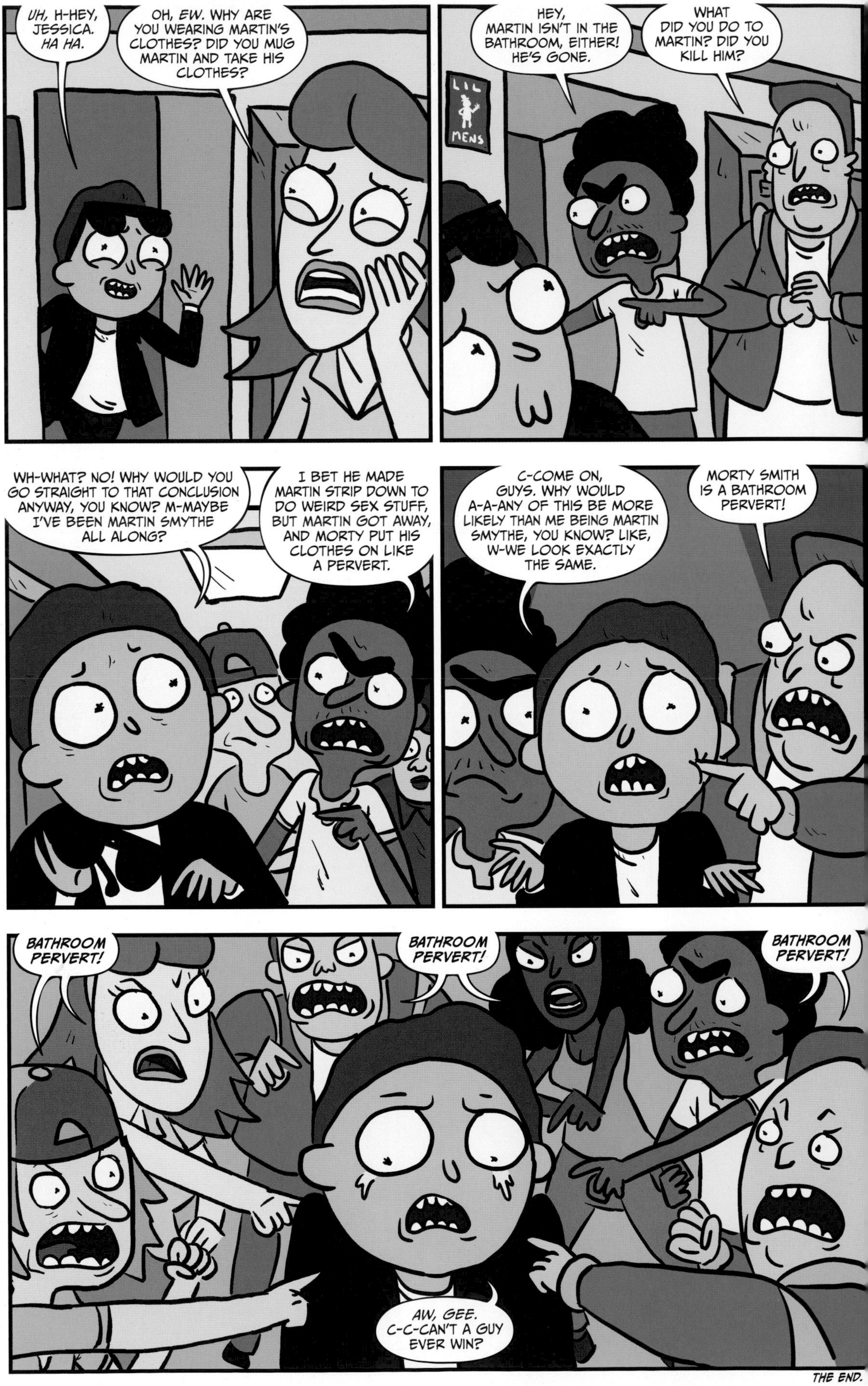
UH, H-HEY, JESSICA. HA HA.
OH, EW. WHY ARE YOU WEARING MARTIN'S CLOTHES? DID YOU MUG MARTIN AND TAKE HIS CLOTHES?
LIL MENS
HEY, MARTIN ISN'T IN THE BATHROOM, EITHER! HE'S GONE.
WHAT DID YOU DO TO MARTIN? DID YOU KILL HIM?
WH-WHAT? NO! WHY WOULD YOU GO STRAIGHT TO THAT CONCLUSION ANYWAY, YOU KNOW? M-MAYBE I'VE BEEN MARTIN SMYTHE ALL ALONG?
I BET HE MADE MARTIN STRIP DOWN TO DO WEIRD SEX STUFF, BUT MARTIN GOT AWAY, AND MORTY PUT HIS CLOTHES ON LIKE A PERVERT.
C-COME ON, GUYS. WHY WOULD A-A-ANY OF THIS BE MORE LIKELY THAN ME BEING MARTIN SMYTHE, YOU KNOW? LIKE, W-WE LOOK EXACTLY THE SAME.
MORTY SMITH IS A BATHROOM PERVERT!
BATHROOM PERVERT!
BATHROOM PERVERT!
BATHROOM PERVERT!
AW, GEE. C-C-CAN'T A GUY EVER WIN?

THE END.

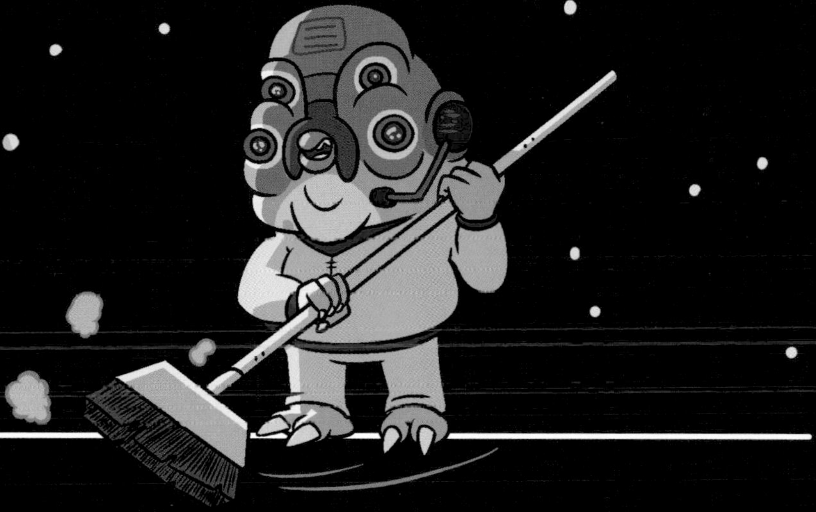

BONUS STORIES

DEATH BECOMES HIM

WRITTEN BY **MAGDALENE VISAGGIO** ILLUSTRATED BY **IAN MCGINTY**

INTRODUCING: GLOOTIE!

WRITTEN BY **KYLE STARKS** ILLUSTRATED BY **MARC ELLERBY**

FEEL BAD INC.

WRITTEN BY **MAGDALENE VISAGGIO** ILLUSTRATED BY **IAN MCGINTY**

WHAT IF RICK WAS ONE OF US?

WRITTEN BY **MAGDALENE VISAGGIO** ILLUSTRATED BY **IAN MCGINTY**

LAST THINGS

WRITTEN BY **MAGDALENE VISAGGIO** ILLUSTRATED BY **IAN MCGINTY**

COLORED BY **SARAH STERN** LETTERED BY **CRANK!**

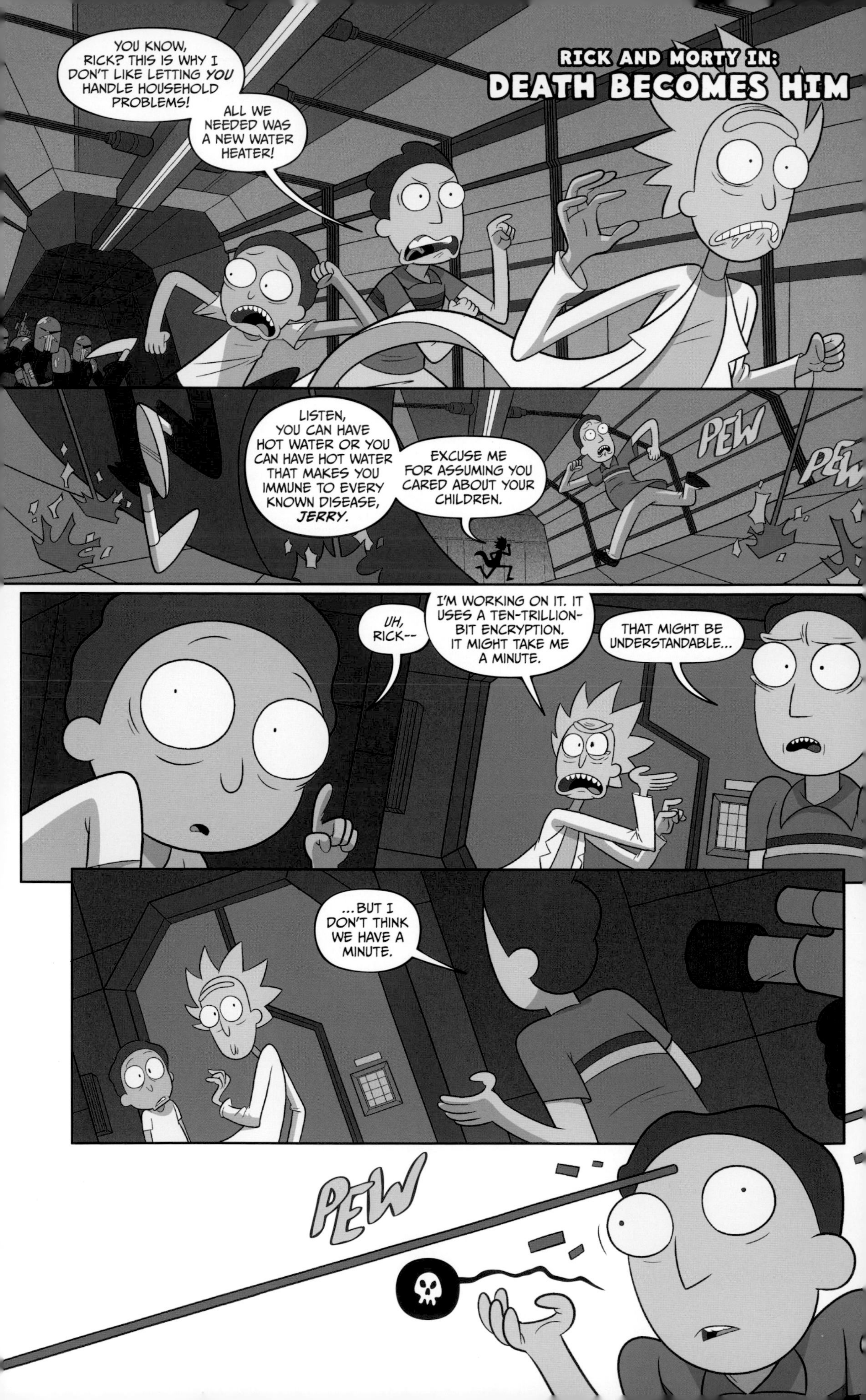
RICK AND MORTY IN:
DEATH BECOMES HIM
YOU KNOW, RICK? THIS IS WHY I DON'T LIKE LETTING YOU HANDLE HOUSEHOLD PROBLEMS!
ALL WE NEEDED WAS A NEW WATER HEATER!
LISTEN, YOU CAN HAVE HOT WATER OR YOU CAN HAVE HOT WATER THAT MAKES YOU IMMUNE TO EVERY KNOWN DISEASE, JERRY.
EXCUSE ME FOR ASSUMING YOU CARED ABOUT YOUR CHILDREN.
PEW
PEW
UH, RICK--
I'M WORKING ON IT. IT USES A TEN-TRILLION-BIT ENCRYPTION. IT MIGHT TAKE ME A MINUTE.
THAT MIGHT BE UNDERSTANDABLE...
...BUT I DON'T THINK WE HAVE A MINUTE.
PEW

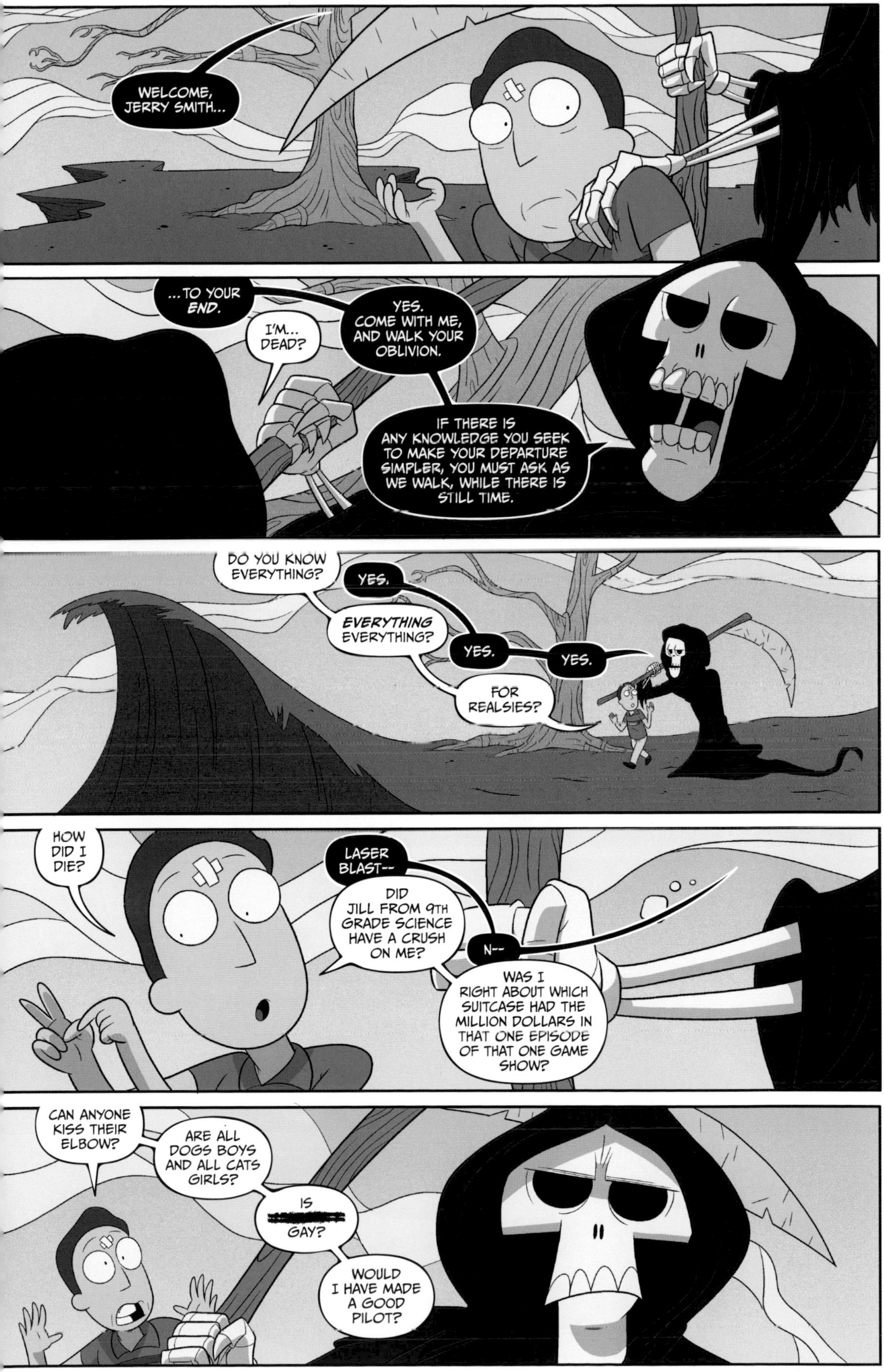

WELCOME, JERRY SMITH...
...TO YOUR *END*.
I'M... DEAD?
YES. COME WITH ME, AND WALK YOUR OBLIVION.
IF THERE IS ANY KNOWLEDGE YOU SEEK TO MAKE YOUR DEPARTURE SIMPLER, YOU MUST ASK AS WE WALK, WHILE THERE IS STILL TIME.
DO YOU KNOW EVERYTHING?
YES.
EVERYTHING EVERYTHING?
YES.
FOR REALSIES?
YES.
HOW DID I DIE?
LASER BLAST--
DID JILL FROM 9TH GRADE SCIENCE HAVE A CRUSH ON ME?
N--
WAS I RIGHT ABOUT WHICH SUITCASE HAD THE MILLION DOLLARS IN THAT ONE EPISODE OF THAT ONE GAME SHOW?
CAN ANYONE KISS THEIR ELBOW?
ARE ALL DOGS BOYS AND ALL CATS GIRLS?
IS [redacted] GAY?
WOULD I HAVE MADE A GOOD PILOT?

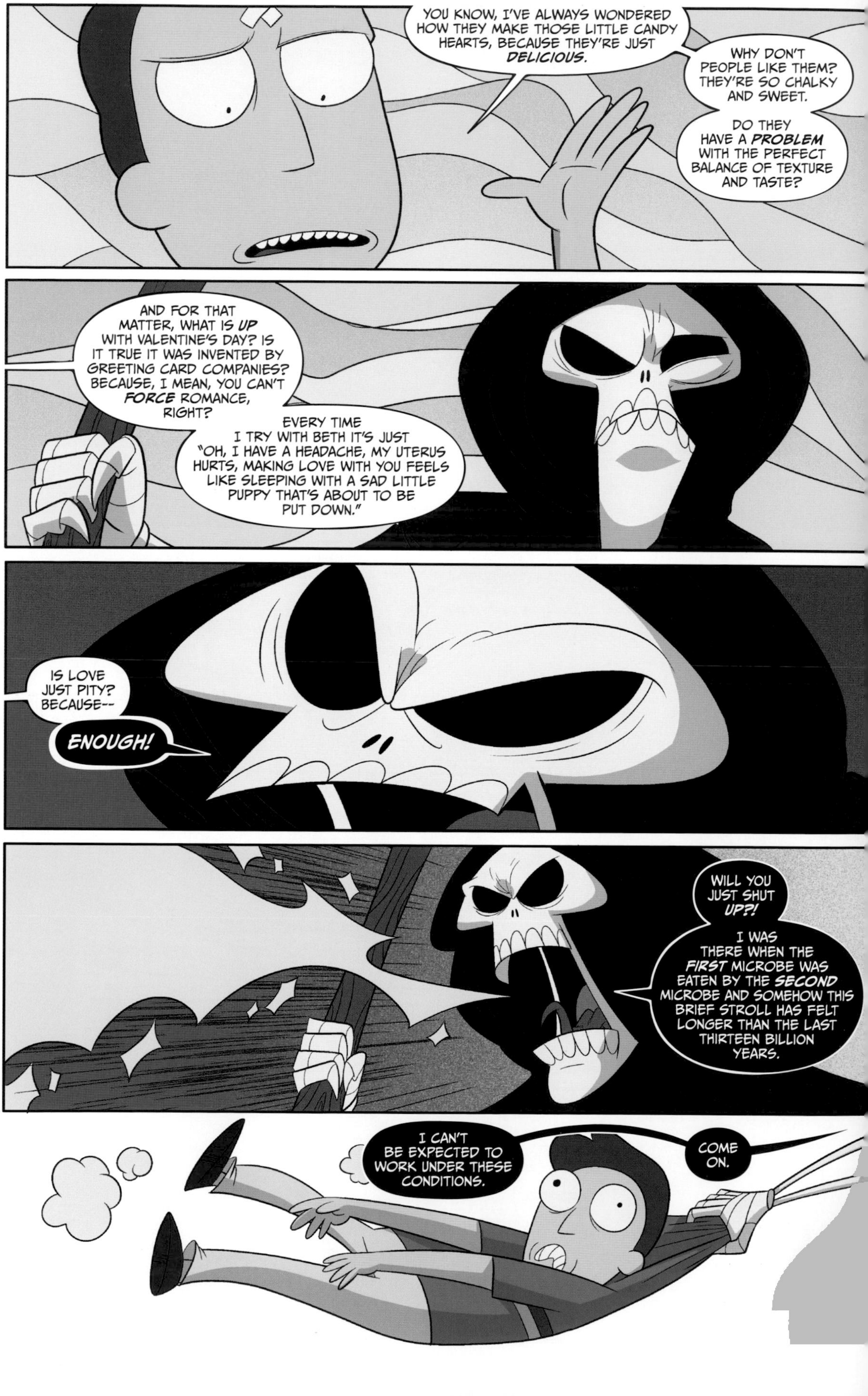
YOU KNOW, I'VE ALWAYS WONDERED HOW THEY MAKE THOSE LITTLE CANDY HEARTS, BECAUSE THEY'RE JUST *DELICIOUS*.
WHY DON'T PEOPLE LIKE THEM? THEY'RE SO CHALKY AND SWEET.
DO THEY HAVE A *PROBLEM* WITH THE PERFECT BALANCE OF TEXTURE AND TASTE?
AND FOR THAT MATTER, WHAT IS *UP* WITH VALENTINE'S DAY? IS IT TRUE IT WAS INVENTED BY GREETING CARD COMPANIES? BECAUSE, I MEAN, YOU CAN'T *FORCE* ROMANCE, RIGHT?
EVERY TIME I TRY WITH BETH IT'S JUST "OH, I HAVE A HEADACHE, MY UTERUS HURTS, MAKING LOVE WITH YOU FEELS LIKE SLEEPING WITH A SAD LITTLE PUPPY THAT'S ABOUT TO BE PUT DOWN."
IS LOVE JUST PITY? BECAUSE--
ENOUGH!
WILL YOU JUST SHUT *UP?!*
I WAS THERE WHEN THE *FIRST* MICROBE WAS EATEN BY THE *SECOND* MICROBE AND SOMEHOW THIS BRIEF STROLL HAS FELT LONGER THAN THE LAST THIRTEEN BILLION YEARS.
I CAN'T BE EXPECTED TO WORK UNDER THESE CONDITIONS.
COME ON.

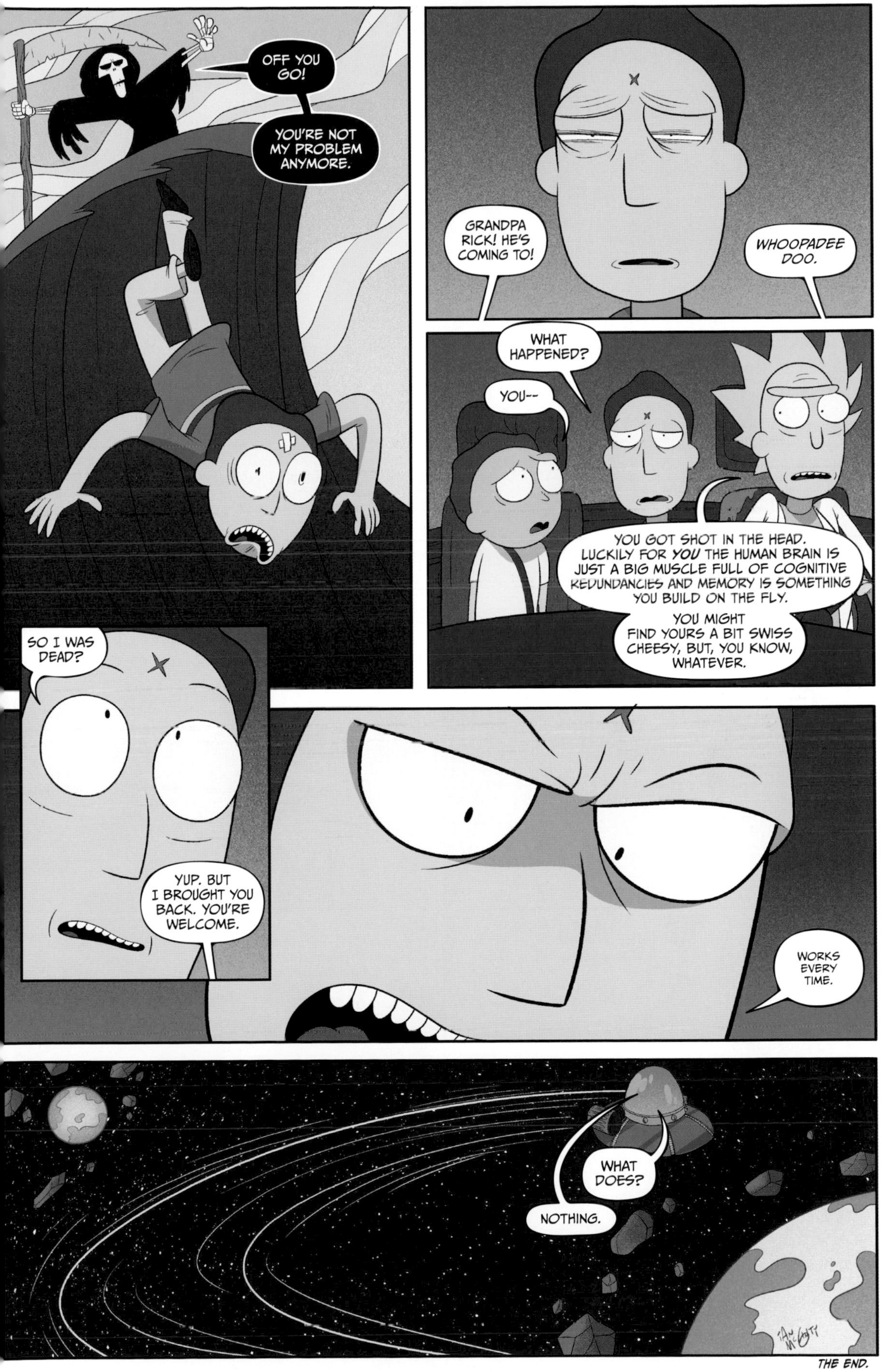
OFF YOU GO!
YOU'RE NOT MY PROBLEM ANYMORE.
GRANDPA RICK! HE'S COMING TO!
WHOOPADEE DOO.
WHAT HAPPENED?
YOU--
YOU GOT SHOT IN THE HEAD. LUCKILY FOR *YOU* THE HUMAN BRAIN IS JUST A BIG MUSCLE FULL OF COGNITIVE REDUNDANCIES AND MEMORY IS SOMETHING YOU BUILD ON THE FLY.
YOU MIGHT FIND YOURS A BIT SWISS CHEESY, BUT, YOU KNOW, WHATEVER.
SO I WAS DEAD?
YUP. BUT I BROUGHT YOU BACK. YOU'RE WELCOME.
WORKS EVERY TIME.
WHAT DOES?
NOTHING.

THE END.

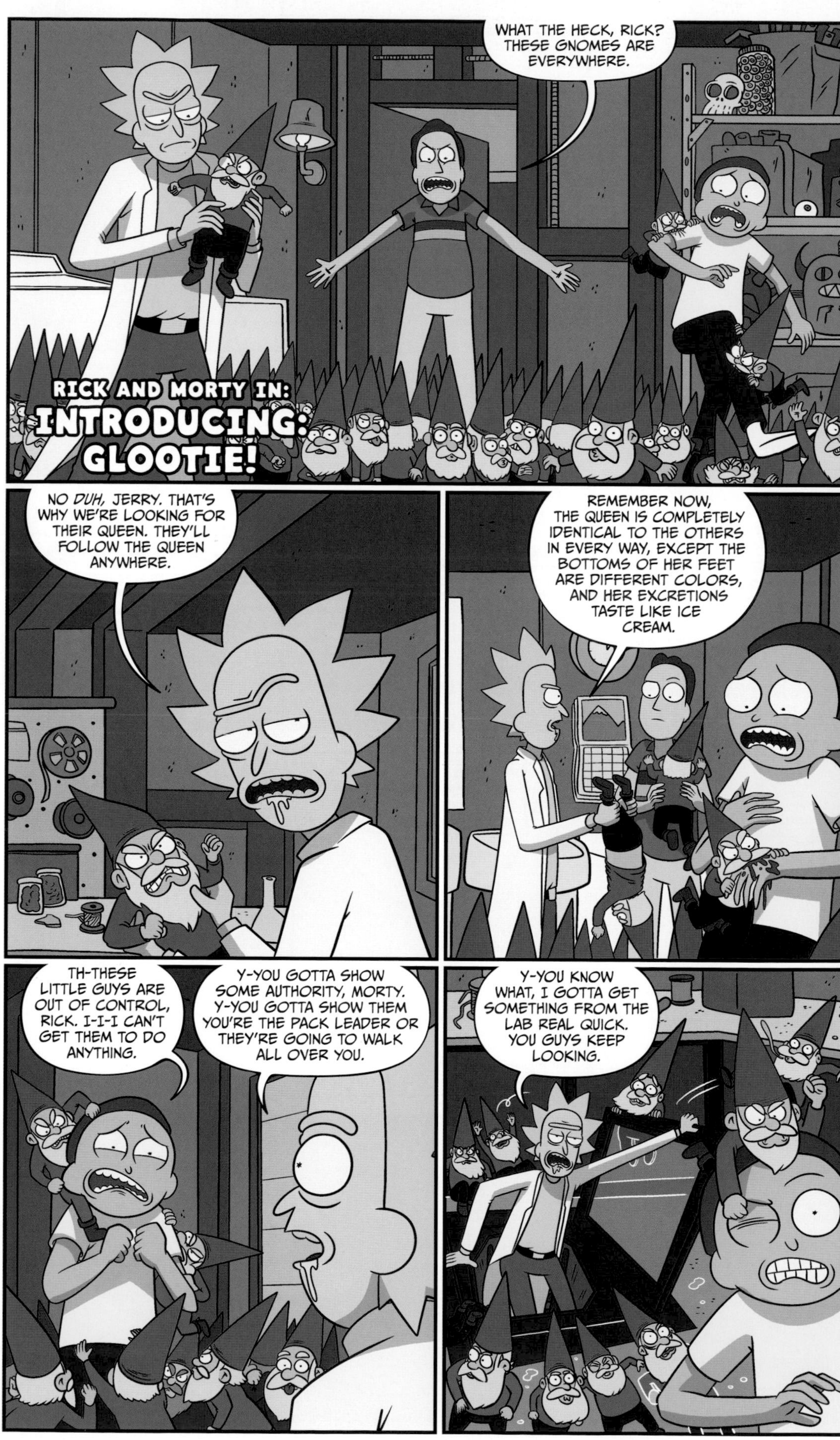
WHAT THE HECK, RICK? THESE GNOMES ARE EVERYWHERE.
RICK AND MORTY IN:
INTRODUCING: GLOOTIE!
NO DUH, JERRY. THAT'S WHY WE'RE LOOKING FOR THEIR QUEEN. THEY'LL FOLLOW THE QUEEN ANYWHERE.
REMEMBER NOW, THE QUEEN IS COMPLETELY IDENTICAL TO THE OTHERS IN EVERY WAY, EXCEPT THE BOTTOMS OF HER FEET ARE DIFFERENT COLORS, AND HER EXCRETIONS TASTE LIKE ICE CREAM.
TH-THESE LITTLE GUYS ARE OUT OF CONTROL, RICK. I-I-I CAN'T GET THEM TO DO ANYTHING.
Y-YOU GOTTA SHOW SOME AUTHORITY, MORTY. Y-YOU GOTTA SHOW THEM YOU'RE THE PACK LEADER OR THEY'RE GOING TO WALK ALL OVER YOU.
Y-YOU KNOW WHAT, I GOTTA GET SOMETHING FROM THE LAB REAL QUICK. YOU GUYS KEEP LOOKING.

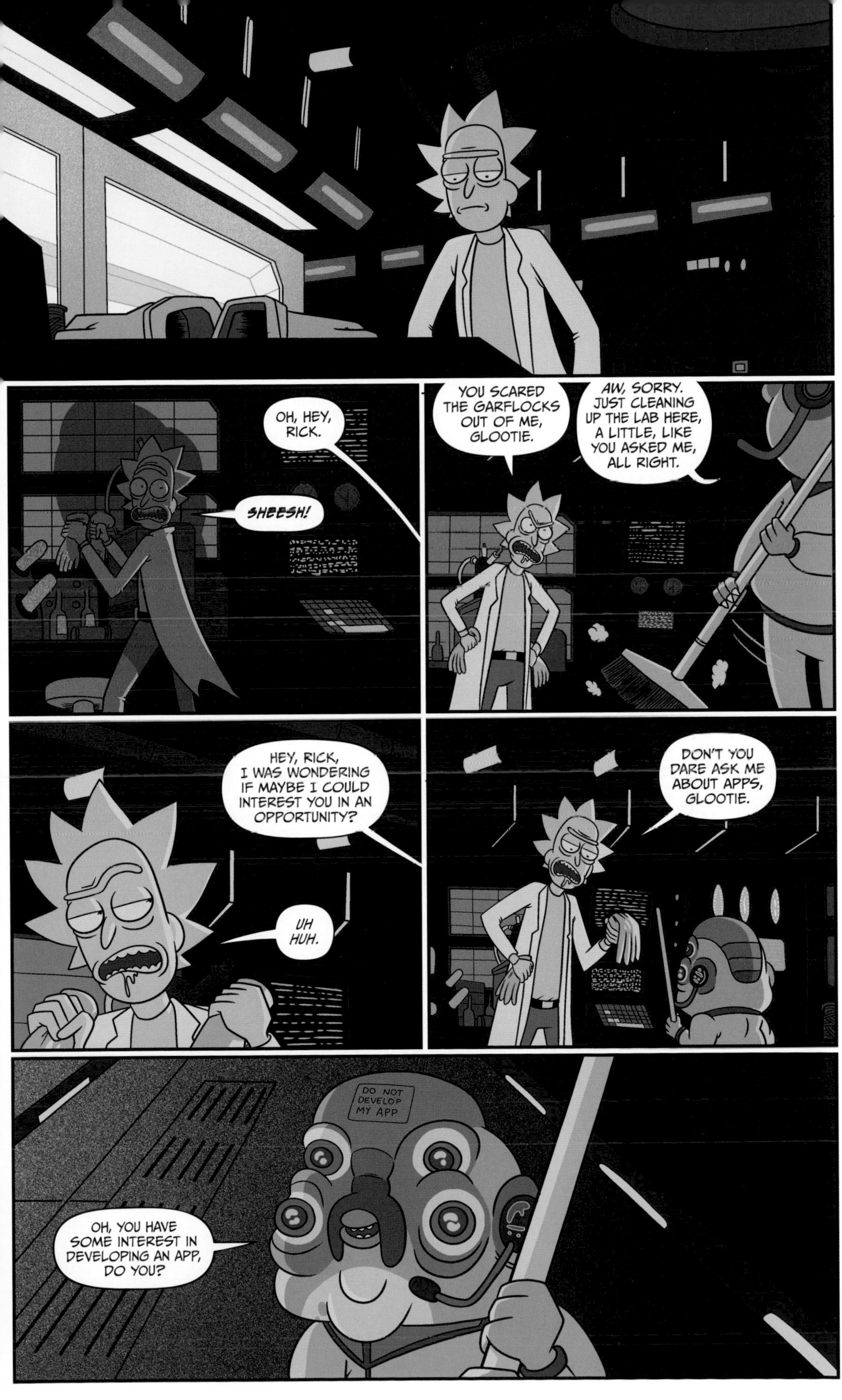
OH, HEY, RICK.
SHEESH!
YOU SCARED THE GARFLOCKS OUT OF ME, GLOOTIE.
AW, SORRY. JUST CLEANING UP THE LAB HERE, A LITTLE, LIKE YOU ASKED ME, ALL RIGHT.
HEY, RICK, I WAS WONDERING IF MAYBE I COULD INTEREST YOU IN AN OPPORTUNITY?
UH HUH.
DON'T YOU DARE ASK ME ABOUT APPS, GLOOTIE.
DO NOT DEVELOP MY APP
OH, YOU HAVE SOME INTEREST IN DEVELOPING AN APP, DO YOU?

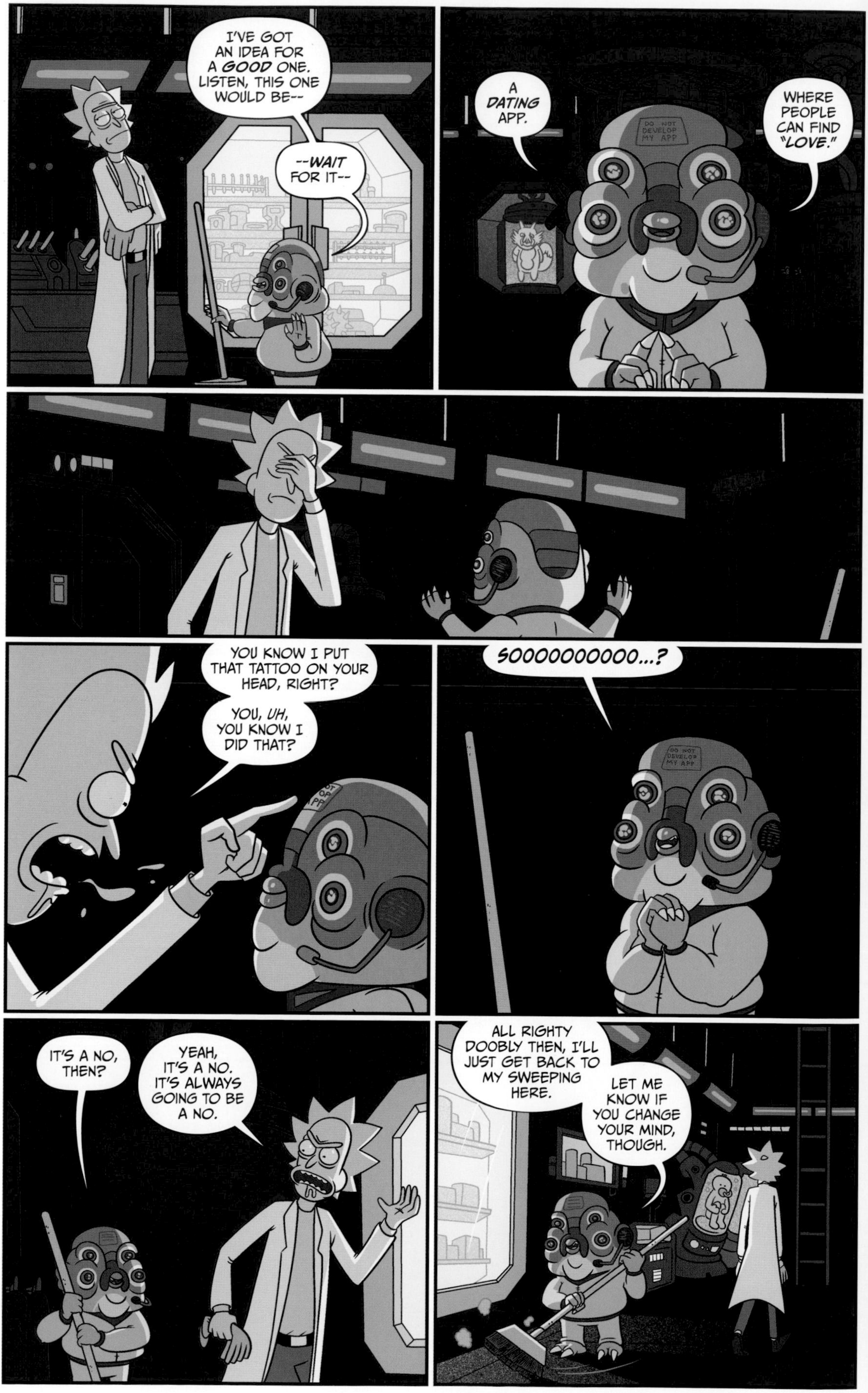

I'VE GOT AN IDEA FOR A GOOD ONE. LISTEN, THIS ONE WOULD BE--
--WAIT FOR IT--
A DATING APP.
DO NOT DEVELOP MY APP
WHERE PEOPLE CAN FIND "LOVE."
YOU KNOW I PUT THAT TATTOO ON YOUR HEAD, RIGHT?
YOU, UH, YOU KNOW I DID THAT?
SOOOOOOOOOO...?
DO NOT DEVELOP MY APP
IT'S A NO, THEN?
YEAH, IT'S A NO. IT'S ALWAYS GOING TO BE A NO.
ALL RIGHTY DOOBLY THEN, I'LL JUST GET BACK TO MY SWEEPING HERE.
LET ME KNOW IF YOU CHANGE YOUR MIND, THOUGH.

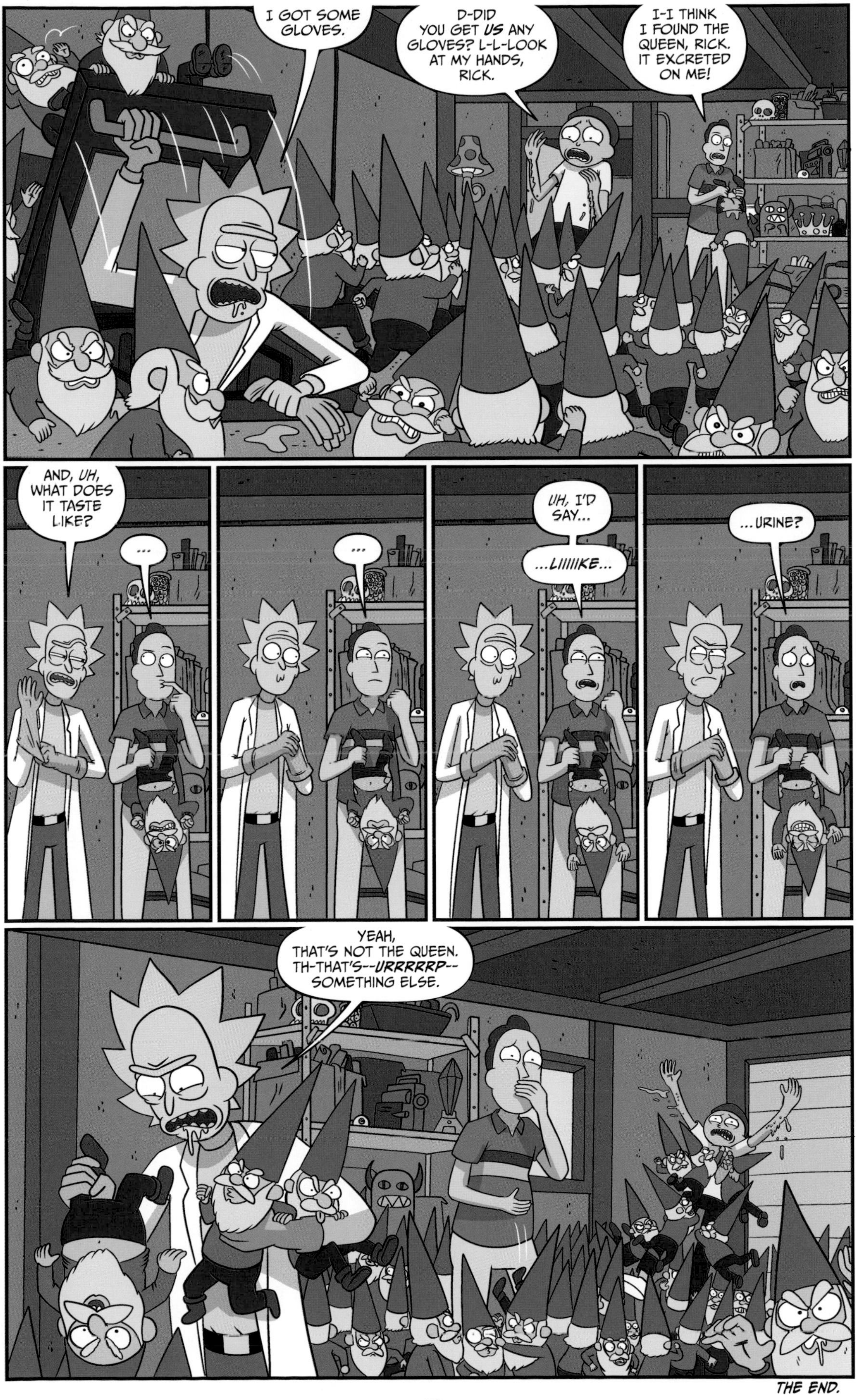
I GOT SOME GLOVES.
D-DID YOU GET *US* ANY GLOVES? L-L-LOOK AT MY HANDS, RICK.
I-I THINK I FOUND THE QUEEN, RICK. IT EXCRETED ON ME!
AND, *UH*, WHAT DOES IT TASTE LIKE?
...
...
UH, I'D SAY...
...LIIIIIKE...
...URINE?
YEAH, THAT'S NOT THE QUEEN. TH-THAT'S--*URRRRRP*-- SOMETHING ELSE.

THE END.

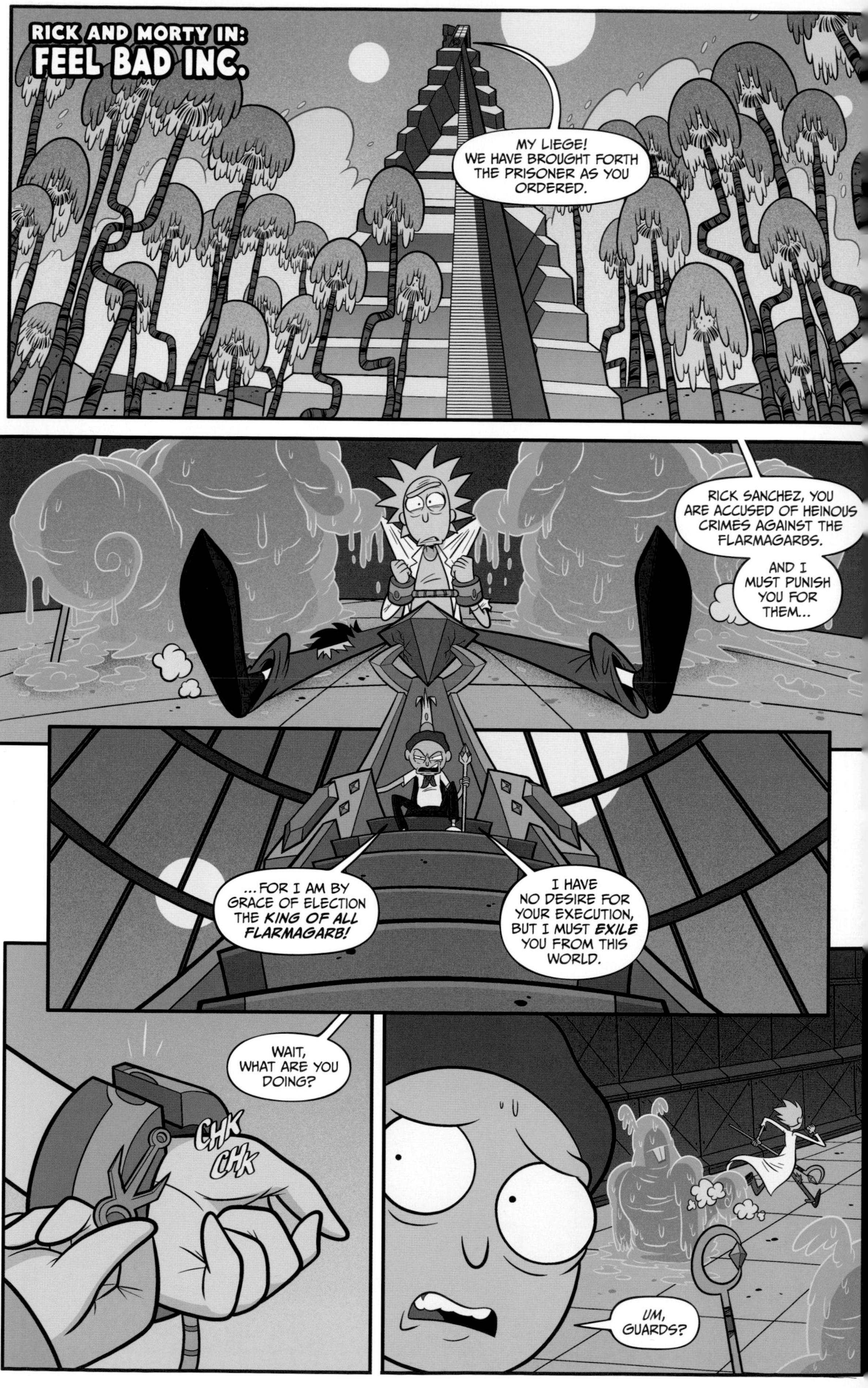
RICK AND MORTY IN:
FEEL BAD INC.
MY LIEGE! WE HAVE BROUGHT FORTH THE PRISONER AS YOU ORDERED.
RICK SANCHEZ, YOU ARE ACCUSED OF HEINOUS CRIMES AGAINST THE FLARMAGARBS.
AND I MUST PUNISH YOU FOR THEM...
...FOR I AM BY GRACE OF ELECTION THE KING OF ALL FLARMAGARB!
I HAVE NO DESIRE FOR YOUR EXECUTION, BUT I MUST EXILE YOU FROM THIS WORLD.
WAIT, WHAT ARE YOU DOING?
CHK
CHK
UM, GUARDS?

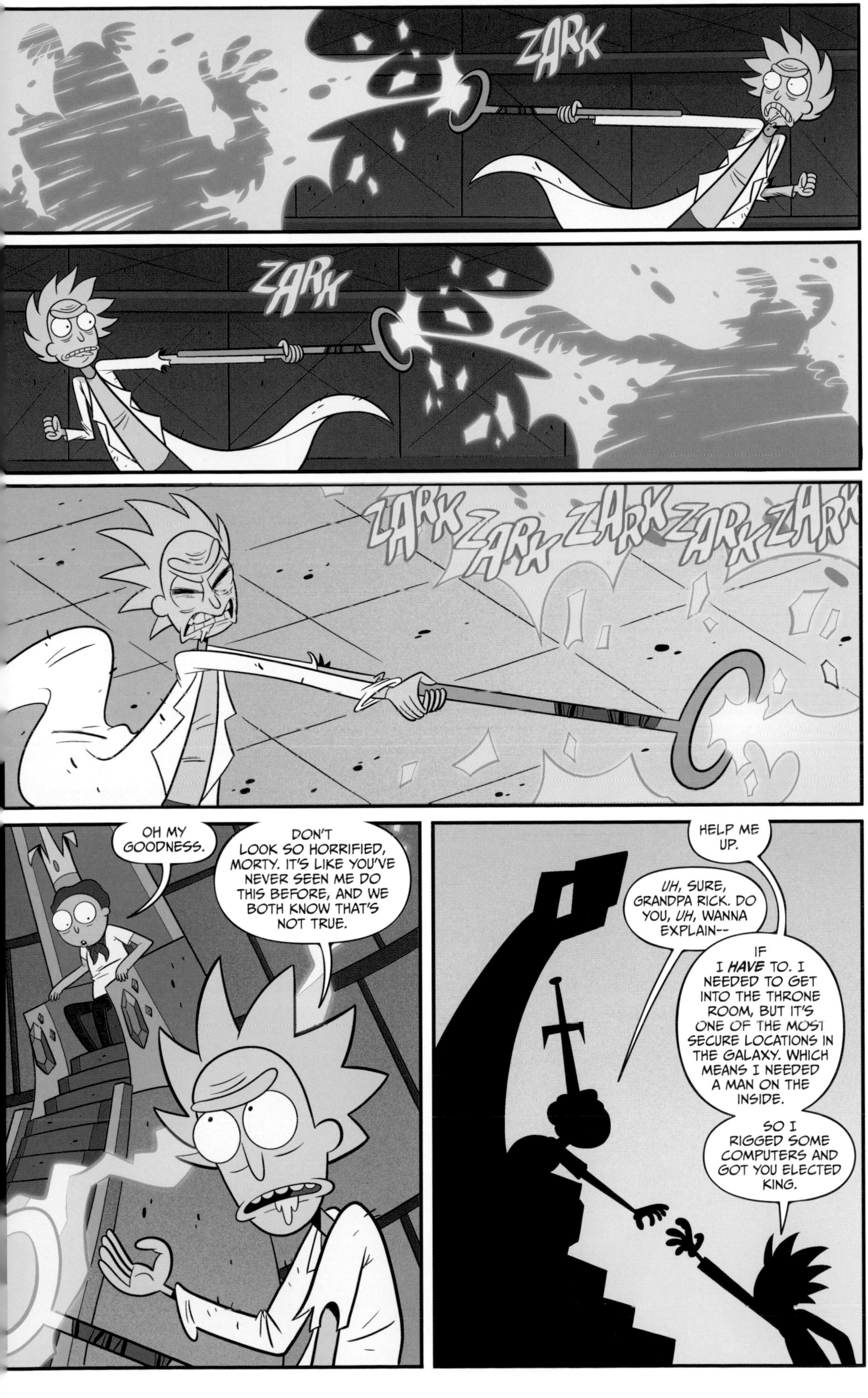
ZARK
ZARK
ZARK ZARK ZARK ZARK ZARK
OH MY GOODNESS.
DON'T LOOK SO HORRIFIED, MORTY. IT'S LIKE YOU'VE NEVER SEEN ME DO THIS BEFORE, AND WE BOTH KNOW THAT'S NOT TRUE.
HELP ME UP.
UH, SURE, GRANDPA RICK. DO YOU, *UH*, WANNA EXPLAIN--
IF I ***HAVE*** TO. I NEEDED TO GET INTO THE THRONE ROOM, BUT IT'S ONE OF THE MOST SECURE LOCATIONS IN THE GALAXY. WHICH MEANS I NEEDED A MAN ON THE INSIDE.
SO I RIGGED SOME COMPUTERS AND GOT YOU ELECTED KING.

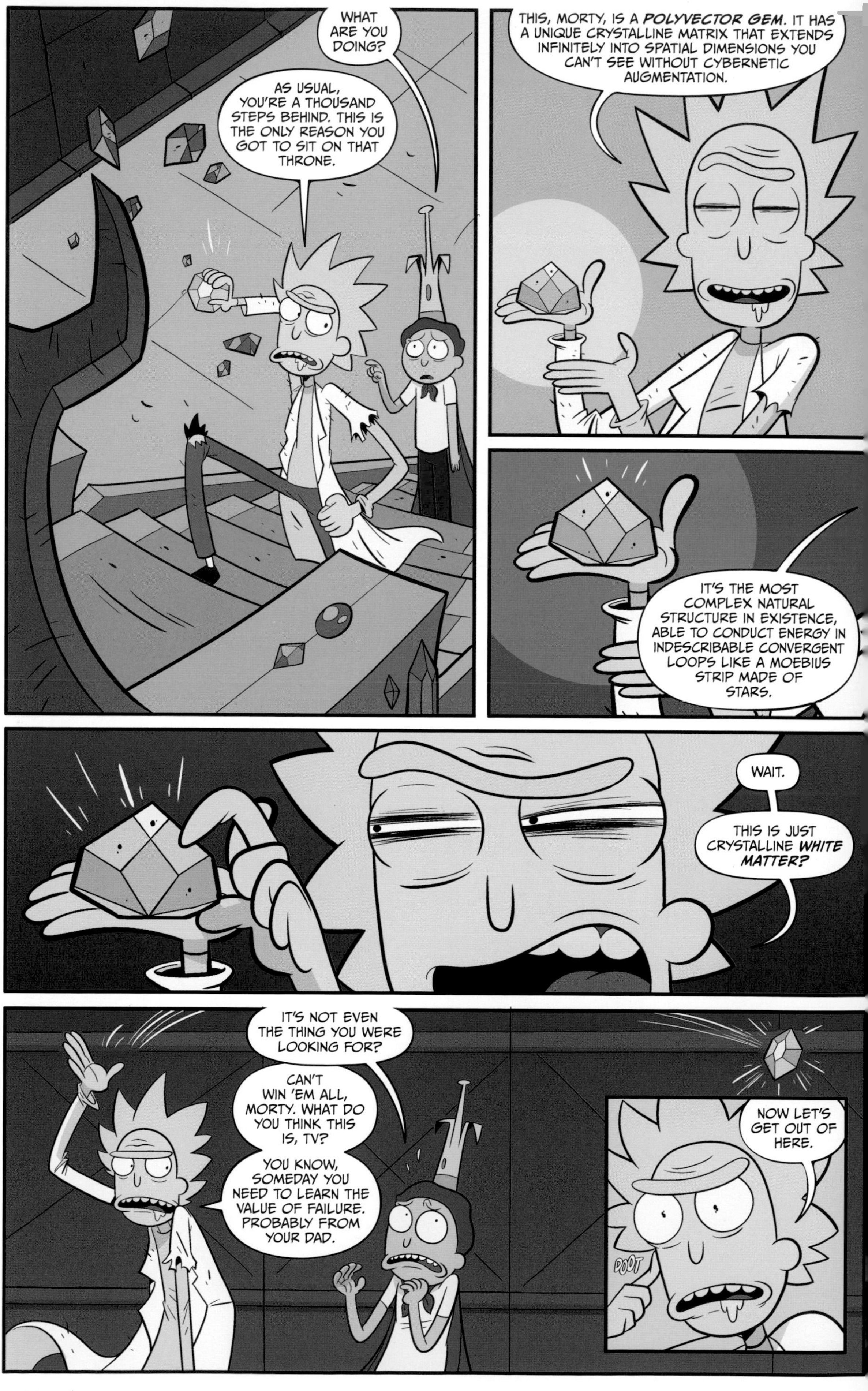
WHAT ARE YOU DOING?
AS USUAL, YOU'RE A THOUSAND STEPS BEHIND. THIS IS THE ONLY REASON YOU GOT TO SIT ON THAT THRONE.
THIS, MORTY, IS A **POLYVECTOR GEM**. IT HAS A UNIQUE CRYSTALLINE MATRIX THAT EXTENDS INFINITELY INTO SPATIAL DIMENSIONS YOU CAN'T SEE WITHOUT CYBERNETIC AUGMENTATION.
IT'S THE MOST COMPLEX NATURAL STRUCTURE IN EXISTENCE, ABLE TO CONDUCT ENERGY IN INDESCRIBABLE CONVERGENT LOOPS LIKE A MOEBIUS STRIP MADE OF STARS.
WAIT.
THIS IS JUST CRYSTALLINE ***WHITE MATTER?***
IT'S NOT EVEN THE THING YOU WERE LOOKING FOR?
CAN'T WIN 'EM ALL, MORTY. WHAT DO YOU THINK THIS IS, TV?
YOU KNOW, SOMEDAY YOU NEED TO LEARN THE VALUE OF FAILURE. PROBABLY FROM YOUR DAD.
NOW LET'S GET OUT OF HERE.
DOOT

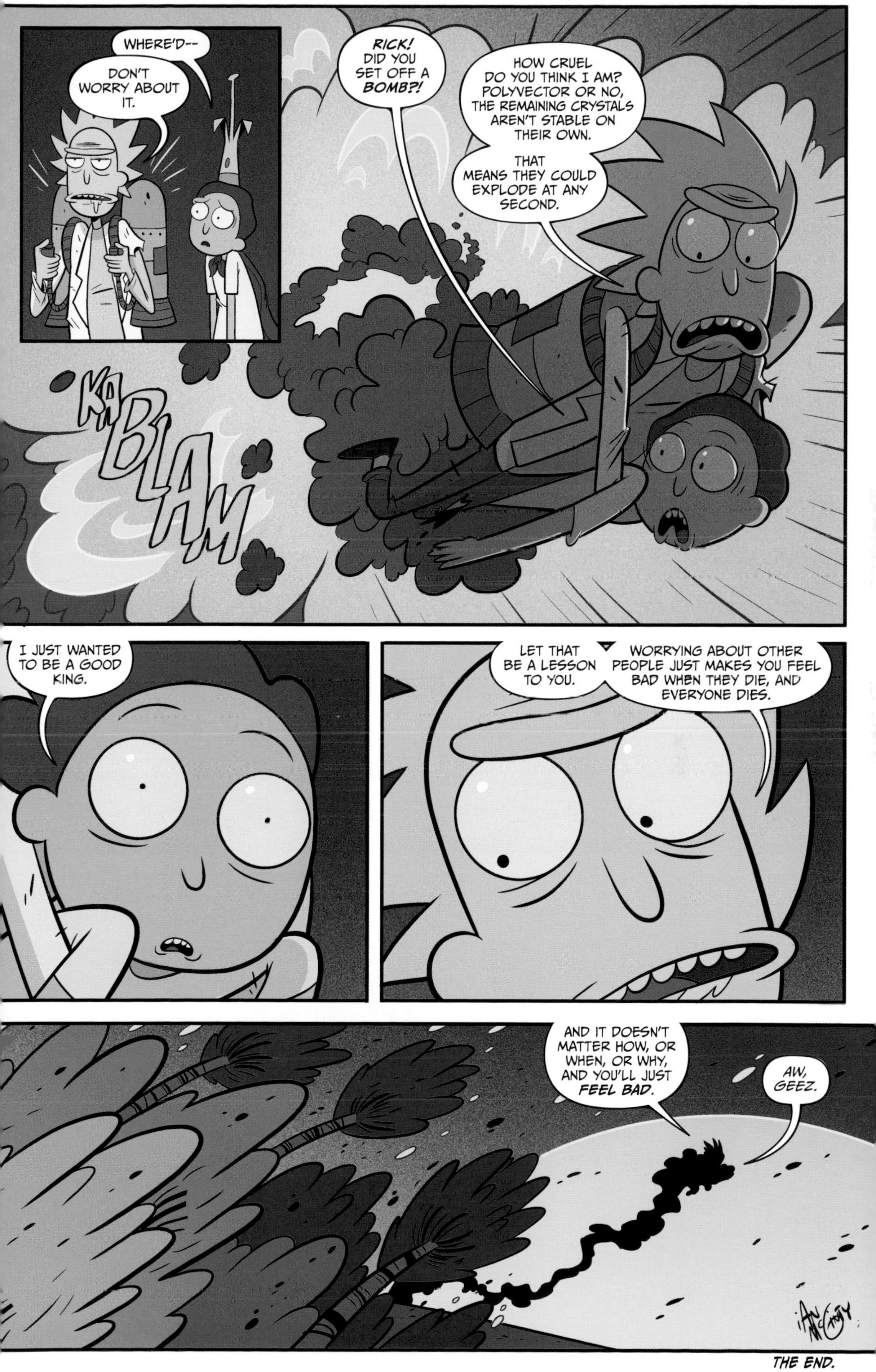
WHERE'D--
DON'T WORRY ABOUT IT.
KA BLAM
RICK! DID YOU SET OFF A BOMB?!
HOW CRUEL DO YOU THINK I AM? POLYVECTOR OR NO, THE REMAINING CRYSTALS AREN'T STABLE ON THEIR OWN.
THAT MEANS THEY COULD EXPLODE AT ANY SECOND.
I JUST WANTED TO BE A GOOD KING.
LET THAT BE A LESSON TO YOU.
WORRYING ABOUT OTHER PEOPLE JUST MAKES YOU FEEL BAD WHEN THEY DIE, AND EVERYONE DIES.
AND IT DOESN'T MATTER HOW, OR WHEN, OR WHY, AND YOU'LL JUST FEEL BAD.
AW, GEEZ.

THE END.

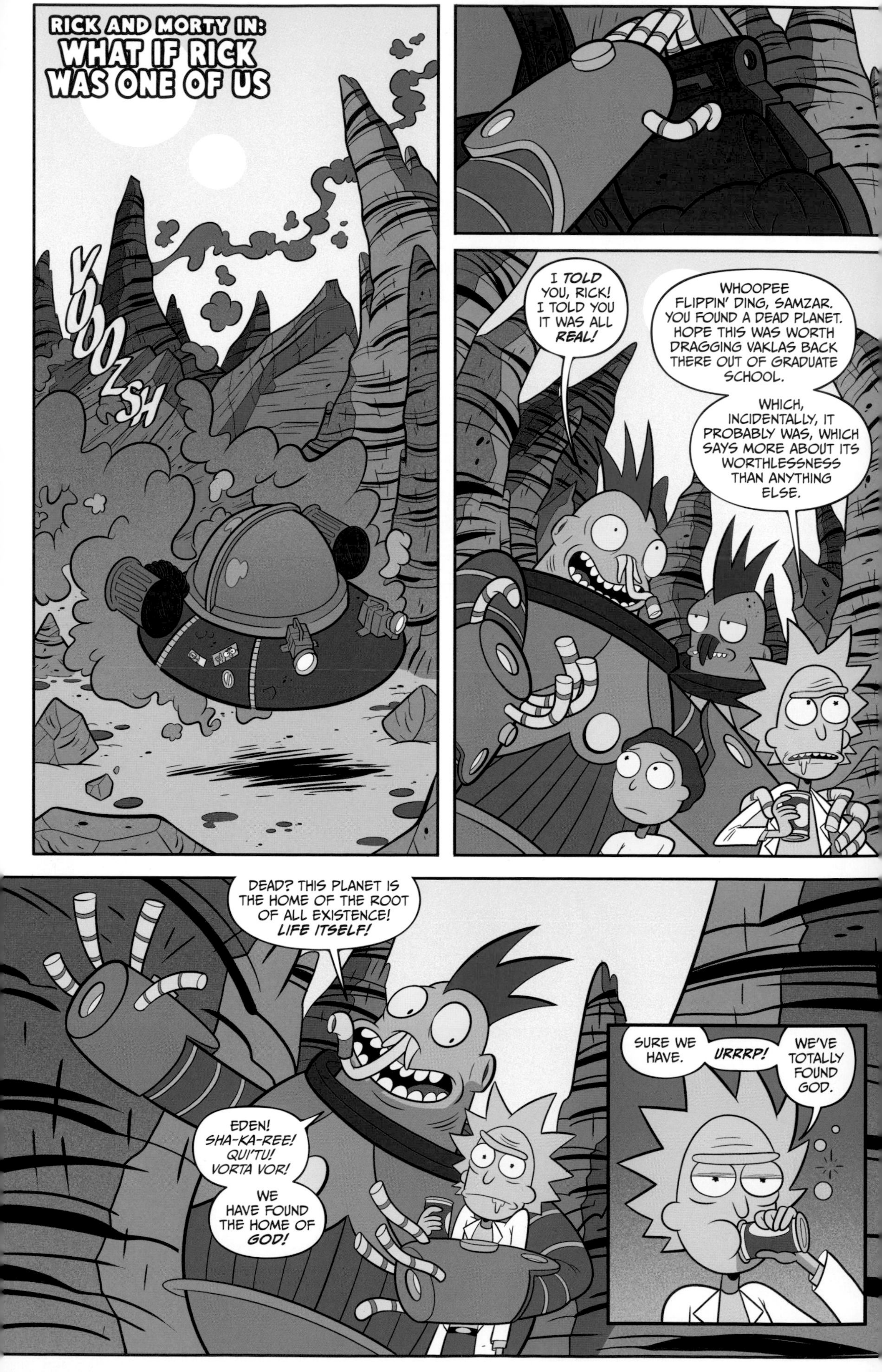
RICK AND MORTY IN:
WHAT IF RICK WAS ONE OF US
YOOOZSH
I *TOLD* YOU, RICK! I TOLD YOU IT WAS ALL *REAL!*
WHOOPEE FLIPPIN' DING, SAMZAR. YOU FOUND A DEAD PLANET. HOPE THIS WAS WORTH DRAGGING VAKLAS BACK THERE OUT OF GRADUATE SCHOOL.
WHICH, INCIDENTALLY, IT PROBABLY WAS, WHICH SAYS MORE ABOUT ITS WORTHLESSNESS THAN ANYTHING ELSE.
DEAD? THIS PLANET IS THE HOME OF THE ROOT OF ALL EXISTENCE! *LIFE ITSELF!*
EDEN! *SHA-KA-REE! QUI'TU! VORTA VOR!*
WE HAVE FOUND THE HOME OF *GOD!*
SURE WE HAVE.
URRRP!
WE'VE TOTALLY FOUND GOD.

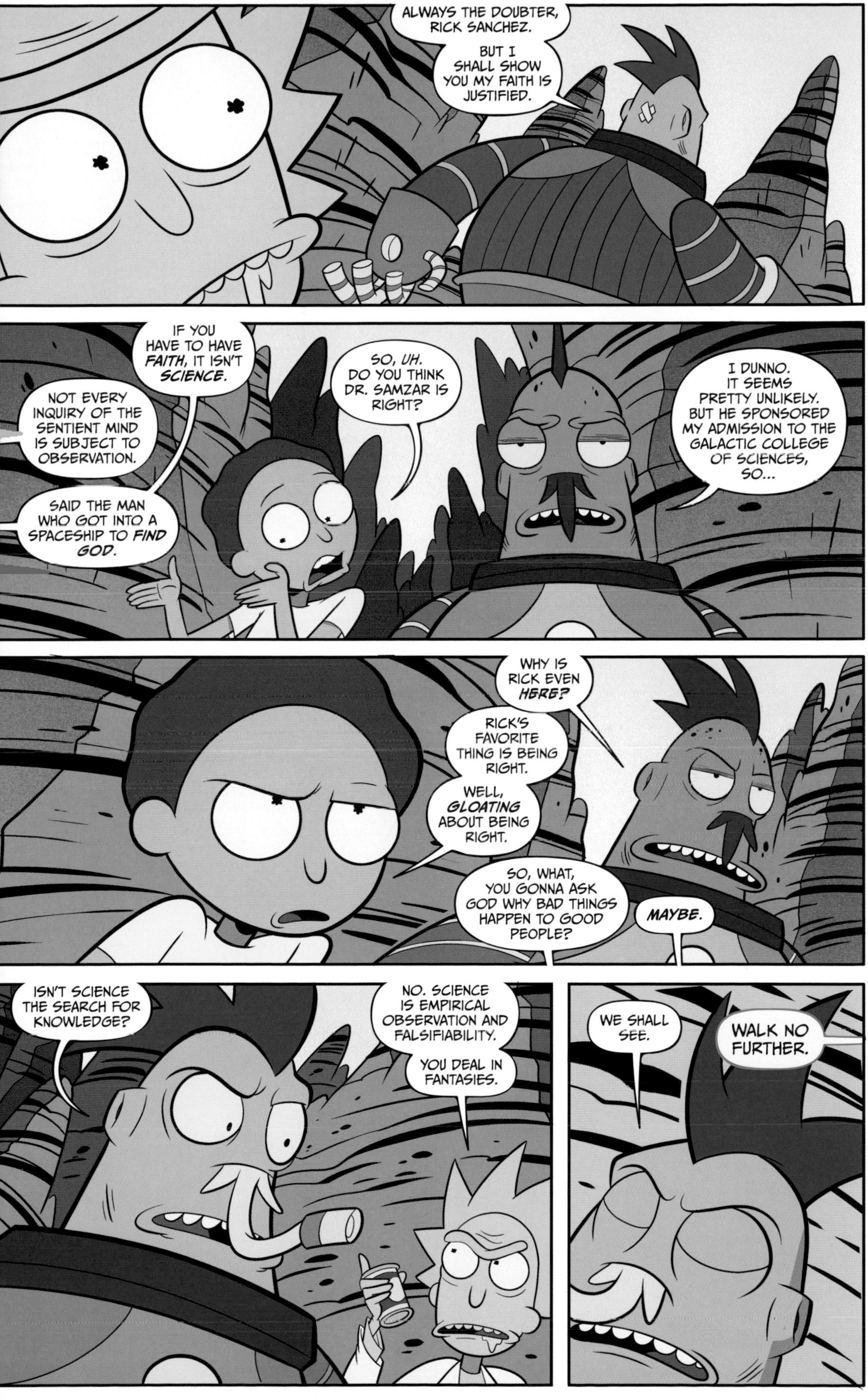
ALWAYS THE DOUBTER, RICK SANCHEZ.
BUT I SHALL SHOW YOU MY FAITH IS JUSTIFIED.
NOT EVERY INQUIRY OF THE SENTIENT MIND IS SUBJECT TO OBSERVATION.
IF YOU HAVE TO HAVE FAITH, IT ISN'T SCIENCE.
SAID THE MAN WHO GOT INTO A SPACESHIP TO FIND GOD.
SO, UH. DO YOU THINK DR. SAMZAR IS RIGHT?
I DUNNO. IT SEEMS PRETTY UNLIKELY. BUT HE SPONSORED MY ADMISSION TO THE GALACTIC COLLEGE OF SCIENCES, SO...
WHY IS RICK EVEN HERE?
RICK'S FAVORITE THING IS BEING RIGHT.
WELL, GLOATING ABOUT BEING RIGHT.
SO, WHAT, YOU GONNA ASK GOD WHY BAD THINGS HAPPEN TO GOOD PEOPLE?
MAYBE.
ISN'T SCIENCE THE SEARCH FOR KNOWLEDGE?
NO. SCIENCE IS EMPIRICAL OBSERVATION AND FALSIFIABILITY.
YOU DEAL IN FANTASIES.
WE SHALL SEE.
WALK NO FURTHER.

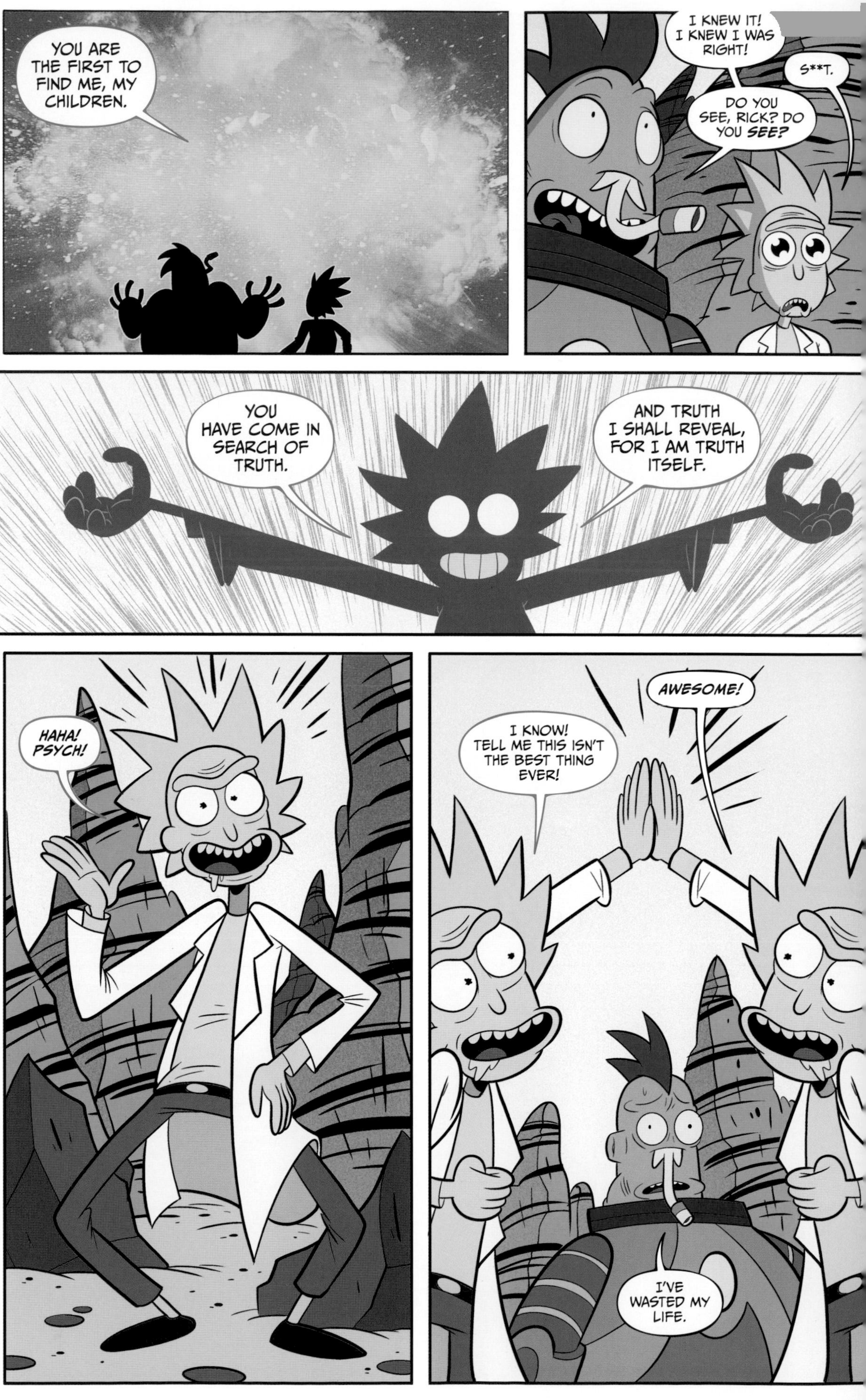
YOU ARE THE FIRST TO FIND ME, MY CHILDREN.
I KNEW IT! I KNEW I WAS RIGHT!
DO YOU SEE, RICK? DO YOU **SEE?**
S**T.
YOU HAVE COME IN SEARCH OF TRUTH.
AND TRUTH I SHALL REVEAL, FOR I AM TRUTH ITSELF.
HAHA! PSYCH!
I KNOW! TELL ME THIS ISN'T THE BEST THING EVER!
AWESOME!
I'VE WASTED MY LIFE.

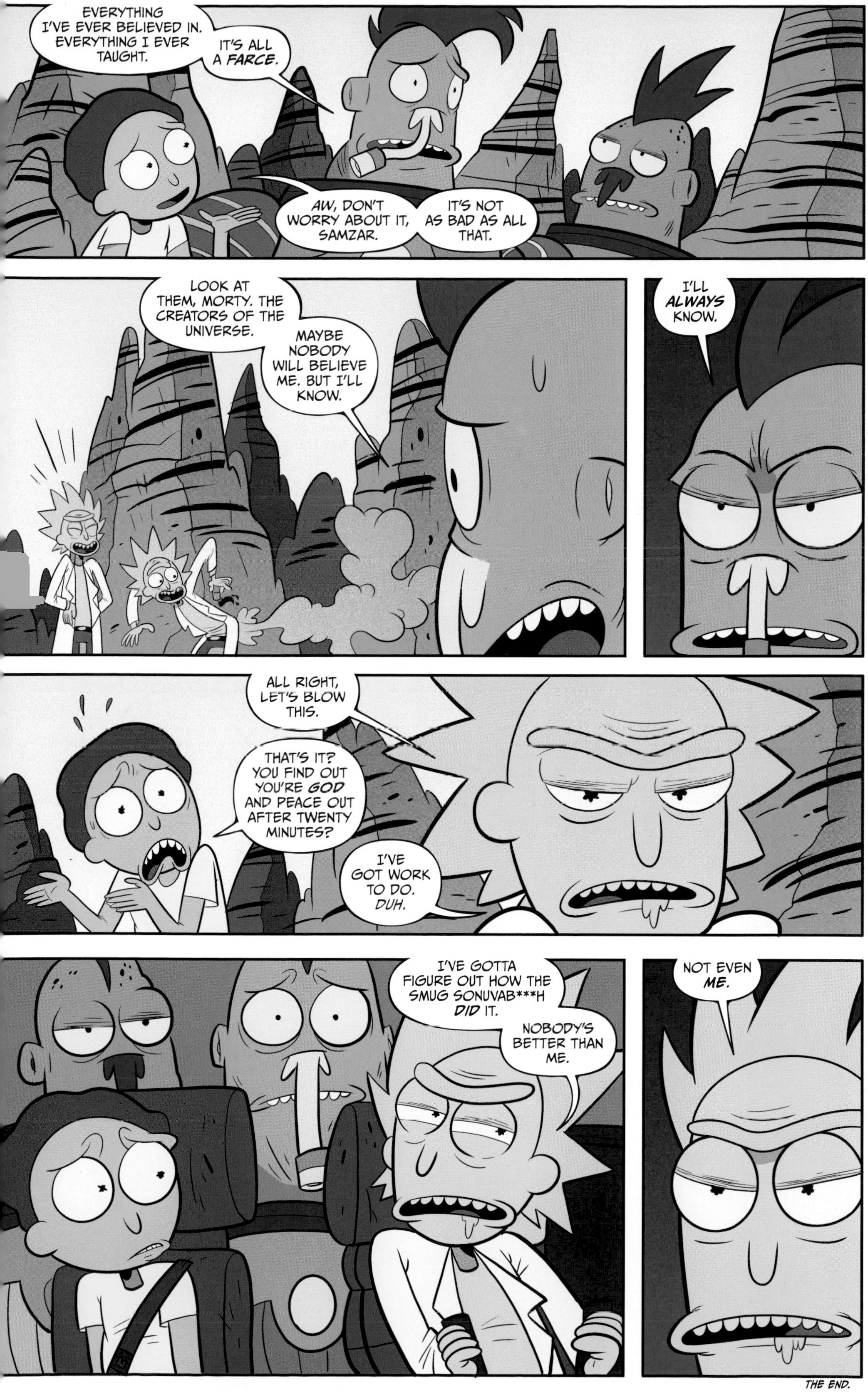
EVERYTHING I'VE EVER BELIEVED IN. EVERYTHING I EVER TAUGHT.
IT'S ALL A FARCE.
AW, DON'T WORRY ABOUT IT, SAMZAR.
IT'S NOT AS BAD AS ALL THAT.
LOOK AT THEM, MORTY. THE CREATORS OF THE UNIVERSE.
MAYBE NOBODY WILL BELIEVE ME. BUT I'LL KNOW.
I'LL ALWAYS KNOW.
ALL RIGHT, LET'S BLOW THIS.
THAT'S IT? YOU FIND OUT YOU'RE GOD AND PEACE OUT AFTER TWENTY MINUTES?
I'VE GOT WORK TO DO. DUH.
I'VE GOTTA FIGURE OUT HOW THE SMUG SONUVAB***H DID IT.
NOBODY'S BETTER THAN ME.
NOT EVEN ME.

THE END.

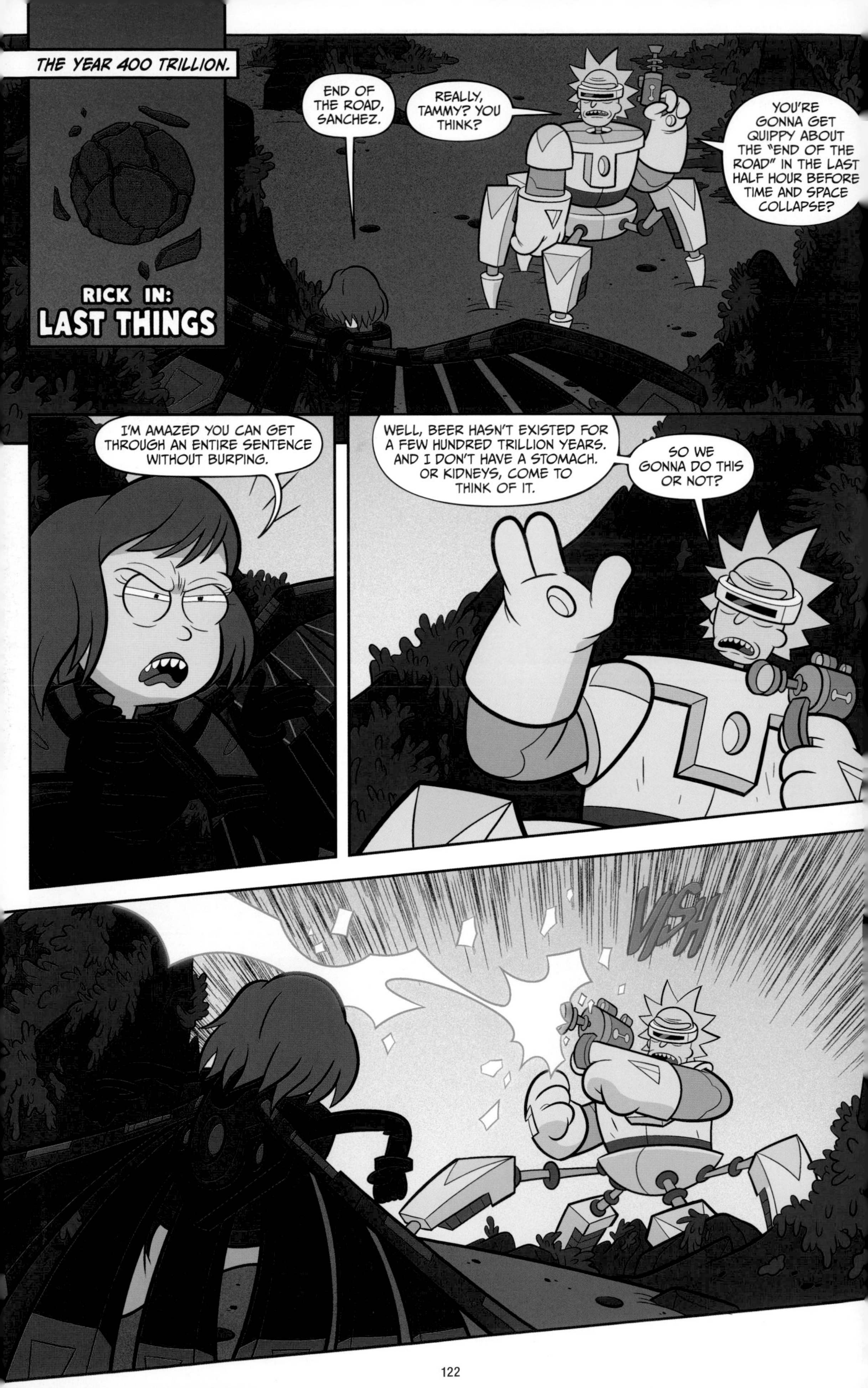
THE YEAR 400 TRILLION.
RICK IN: LAST THINGS
END OF THE ROAD, SANCHEZ.
REALLY, TAMMY? YOU THINK?
YOU'RE GONNA GET QUIPPY ABOUT THE "END OF THE ROAD" IN THE LAST HALF HOUR BEFORE TIME AND SPACE COLLAPSE?
I'M AMAZED YOU CAN GET THROUGH AN ENTIRE SENTENCE WITHOUT BURPING.
WELL, BEER HASN'T EXISTED FOR A FEW HUNDRED TRILLION YEARS. AND I DON'T HAVE A STOMACH. OR KIDNEYS, COME TO THINK OF IT.
SO WE GONNA DO THIS OR NOT?
VISH

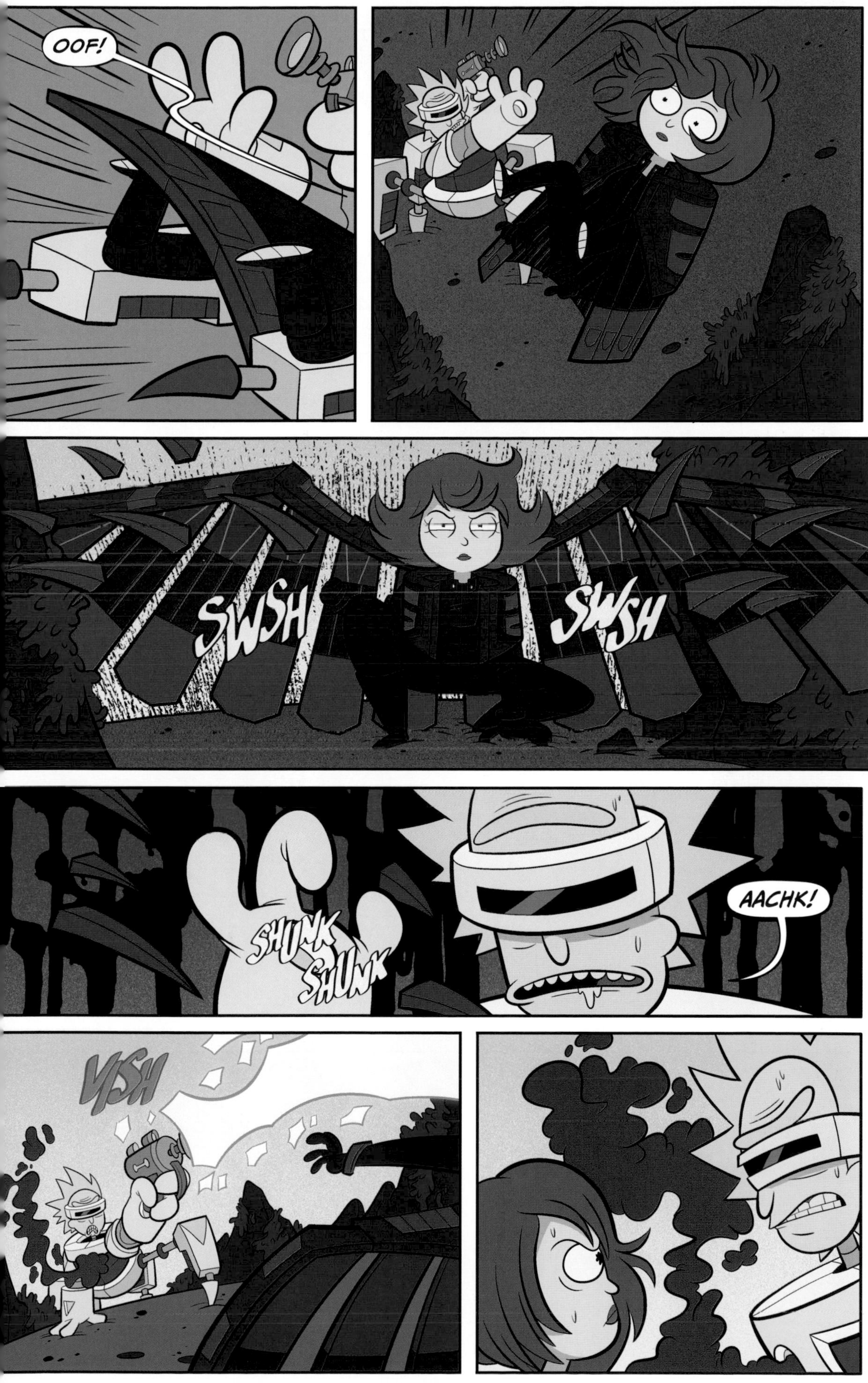
OOF!
SWSH
SWSH
SHUNK
SHUNK
AACHK!
VISH

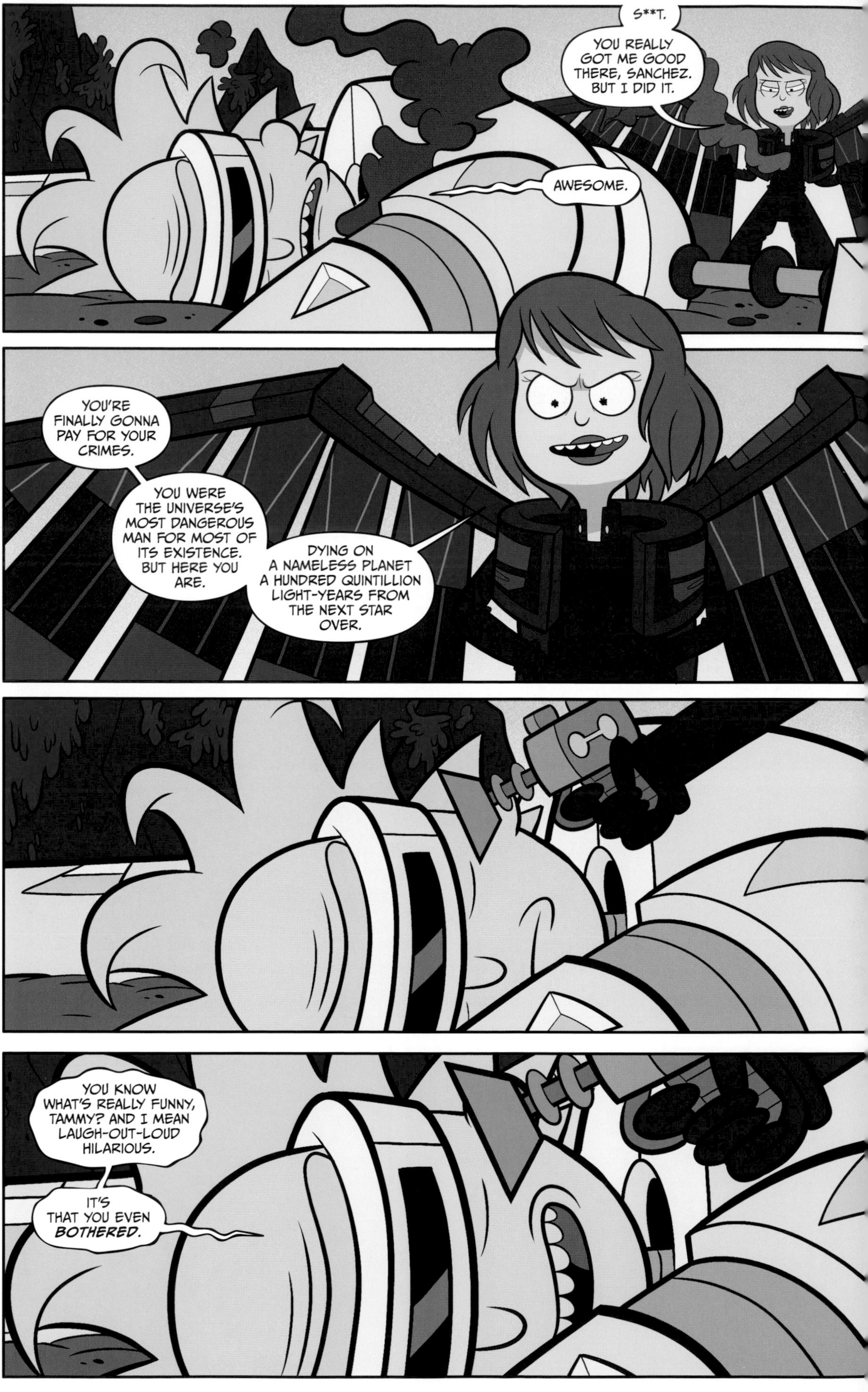
S**T.
YOU REALLY GOT ME GOOD THERE, SANCHEZ. BUT I DID IT.
AWESOME.
YOU'RE FINALLY GONNA PAY FOR YOUR CRIMES.
YOU WERE THE UNIVERSE'S MOST DANGEROUS MAN FOR MOST OF ITS EXISTENCE. BUT HERE YOU ARE.
DYING ON A NAMELESS PLANET A HUNDRED QUINTILLION LIGHT-YEARS FROM THE NEXT STAR OVER.
YOU KNOW WHAT'S REALLY FUNNY, TAMMY? AND I MEAN LAUGH-OUT-LOUD HILARIOUS.
IT'S THAT YOU EVEN *BOTHERED*.

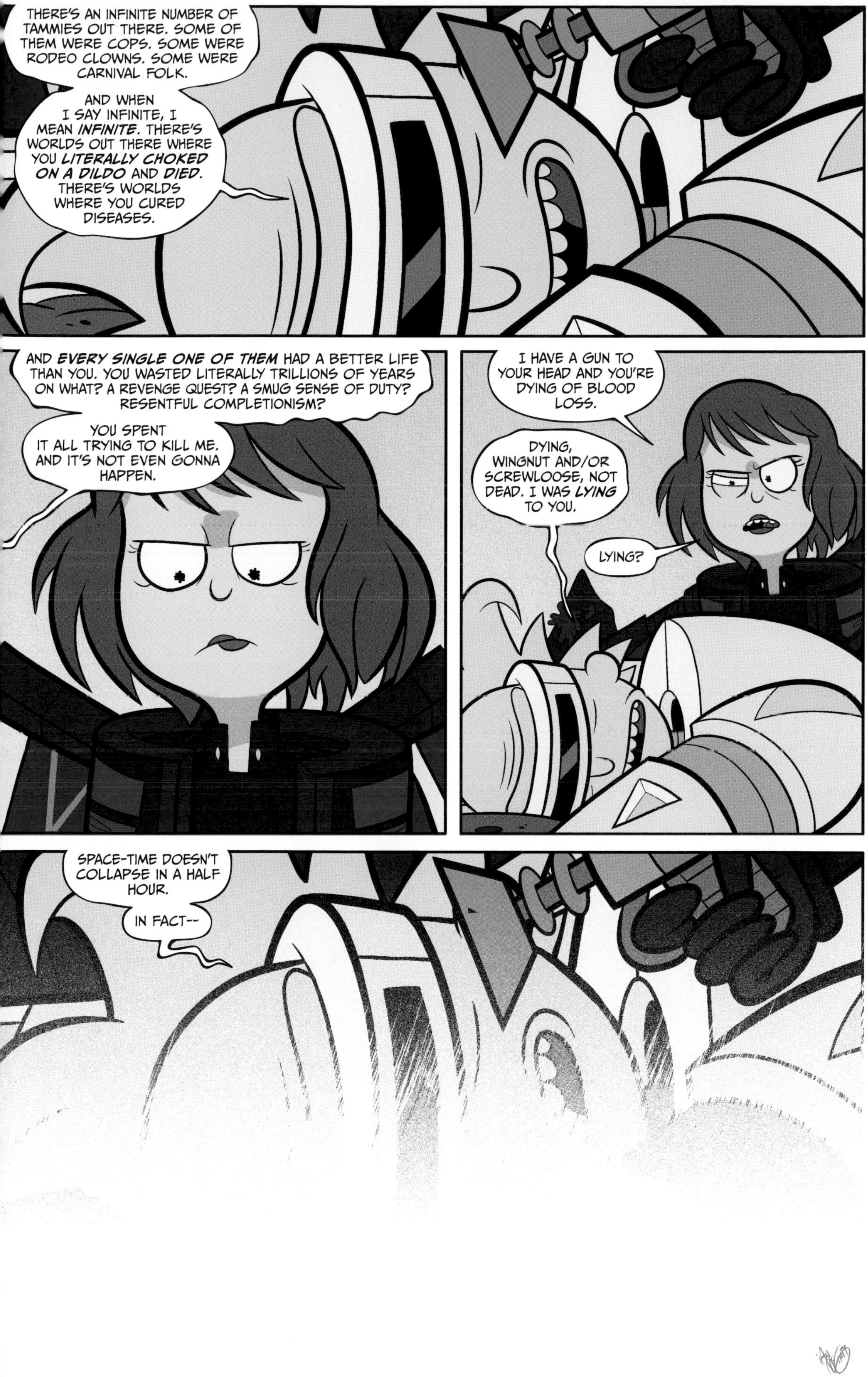
THERE'S AN INFINITE NUMBER OF TAMMIES OUT THERE. SOME OF THEM WERE COPS. SOME WERE RODEO CLOWNS. SOME WERE CARNIVAL FOLK.
AND WHEN I SAY INFINITE, I MEAN INFINITE. THERE'S WORLDS OUT THERE WHERE YOU LITERALLY CHOKED ON A DILDO AND DIED. THERE'S WORLDS WHERE YOU CURED DISEASES.
AND EVERY SINGLE ONE OF THEM HAD A BETTER LIFE THAN YOU. YOU WASTED LITERALLY TRILLIONS OF YEARS ON WHAT? A REVENGE QUEST? A SMUG SENSE OF DUTY? RESENTFUL COMPLETIONISM?
YOU SPENT IT ALL TRYING TO KILL ME. AND IT'S NOT EVEN GONNA HAPPEN.
I HAVE A GUN TO YOUR HEAD AND YOU'RE DYING OF BLOOD LOSS.
DYING, WINGNUT AND/OR SCREWLOOSE, NOT DEAD. I WAS LYING TO YOU.
LYING?
SPACE-TIME DOESN'T COLLAPSE IN A HALF HOUR.
IN FACT--

DAN HARMON is the Emmy® winning creator/executive producer of the comedy series *Community,* as well as the co-creator/executive producer of Adult Swim's *Rick and Morty*™.

JUSTIN ROILAND grew up in Manteca, California, where he did the basic stuff children do. Later in life he traveled to Los Angeles. Justin also really hates writing about himself in the third person. I hate this. That's right. It's me. I've been writing this whole thing. Hi. The cat's out of the bag. It's just you and me now. There never was a third person.

KYLE STARKS is an Eisner-nominated comic creator from Southern Indiana, where he resides with his beautiful wife and two amazing daughters. Check out his creator-owned work: *Assaination Nation, Kill Them All,* and *Sexcastle.*

TINI HOWARD is a writer and swamp witch from the Carolina Wilds. Her work includes *Rick and Morty*™: *Pocket Like You Stole It, Assassinistas, Euthanauts,* and she is now a Marvel exclusive writer. She lives with her husband, Blake, and her son, Orlando, who is a cat.

MAGDALENE VISAGGIO is the Eisner and GLAAD Media Award-nominated writer behind *Kim & Kim, Eternity Girl, Dazzler: X Song, Transformers vs Visionaries,* and *Morning in America.* A lifelong comics reader, she studied English at Virginia Commonwealth University and did graduate work in Ethics & Moral Theology at Seton Hall before dropping out to focus on writing comics where people hit each other with guitars. When not writing, she's probably passed out on her couch at three in the morning with a cat on top of her while Netflix asks if she wants to continue watching *Star Trek: The Next Generation.* She lives in Manhattan.

MARC ELLERBY is a comics illustrator living in Essex, UK. He has worked on such titles as *Doctor Who, Regular Show,* and *The Amazing World of Gumball.* His own comics are *Chloe Noonan: Monster Hunter* and *Ellerbisms.*

PHILIP MURPHY is an Irish cartoonist whose past work include titles such as *Teen Titans Go!, The Powerpuff Girls, Star Trek vs Transformers.* He's a big fan of cartoons, movies, and video games, both retro and new, so getting the chance to adapt the characters into comics and play around in their universe is a dream come true.

IAN MCGINTY is an artist, writer, and designer. He is the creator of *Welcome to Showside* and worked on Nickelodeon's *INVADER ZIM* movie, *Rocko's Modern Life, Adventure Time,* and more.

SARAH STERN is a comic artist and colorist from New York. Find her at sarahstern.com or follow her on Twitter at @worstwizard.

CHRIS CRANK letters a bunch of books put out by Image, Dark Horse, and Oni Press. He also has a podcast with Mike Norton (**crankcast.net**) and makes music (**sonomorti.bandcamp.com**).

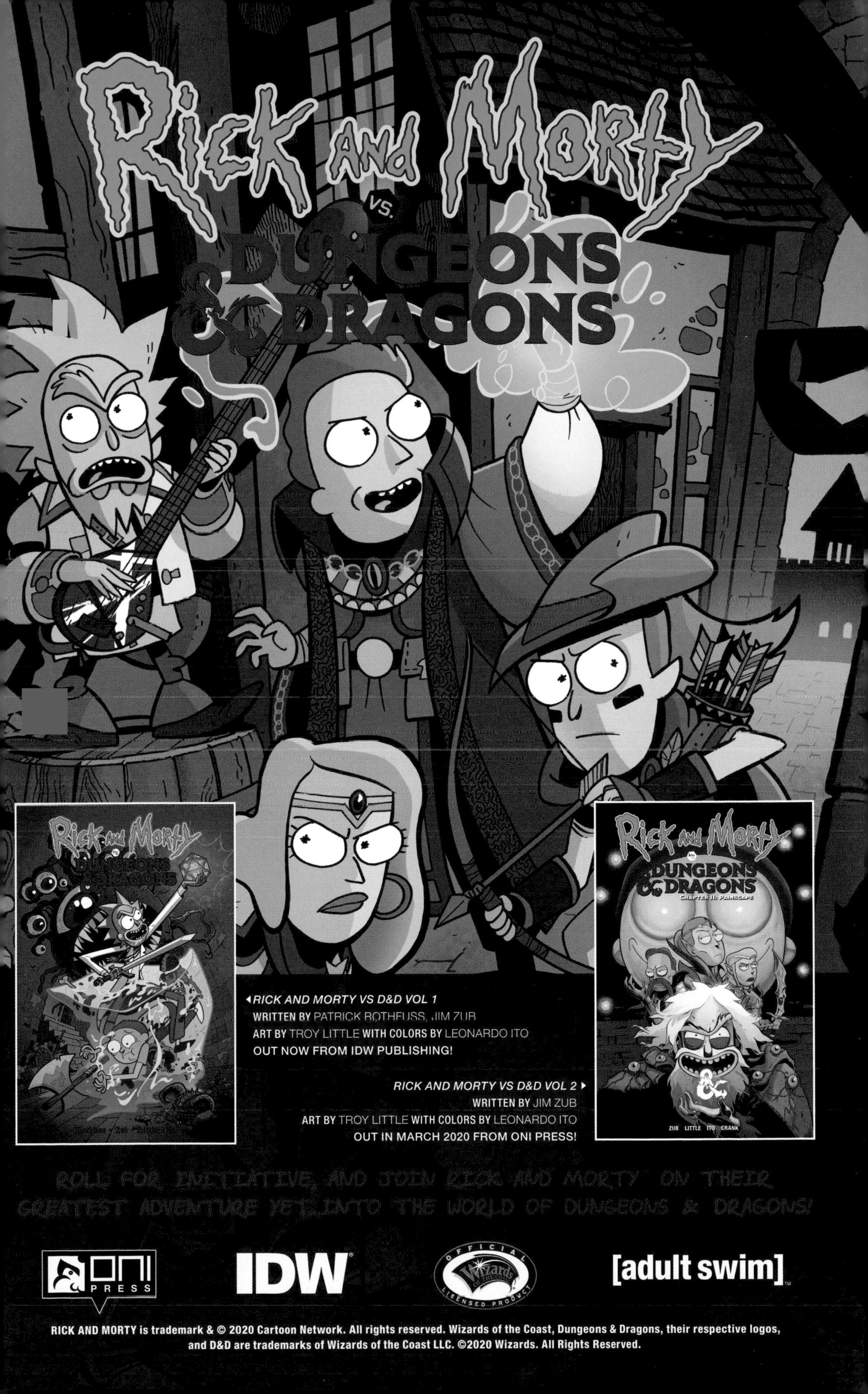

RICK AND MORTY VS. DUNGEONS & DRAGONS
◂ RICK AND MORTY VS D&D VOL 1
WRITTEN BY PATRICK ROTHFUSS, JIM ZUB
ART BY TROY LITTLE WITH COLORS BY LEONARDO ITO
OUT NOW FROM IDW PUBLISHING!
RICK AND MORTY VS D&D VOL 2 ▸
WRITTEN BY JIM ZUB
ART BY TROY LITTLE WITH COLORS BY LEONARDO ITO
OUT IN MARCH 2020 FROM ONI PRESS!
DUNGEONS & DRAGONS
CHAPTER II: PAINSCAPE
ZUB LITTLE ITO CRANK
ROLL FOR INITIATIVE, AND JOIN RICK AND MORTY ON THEIR GREATEST ADVENTURE YET INTO THE WORLD OF DUNGEONS & DRAGONS!
ONI PRESS
IDW
OFFICIAL Wizards OF THE COAST LICENSED PRODUCT
[adult swim]
RICK AND MORTY is trademark & © 2020 Cartoon Network. All rights reserved. Wizards of the Coast, Dungeons & Dragons, their respective logos, and D&D are trademarks of Wizards of the Coast LLC. ©2020 Wizards. All Rights Reserved.

MORE BOOKS FROM ONI PRESS

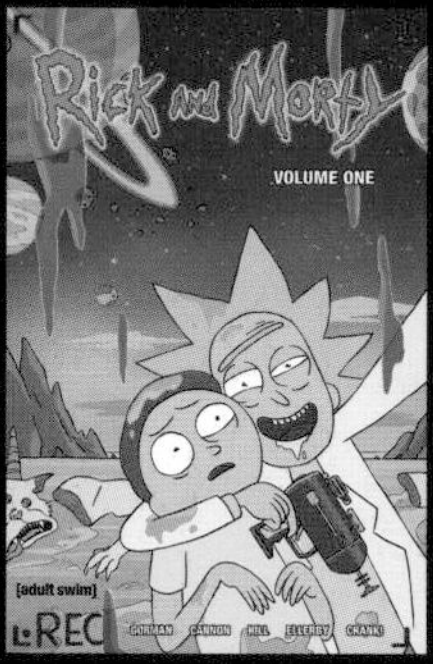
Rick and Morty
VOLUME ONE

RICK AND MORTY™, VOL. 1
By Zac Gorman, CJ Cannon, Marc Ellerby, and more
128 pages, softcover, color
ISBN 978-1-62010-281-7

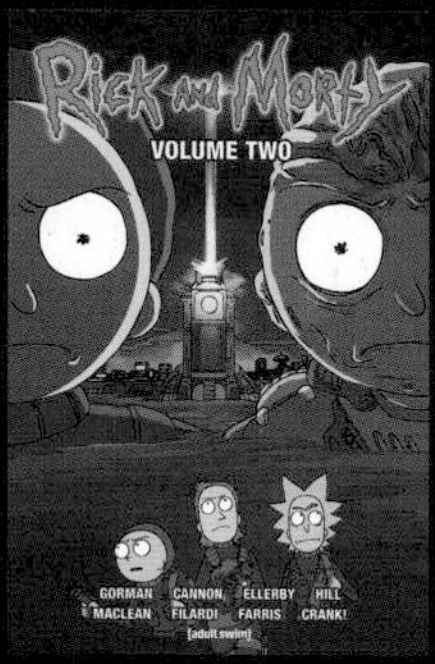
Rick and Morty
VOLUME TWO

RICK AND MORTY™, VOL. 2
By Zac Gorman, CJ Cannon, Marc Ellerby, and more
128 pages, softcover, color
ISBN 978-1-62010-319-7

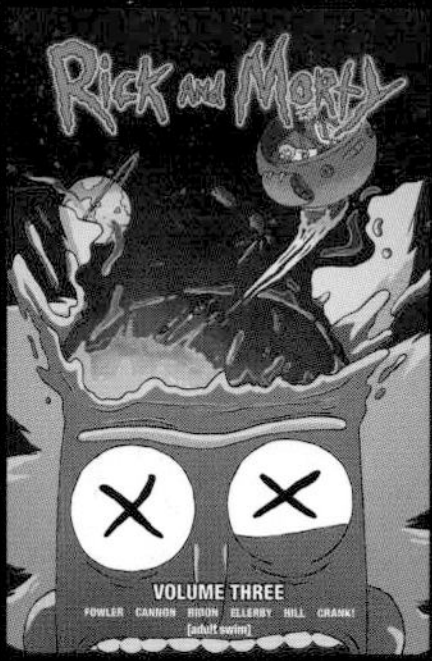
Rick and Morty
VOLUME THREE

RICK AND MORTY™, VOL. 3
By Tom Fowler, CJ Cannon, Marc Ellerby, and more
128 pages, softcover, color
ISBN 978-1-62010-343-2

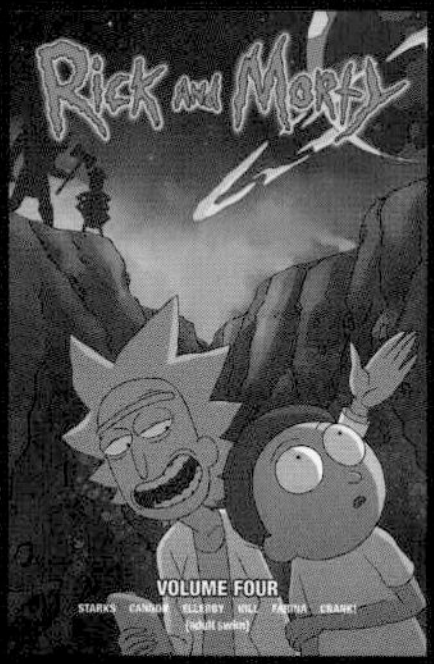
Rick and Morty
VOLUME FOUR

RICK AND MORTY™, VOL. 4
By Kyle Starks, CJ Cannon, Marc Ellerby, and more
128 pages, softcover, color
ISBN 978-1-62010-377-7

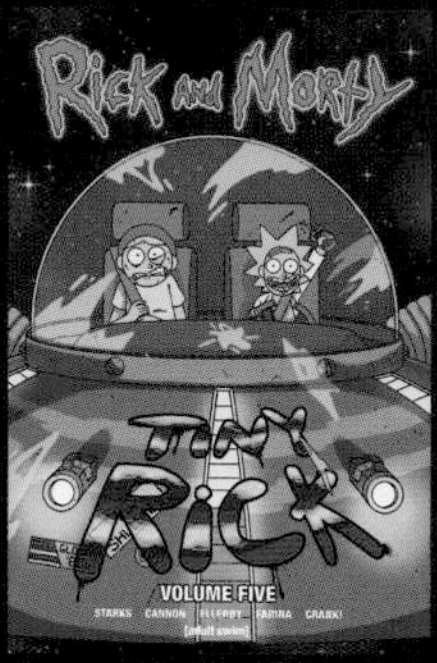
Rick and Morty
TINY RICK
VOLUME FIVE

RICK AND MORTY™, VOL. 5
By Kyle Starks, CJ Cannon, Marc Ellerby, and more!
128 pages, softcover, color
ISBN 978-1-62010-416-3

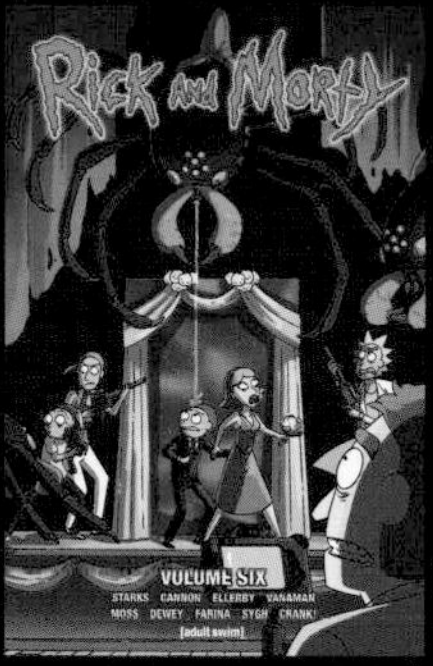
Rick and Morty
VOLUME SIX

RICK AND MORTY™, VOL. 6
By Kyle Starks, CJ Cannon, Marc Ellerby, and more
128 pages, softcover, color
ISBN 978-1-62010-452-1

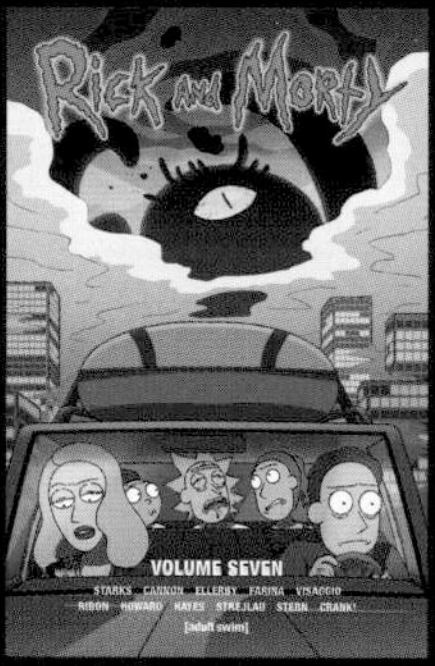
Rick and Morty
VOLUME SEVEN

RICK AND MORTY™, VOL. 7
By Kyle Starks, CJ Cannon, Marc Ellerby, and more
128 pages, softcover, color
ISBN 978-1-62010-509-2

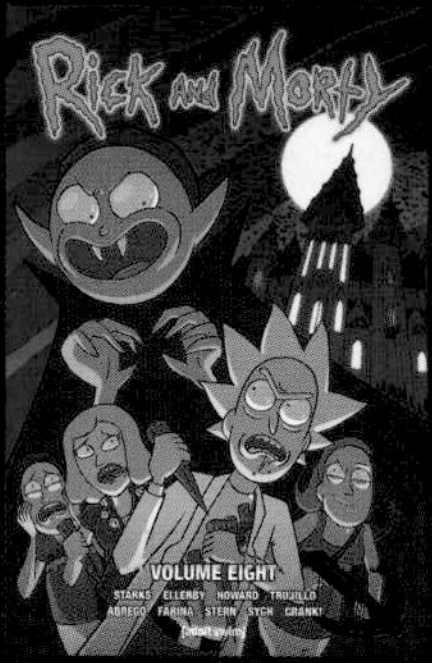
Rick and Morty
VOLUME EIGHT

RICK AND MORTY™, VOL. 8
By Kyle Starks, Tini Howard, Marc Ellerby, and more
128 pages, softcover, color
ISBN 978-1-62010-549-8

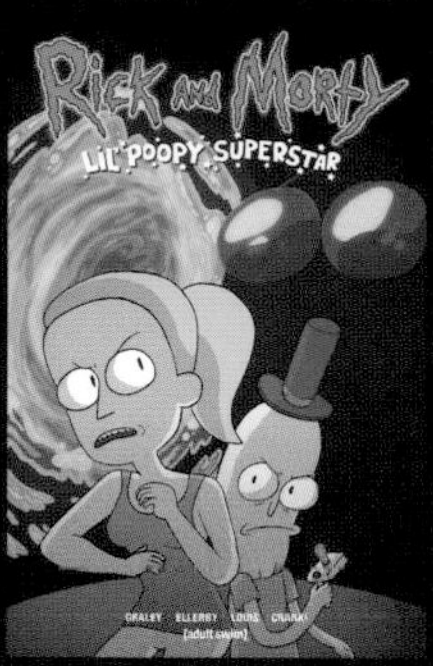
Rick and Morty
LIL' POOPY SUPERSTAR

RICK AND MORTY™: LIL' POOPY SUPERSTAR
By Sarah Graley, Marc Ellerby, and Mildred Louis
128 pages, softcover, color
ISBN 978-1-62010-374-6

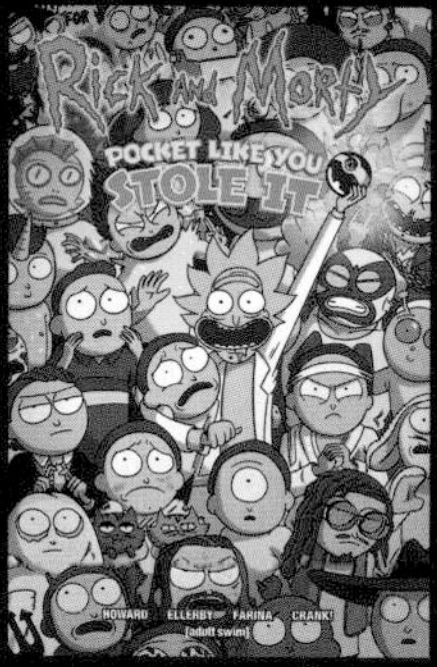
Rick and Morty
POCKET LIKE YOU STOLE IT

RICK AND MORTY™: POCKET LIKE YOU STOLE IT
By Tini Howard, Marc Ellerby, and Katy Farina
128 pages, softcover, color
ISBN 978-1-62010-474-3

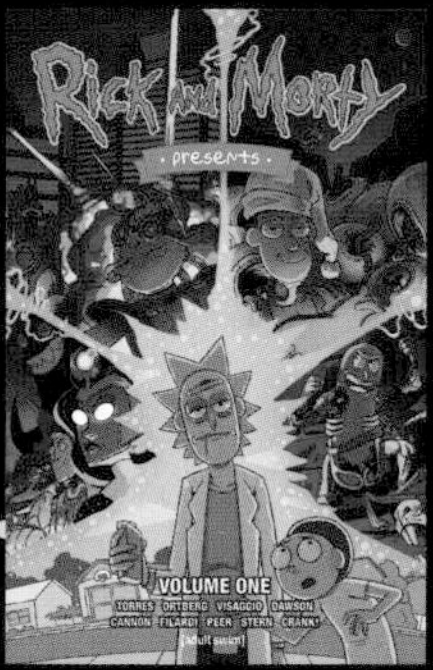
Rick and Morty
presents
VOLUME ONE

RICK AND MORTY™ PRESENTS, VOL. 1
By J. Torres, Daniel Ortberg, CJ Cannon, and more
136 pages, softcover, color
ISBN 978-1-62010-552-8

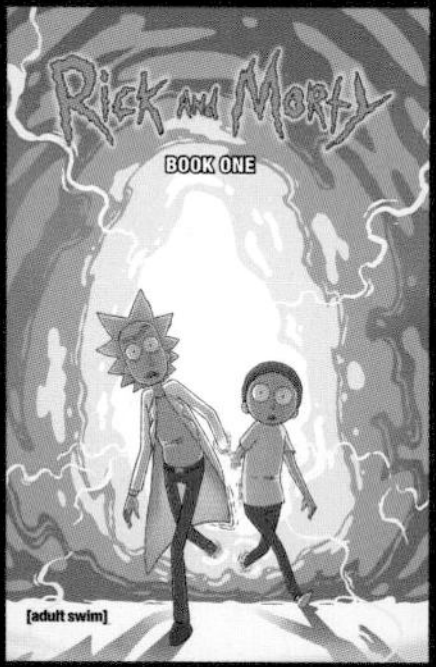
Rick and Morty
BOOK ONE

RICK AND MORTY™ DELUXE EDITION, BOOK ONE
By Zac Gorman, CJ Cannon, Marc Ellerby, and more
296 pages, hardcover, color
ISBN 978-1-62010-360-9

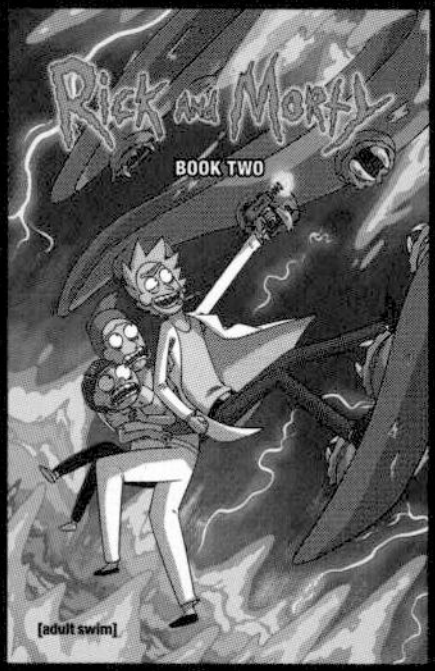
Rick and Morty
BOOK TWO

RICK AND MORTY™ DELUXE EDITION, BOOK TWO
By Tom Fowler, Kyle Starks, CJ Cannon, Marc Ellerby, and more
288 pages, hardcover, color
ISBN 978-1-62010-439-2

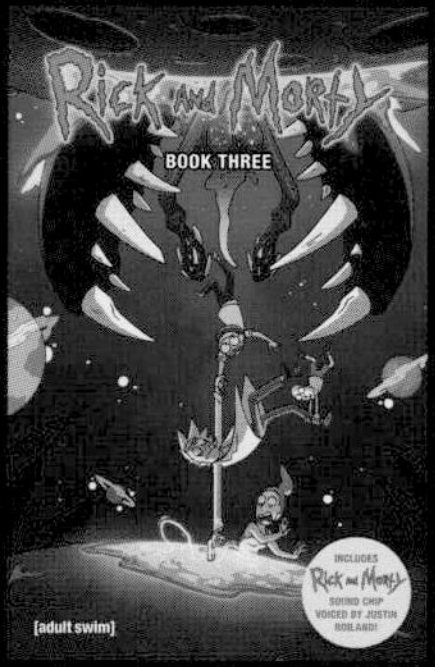
Rick and Morty
BOOK THREE

RICK AND MORTY™ DELUXE EDITION, BOOK THREE
By Kyle Starks, CJ Cannon, Marc Ellerby, Sarah Graley, and more
288 pages, hardcover, color
ISBN 978-1-62010-535-1

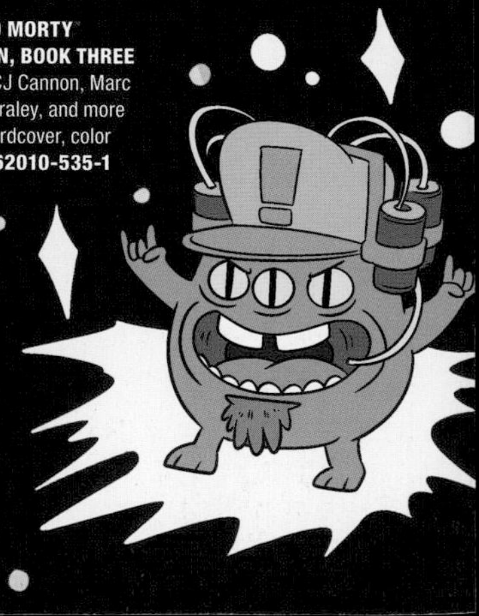

ONI PRESS

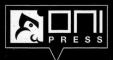

For more information on these and other fine Oni Press comic books and graphic novels visit **www.onipress.com.** To find a comic specialty store in your area visit **www.comicshops.us.**